GREEN SKY

INNOVATION

Make the Future of Ministry

by Liam Savage

www.greenskyinnovation.com

Paperback ISBN: 979-8-218-06233-0

Cover art by Liam Savage

Interior design and typesetting by *waynekehoe.com*

Author photo by Merritt Franzmann

Contents

Introduction 7

The Kingdom Builder's Perspective 10
INNOVATE FOR THE PURPOSE OF BUILDING GOD'S KINGDOM.

One Body, One Mission 12
Reaching Out Your Hand 18
The Beauty of Complexity 23
The Greatest Commandment 28
Poem: The Man with a Vision for the Sea 35

The Philosopher's Perspective 46
UNCOVER THE UNSEEN REALITIES THAT AFFECT INNOVATION.

Parable: The Seed and the Shell 47
Unseen Problems 55
The Systems We Inhabit 61
The Systems We Create 78
Asking the Right Questions 92

The Beginner's Perspective 102
GO BACK TO BEING A BEGINNER TO DISCOVER THE TRUTH.

Parable: The Cave 103
See the World as You Do 114
See the World as Others Do 119
How Culture Shapes Your World 125
See the World as It Is 133
Making Sense of It All 139

The Storyteller's Perspective 148
CONNECT YOUR INNOVATIONS TO THOSE WHO NEED THEM MOST.

Parable: The Half-Circle Wall 149
Wrestle with Your Why 153
You Can Only Choose One 160
Marketing Your Ministry 166
Crafting the Journey 171

The Culture Maker's Perspective 182
CREATE AN ENVIRONMENT WHERE INNOVATION FLOURISHES.

Parable: Winnie the Pooh 183
Leading from Behind 186
Pilots, Doctors, and Ministers 192
Changing the Culture 198
Destructive Peace vs. Constructive Conflict 205
Your Ministry Is Your People 210
Doing Our Best Work Together 219

The Host's Perspective 234
UNLOCK INNOVATIVE COLLABORATION ON YOUR TEAM AND OTHERS.

Parable: A Tale of Two Tables 235
Together as One 240
Crafting Memories 246
The Hidden Power of Facilitation 255

The Learner's Perspective …… **262**

ENSURE YOUR INNOVATION REMAINS RELEVANT TODAY AND TOMORROW.

Parable: The Perfect Man …… 263
The Work of Unlearning …… 268
Celebrating Failure …… 272
Faster and Smaller Is Better …… 275
Growing in the Right Direction …… 278
Why We're Never Finished …… 282

Afterword: Keep Going …… **290**

Acknowledgements …… **295**

Index

Authors, Books, and People …… 296
Concepts and Keywords …… 300

Introduction

God is the ultimate innovator and we are created in His image to see through His eyes as we carry the Gospel to an ever-changing world. Many books promise the secrets of success to help businesses and ministries improve. But few capture the true purpose. We innovate to glorify God.

Innovating is not simply coming up with ideas—that is creativity. It is not just bringing those ideas to life—the act of invention. Innovation is creating new *value*. It is making something new that people want or helps them in some way. Innovation is both creativity and invention applied in the right direction.

In this book, you will learn seven perspectives of a ministry innovator. We will explore being a kingdom builder, philosopher, beginner, storyteller, culture maker, host, and learner. These perspectives are foundational to understanding and effectively practicing innovation. This book is all about the way we see. *Green Sky* is the title because we typically think of the sky as blue and the land as green. But if the foundation we stand on is in heaven, then our point of view should be upside down as we look at the world from God's perspective and with His vision.

My goal is not to give you magical solutions that will solve your ministry's problems and guarantee success. Rather, my desire is to shape you into the kind of innovator who can create innovative solutions for yourself and others. By embracing these perspectives, we can grow the strength of the Church in the area of innovation so we can spread the Gospel in new ways.

Ministry is the highest application of innovation because we have the most valuable message for the world. Creating new value around the Gospel means making better and easier ways for people to encounter the Good News and embrace it. Ministry innovation is the practical work of making disciples of all nations as Jesus commanded.

Ministry innovation is the practical work of making disciples of all nations.

Innovation might not be new, but new skills are needed. When Solomon was preparing to build the Lord's temple, he wrote to the king of Tyre for help. There were many things Solomon needed, including the timber to construct the temple. But the first thing he asked for was someone skilled (2 Chronicles 2:7).

In the letter that King Hiram wrote back he said, "I have sent a skilled man, who has understanding, . . . He is trained to work in gold, silver, bronze, iron, stone, and wood, and in purple, blue, and crimson fabrics and fine linen, and to do all sorts of engraving and execute any design that may be assigned him with your craftsman" (2 Chronicles 2:13–14). The Bible says this man "was full of wisdom, understanding, and skill" (1 Kings 7:14).

Because Solomon was wise, he recognized how great the task was in front of him and knew he needed help. He needed an innovator skilled in many areas to direct the work and practically carry it out.

The temple was a physical building—"a house for the name of the LORD" (2 Chronicles 2:4) —where the people of Israel would make their offerings. Innovating that building was an act of worship and a testimony of the Lord's fame to the world.

Today we live in a new reality. Every believer is a temple who bears the name of the Lord to the world (1 Corinthians 6:19). We as the Body of Christ testify to the great message of redemption and victory Jesus won for us on the cross.

The Church around us needs innovators as much as Solomon once did. The tools of our trade are different—no longer the hard skills of metal work, dyes, and engraving needed for physical buildings. Now we need the soft skills of kingdom building, storytelling, learning, and culture-making. We need the seven perspectives described in this book and probably many more as our work continues to grow and change.

Solomon's craftsman applied his skills to construct a physical temple, but today we build into the people, processes, and projects that carry the Gospel to a waiting world. We build the Body of Christ and invite all who do not yet know Jesus to join us in God's kingdom.

Innovation is the natural result of reflecting God's infinite creativity and sharing in His tireless pursuit of the lost. While our calling has not changed, the world around us looks different every day. Navigating it with excellence requires Spirit-led understanding and a willingness to change and improve our methods.

My prayer is that we will be people who are skilled, wise, and ready—innovators who answer the call to build God's Church.

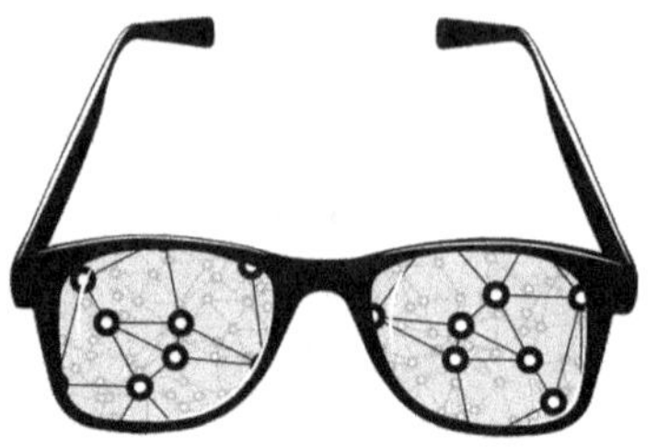

The Kingdom Builder's Perspective

INNOVATE FOR THE PURPOSE OF BUILDING GOD'S KINGDOM

*"We may have all come on different ships,
but we're in the same boat now."*

—Martin Luther King Jr., American activist

Ministry innovation is different from innovation anywhere else because we are applying it to building God's kingdom. It is exercising the creativity and intelligence God has given us, but not for our own gain. The world focuses on innovation to get ahead, to make more money, or to make themselves or their inventions famous. We are called to make God famous and proclaim His name to the ends of the earth.

We have the privilege of working alongside God because we were first called into relationship with Him. Our understanding of God determines our understanding of everything. It shapes how we perceive ourselves, the purpose of our existence, and our relationships. A person's decision to join God's family or to reject God's offer of grace is the most important choice anyone will ever make.

We are reminding ourselves of these truths because they are foundational. God wants a relationship with each of us. He knows us. He loves us. He created us with a purpose. He has designed us to be a part of the Body of Christ. You and I are citizens of God's kingdom and only tourists here on Earth.

Being part of the Church is not about going to a building on Sundays or following the Bible's rules in order to be a good

Christian. It is about fulfilling God's design to be in relationship with each other and operate in unity to accomplish His mission.

Every member of the Body is needed and we are called to love and serve one another.

As ministry organizations, partnering with others can be challenging and humbling. It can feel faster and safer to innovate alone. But functioning independently from one another is not God's design. We are not intended to compete, but to collaborate.

Who else is out there working towards the same goals? Who has the answers you need, the capacities you lack, or the ideas you might never come up with on your own? God's kingdom is the most beautifully complex and diverse network in the world. We have access to everything we need and more if we work in partnership.

Spreading the Gospel is ultimately God's work, and we are simply joining Him in that process. It is His kingdom we are building, so let's innovate according to His kingdom values.

ONE BODY, ONE MISSION

> *For as in one body we have many members, and the members do not all have the same function, so we, though many, are one body in Christ, and individually members one of another.*
>
> Romans 12:4–5

The Bible describes us as one body, diverse but united. We are one whole person, the bride of Christ. We often refer to this as the Global Church—capital C to show that it includes all believers and all churches. We are family! Wherever you are today, whatever language you primarily speak or culture you were born into—we are connected by the blood of Christ. God's Word says we are brothers and sisters because we have all been adopted by God the Father. This metaphor of being one body is beautiful and a picture of heaven.

I wish that being the Church was easy all the time. It seems like there is always that one person who makes it difficult to love the *whole* Church. You know who I'm talking about. That one person who is difficult to connect with. Let's call him Carl. If you're honest, maybe you go out of your way to avoid Carl on a Sunday morning. He's not the person you invite over to your house when you have the choice. Maybe his opinions are so different from yours that it's hard to talk to him. Worse, maybe he's opposing you, gossiping about you, or taking credit for your work.

But Carl is part of God's plan for the Church too. God designed our very DNA. He knit us together in our mother's womb. He obviously knew there would be a few people like Carl who would be harder to get along with than others.

God knew that the Church is a bunch of broken, sinful, messy people together in one place. This inevitably leads to some hurt feelings or even deeper pains. So what was He thinking? How are we supposed to be one body and one big family when there are people we don't even like in our midst?

To answer that question we have to stop focusing on ourselves, step back, and look at the big picture. All of creation exists to glorify God. That includes us as humans who are created in the very image of God. Remember Carl? He is made in the image of God in his own unique way. You and Carl both have an important job as members of the Body: to take the Good News of Jesus's resurrection to the ends of the earth. The Church is God's chosen medium for the Gospel.

Medium is where we get the word *media*: a format for conveying messages. Books, TV, the Internet, our voices, radio waves . . . these are all mediums. They are ways to send information. God's chosen method of communication for His Gospel is us! The Church—His Body—is the way He is sending a message to the world. Not all mediums are equal. A handwritten note is a much more heartfelt way to send a message to a friend than a brief email. That should make us wonder: Why did God choose the Church to be His medium? God sent His own Son to deliver His message face to face.

Why send the Good News through flawed human beings? It seems like there must be a better way. But in His infinite wisdom, God sent us out to carry the Gospel. We can rest in the knowledge that this is the best solution and that He will lead us.

I have personally experienced the impact of the Church as a medium for the Gospel many times in my life. While traveling to Central Asia to spend time with a church movement there, a man I had never met before named Daniyar picked me up from the small airport at 4:00 a.m. Getting into his car, I said, "I'm sorry it is so early for you! You had to get up in the middle of the night and drive so far to pick me up."

Daniyar had driven two hours to come get me, and I was unsure if I would have done the same for a perfect stranger. But Daniyar replied instantly with the little English he knew, "I am happy to pick you up; you are my brother! You are family! I love you."

I was stunned. What sacrificial love to go out of his way and be so inconvenienced for me, receiving nothing in return. He communicated the Gospel to me in that moment more clearly than five hundred sermons now long forgotten.

This exchange made me realize that something beyond my understanding unites Daniyar and me. God designed the Church this way on purpose. As we give of ourselves sacrificially for our neighbors, we create undeniable experiences of the power and truth of God's love. This is why God created us differently, even though it might feel easier if we were all the same. It is far simpler to love people who are like us. We connect better with those who think like we do or respond the way we expect. But the power of the Gospel shows when we love those who are different from us. This is the work of unity, and it is a central task for all believers.

The power of the Gospel shows when we love those who are different from us.

Unity requires empathy. We naturally have empathy for those we care about. Think about your family or close friends. You defend them and think well of them. You assume the best of their intentions and actions. When they make a mistake, you comfort them and help them back on their feet. You're their biggest fan and supporter in every endeavor, wanting them to succeed and truly believing they will.

Now consider this: God calls us to extend this kind of empathy even to strangers and to our enemies. We are to love the unlovable both inside and outside the Church. That is what Christ did on the cross. He loved us when we were far from Him. He forgave us when we were actively His enemies with no desire to change our actions or behavior. Jesus loved us first and gave up everything—His very life!—so we could be reconciled to God.

Loving, reconciling, understanding—this is hard work. But it is the work Christ did for us and the work He calls and empowers us to do for others. We are not only to love the people we like, but even the people who don't like us. We are to choose unity daily, not just with those we agree with, but also with those who disagree with us. It is impossible to do this on our own, so when we do, that is a testimony to the Gospel's power.

Carl and I may be completely different, but the Gospel has succeeded so long as we can still love each other as brothers in Christ at the end of the day. We can stay in relationship by keeping God's intended purpose for our lives at the forefront. Carl's win is my win and his challenges are my challenges because we are connected in the kingdom of God. I have the important job of loving and remaining unified with Carl. I can do this because any difference of opinion or difference in personality is far less important than the unity of the Gospel.

My mission and your mission as Christ followers is to live out the Gospel in front of a watching world. Nothing could be more powerful than seeing radically different people come together and live in unity as the body of Christ. The world is so hungry for this, but only the Gospel has the power to accomplish it.

I know this is a struggle because I have lived it. Sometimes even the best motivations can lead us to places of disunity. I teach an online course called the Innovation Launchpad. I worked hard to design the course and ensure the content would serve people in ministries. Feedback from students was encouraging, and soon more people wanted to join from around the world. I wanted to focus on the project full-time and make it bigger and better. I saw so much potential and wanted to give it away to everyone as fast as I could. The problem was that no one wanted to help me.

For a while, I felt frustrated, misunderstood, and unsupported. In my impatience, I considered striking out on my own. I imagined greater success if no one was holding me back or telling me what to do. I believed I could serve the Church better if I took the Launchpad and left. Some of these were good intentions, but they led me to a place of discontent and disunity. Notice how much this story focuses on myself. There are a whole lot of "I's" and "me's" in this paragraph and not even one "we."

Ultimately, I decided not to leave because unity is one of God's values. I had to admit to myself that despite seemingly noble motivations, my plan was divisive. It was better for the sake of the Gospel to work with others instead of trying to succeed on my own. So I accepted the "slowness" of staying where I was instead of seeking escape. I refocused on winning people over to the idea rather than dismissing them for not understanding.

The project always belonged in God's hands, not mine. I needed to be obedient and choose to remain in unity, trusting God to bring fruit from the project in His timing. This was absolutely the right decision, and I can tell you that since then the Launchpad has grown and an amazing team has come around to support it. But even if this hadn't happened, unity was the right choice because it is God's design.

The alternative to ministering together is working alone. But that is not the example Jesus left for us. When Christ began His earthly ministry, He assembled a diverse team of disciples and welcomed many followers to work together with Him to further the mission. Certainly Jesus could have traveled faster and easier by Himself. Dinner and lodging for thirteen? That can be complicated! But Jesus modeled that the challenges of working with a team are an essential part of His plan.

To not collaborate is to cut oneself off from what is ours by design and deny ourselves the richness that is the Body of Christ. Working together in unity is absolutely necessary for the ministry God has called us to. Of course there are small problems we can solve on our own. But the big ones, we most certainly cannot. The Church is called to care for many people and needs. Everything from a single mom having enough money to support her family to religious freedom being available in every country and everything in between.

Some problems have a clear and simple solution, while others are so complex they feel impossible to answer. If our goal is to innovate in response to the biggest kingdom problems, we must collaborate. We will need to invite people in, hear them out, inspire them, and also learn from them. Transformational change is the work of the whole Church—the whole Body.

No one part can accomplish God's plan alone. There are many things that can't be done by one person, church, or organization. God knew that in advance. That's why He sent Jesus to die for *all* of us, so that *none* of us have an excuse to exclude anyone. Each of us has the same right and privilege to participate in God's work of being kingdom builders.

Messy though relationships and working together might be . . . it is the right messiness. It is the complexity we are supposed to be dealing with. It is a struggle to fight our pride and instead bring ourselves to God as a living sacrifice—choosing to lay down our desires, our hopes, and our hard work. But it is the right struggle because it aligns us with His perfect design for our lives.

Unity in the Global Church is our greatest source of innovation. If the only thing you ever do is to seek unity, that in itself would be an innovative step for the Church and worth your time and effort.

Jesus didn't leave behind a creed, He left behind a Church. We are a community of sinful people, saved by grace, who are empowered to show grace to each other daily. Living in unity is not just a nice idea, it is an active choice and a discipline we must practice.

Unity in the Global Church is our greatest source of innovation.

REACHING OUT YOUR HAND

When Christ died on the cross, God made a way to reconcile humanity to Himself. He reached out His hands to us far before we ever wanted to reach back to Him. This picture of an outstretched hand is powerful for our work as kingdom innovators. It reminds us to reflect God's generosity in our relationships. You reach out your hand all the time. When you meet someone new, you give them a handshake. You extend your hand when giving a gift or offering something. As you interact with others, consider: Are you reaching out your hand or pulling it back?

We all exist in a global network of relationships and connections that offer incredible opportunities for our ministries. But sometimes, organizations don't know how to access them. Ministries are most often hierarchies operating in a network world.

A hierarchy is a common structure you have encountered many times in your life. In a family, parents are in charge of their children. In a school, teachers lead students and a principal oversees the teachers. In a business, even the CEO reports to a board of directors. Whether you are in a large organization or a small team, there is some kind of power structure with someone at the top. That's what being in a hierarchy means.

This kind of structure is designed for efficiency and has clear lines of authority for managing people and decisions. You know based on your title or your responsibilities exactly where you fall in the hierarchy and who is above and below you.

Hierarchies are not the only way to get things done. Consider some of the memorable figures in history who brought great change: Martin Luther King Jr., Nelson Mandela, Martin Luther, and Mahatma Gandhi, to name a few.

These men were central to the Civil Rights movement in the United States, abolishing apartheid in South Africa, Europe's religious Reformation, and India's rejection of British colonialism. These heroes were not solely responsible for the transformational changes they are remembered for. They were leaders of movements whose words inspired and actions set an example.

But it was the collective impact of millions of individuals united by a common cause that changed the course of history.

A network of people is what can ultimately change institutions. Alone, it is almost impossible to directly affect a government, society, or organization. But many people collectively motivated can bring about incredible reform.[1]

The behaviors and results of change-making movements might seem mysterious. But it is actually something that has been extensively researched. The study of networks falls within a branch of mathematics called *graph theory*. Math cannot account for the spark that ignites a successful movement, but it can tell us how information and ideas will spread through that network and predict how it will behave and grow.

A network at its most basic level is a set of relationships. There are many terms to describe the parts of a network. For example, members are called *nodes*. A connected group of nodes is called a "cluster." Your "centrality" within the network refers to how often information flows through you as the shortest path between other nodes.

It is not essential for you to know all the terms, though you may find it interesting to study on your own. What is important are the implications of network theory for ministry and how they differ from how we usually operate.

Hierarchies accomplish work based on authority. *Networks* accomplish things based on influence. Hierarchies require people to be present (usually by paying them), but participation in a network is voluntary. For example, you are not paid to be someone's friend or to serve at church. You do those things of your own free will and can stop doing those things if you wish.

---

1 I learned so much about network theory from the book *Cascades* by Greg Satell and highly recommend it for further reading! Greg Satell, *Cascades: How to Create a Movement that Drives Transformational Change* (New York: McGraw Hill, 2019).

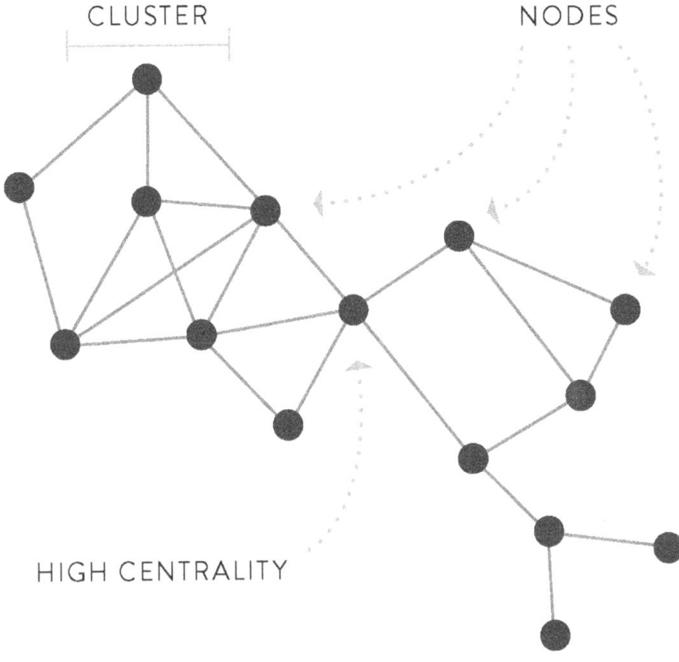

Networks feel very unstructured. Nobody is the boss, and no one can force you to participate. Instead, networks are built on the strength of relationships and influence is the currency. You gain influence by participating and by being connected to other parts of the network.

Networks are powerful because they are flat, unlike hierarchies. Your job title or position doesn't matter once you enter the network. Everyone has an equal chance to participate and build relationships and influence. You might be a small ministry, but you have the same access to the network and its resources that everyone else does.

Being a network influencer helps you be a better kingdom builder because it puts you into relationships with people and organizations you can partner with. When we try to do ministry by ourselves, it is hard to succeed. But if we are intentional about building genuine relationships and investing in others, they will be there with us—shoulder to shoulder—as we pursue our mission. Networks position us to collaborate for the sake of God's kingdom.

We may be tempted to approach networks thinking only of what we can get out of them. They represent real opportunities and benefits. But we must not participate selfishly.

It is the same as building any relationship in your life. It takes time and effort to be a good friend. You don't count the cost. What matters is being present and genuinely caring about people. It is the same in a network. Eventually the trust you've built turns into influence. You earn the right to guide the network's direction by speaking into the lives of the people within it.

We will become much more effective ministries when we recognize the realities of the network world and how to navigate it well. Otherwise, it's like being part of a game you don't know the rules to and don't even know you're playing.

You are probably part of more networks than you realize. There are connections between you and other people at your church, in your job, and even between you and me right now. Although we are in different places and might not have met, we would probably find we have many common relationships through our networks.

Christianity itself is a global movement we as believers are all a part of. Jesus didn't give us a handbook for spreading religious beliefs to non-Christians. Instead, He recruited disciples and left them with this command: "Go therefore and make disciples of all nations, baptizing them in the name of the Father and of the Son and of the Holy Spirit, teaching them to observe all that I have commanded you" (Matthew 28:19–20).

Jesus's master plan was to create a movement to spread the Gospel throughout the world. That is the work we are participating in. Your ministry has a specific way you are responding to Christ's Great Commission. Accomplishing that purpose will require you to activate people to recognize the problem you see and equip them to respond.

Creating and navigating networks is essential if we hope to see our ministry impact continue into the future. Will the change you are working towards last after you are gone? Or does your vision depend on you and end if you step away? These are challenging questions that should cause us to seriously examine our methods. We can work hard to do what God has called us to, but if we haven't invited others to share in that vision alongside us, it may not last.

Creating and navigating
networks is essential.

Jesus ensured His followers were trained and equipped so the work of disciple making would endure. Networks give us similar opportunities, and they are absolutely worth the investment. We can be better kingdom builders and better ministry innovators by participating in networks. We can create movements that build and sustain our mission. All we have to do is reach out.

THE BEAUTY OF COMPLEXITY

In her TED talk "Isolation Is Your Dream-Killer, Not Your Attitude," author Barbara Sher tells a powerful story of how dreams can come true. She was leading a conference event and asked if anyone in the audience had an impossible dream they would be willing to share.

A woman stood and said she had always wanted to go on a cruise, but had three reasons she could not go. The first was that she had no money and the second was that she had a daughter at home who needed full-time care. She had a third reason, but didn't want to share it.

Barbara asked if anyone in the audience might be able to help. A man stood up and ran to the front saying, "I just won a single cruise ticket, but my wife won't let me go by myself. You can have it." Then a nurse stood up and said, "I need to volunteer hours for community service, but I haven't found an opportunity yet this year. I could come and take care of your daughter."

Barbara then said to the woman with the dream: "Well, it looks like your first and second obstacles are taken care of, what was the third reason, the one you didn't want to say?" The woman shared that her daughter's ex-husband was stalking her and she needed to be home all the time to protect her daughter. A man in the back of the room says, "What's his name? I'm a cop."[2]

This shows what networks and relationships can accomplish. One of the greatest obstacles in ministry is that we often remain isolated from help that is all around us. People are naturally helpful when they hear of a need. I'm sure you can think of many times you have gone out of your way for someone, maybe even a stranger. When you put enough people together, their skills, connections, and resources can meet almost any need.

God intentionally puts us together in community for this very reason. The Church is designed to be a place where people care for the needs of each other. People come from different backgrounds and have jobs, knowledge, and skills that can all contribute to helping others. Amazing complexity is represented that can combine in countless ways to produce unique solutions to the challenges we face.

I've experienced the beauty of complexity at events called *hackathons* where software developers gather to design technology-focused

---

2 Barbara Sher, "Isolation Is Your Dream-Killer, Not Your Attitude," TEDx Prague 2015, *https://www.youtube.com/watch?v=H2rG4Dg6xyI*.

solutions to meet specific needs. Hackathons were not originally ministry events, but people began to use this model to solve kingdom problems.

Challenges presented at Christian hackathons might range from fighting human trafficking to using artificial intelligence to translate the Bible into every language. Small teams form around ideas and work intensely to develop solutions in just twenty-four to forty-eight hours. Prizes are offered for the best ideas.

At one hackathon I attended, I worked with a teacher who realized she could apply her research thesis about cross-grade learning to ministry. In response to the challenge of developing Scripture engagement solutions for children, our team worked on a cross-word puzzle game that incorporated peer-to-peer evangelism.

I might never have crossed paths with this teacher in my daily ministry work or learned about the effectiveness of older children teaching younger ones. The connection we made at the event led to partnership opportunities years later.

At hackathons, technology people, business people, and ministries are all represented. Imagine the amazing solutions that might emerge if we widened the circle even further. What ideas might artists, architects, writers, or nurses contribute? God's kingdom includes every profession and every skill set. But we don't always activate those people to help us in ministry.

Hackathons are examples of network theory in action. What I experienced working on those teams points to a very important principle: *diversity is the foundation for innovation.* We often believe only a few special people are gifted innovators. We think of those once-in-a-generation geniuses who create inventions that change the world. We call that innovation and admire it from a distance.

But the truth is that we are stronger and smarter operating in a network than we are as a lone genius. Innovation flourishes when we leverage our strengths in community.

A clear illustration of how diversity leads to innovation is global economics. Harvard professor Ricardo Hausmann studies the economies of nations and the network dynamics between them. Countries behave a lot like people. There are many countries in the world, and they're not all the same. Some seem smarter than others, are richer than others, or can do what others cannot. Some countries are able to innovate and solve huge problems, while others struggle to overcome basic challenges.

A few countries have been able to send people to outer space, while in other countries most citizens will never be able to afford traveling outside their nation's borders. But why is that? What makes one country's economy and potential so different from another's? The answer lies in diversity.

The countries who are most advanced have the most complex economies and the most diverse population in terms of knowledge and skills. This makes sense, of course. People who are farmers lack the technical skills and training to be airplane engineers. And if you're living in an agricultural society, you probably don't have specialized factories that produce jet engines and the parts needed to build airplanes. Instead, your country imports airplanes from a country that does produce them, and you export the food you grow in exchange.

Here's where it gets interesting, though. The countries that produce airplanes might seem unique. After all, they can build something that other countries can't. But it turns out that these countries don't just make airplanes. They also have farmers and fishermen and textile producers just like nations with simpler economies. In fact, the advanced countries do all the same things that primarily agricultural ones do.

The most innovative nations have the broadest range of activities represented in their economy. That diversity is the secret to their success. It is what allows them to build innovations like airplanes or Internet satellites or rockets to take their people to space.

Hausmann's work shows that when countries have lots of different industries, they can eventually produce something few others can. Interestingly, he also shows that there is a path of connections from one industry to the next.[3] It is difficult to jump from one area of knowledge to another without taking all the steps required in between. You can't go from farming directly to producing airplanes. But if you branch out and build up all the adjacent industries, eventually jets are inevitable.

The link between diversity and innovation is a universal principle that applies both to economics and to ministry. Innovation is not the work of an individual, but the result of diversity.

One person's skills are less important than how many different skills we have represented. You don't need one genius; you need lots of people with different knowledge and experiences that can combine in interesting ways.

Innovation is not the work of an individual, but the result of diversity.

Cross-connections between diverse areas create new potential for innovative solutions. The more pieces you have, the more combinations and solutions are possible. Innovation is less like assembling a puzzle and more like building with LEGO bricks. To make a puzzle, the pieces all fit together in one specific way to make the final picture. But with LEGO pieces, there are infinite combinations to make all sorts of different things using the same pieces. The key is having enough pieces to build what you are envisioning.

---

3 Ricardo Hausmann, "Ricardo Hausmann on Economic Complexity and Productive Knowledge," April 8, 2013, *https://www.youtube.com/watch?v=0JC24CBVsdo*.

Whether on your team or in your organization, diversity is what makes innovation thrive. If you find yourself lacking in some area, lean on your networks to find it. Being part of a network is better than being a genius.

By connecting people together, we create extraordinary potential. There are answers to our problems in industries very far from ministry and ideas hidden with people we might never expect. The solutions we need may have already been invented, and we just need to find and apply them.

The best news is that we are already part of the most diverse network in the world. God's kingdom is a nation without borders. It is a kingdom with every kind of person bringing their unique gifts and skills to serve God's mission. It is a network of billions.

The Global Church should be the greatest source of innovation the world has ever seen! We can accomplish *anything* as the Body of Christ. We have the diversity that is needed and God's kingdom values of unity and love to help us navigate the complexity of collaboration. So let's unlock this innovative potential and step fully into the network of the Global Church.

THE GREATEST COMMANDMENT

> *"Teacher, which is the greatest commandment in the Law?"*
>
> *Jesus replied: "'Love the Lord your God with all your heart and with all your soul and with all your mind.' This is the first and greatest commandment. And the second is like it: 'Love your neighbor as yourself.' All the Law and the Prophets hang on these two commandments."*
>
> *Matthew 22:36–40, NIV*

Jesus made one thing very clear: love is the only thing that is going to make any of this work. We can talk about network theory and the strength of collaboration and how nothing should be impossible for the Church. But when you look around at the churches in your community, that might not be the reality you see.

We're really good at building our own little kingdoms. We are always making an effort to distinguish ourselves from others, and in doing so we create distance and draw lines. We set up conflicts, take sides, and stand behind labels. Just look at how many denominations there are within Christianity.

Throughout history, Christians have been so divided about theology or religious practice that the only solution they could come up with was to start a new branch of their own religion! This is still happening today. Churches fall apart over disagreements, and people leave to follow a new leader. But this is not what God wants for His Body.

The Bible tells us to "aim for restoration, comfort one another, agree with one another, live in peace; and the God of love and peace will be with you" (2 Corinthians 13:11). Disunity damages our ability to live in community with each other and to share the Gospel with others.

OneHope, the international non-profit I work for, partners with the Global Church to reach the next generation with God's Word. We reach more than 100 million children and youth each year, and this work is only possible in a spirit of unity. To help us and our partners develop effective Scripture engagement programs, we conduct research. Our *Global Youth Culture* study[4] revealed some interesting insights on how the next generation views the Church.

From the inside, we know the Church can lack unity. But interestingly, from the outside we can be perceived as a united whole. As

---

4 *Global Youth Culture* surveyed 8,394 teens in 20 countries and 14 languages. Access the research at *globalyouthculture.net.*

part of the *Global Youth Culture* research, we conducted in-depth interviews with teens in the U.S. Some young people said they had no religion, don't believe God exists, and would not come to church even if invited. But this was not because God, religion, or the church were foreign to them.

Nearly all American teens we talked to had some experience of Christianity within their family or close community. But some didn't like what they saw. Some teens talked about Christians who were judgmental, pushy, and hypocritical. They said churches were uncomfortable and weird with everyone singing and doing the same thing at the same time.

Many teens viewed the Bible as a dusty old book that, at best, has nothing to do with life today and, at worst, is used to manipulate and brainwash people. Some saw religion as controlling and for the weak or stupid.

It was sad to hear what these teens thought of the Body of Christ. Some of them had been genuinely hurt by Christianity in the past and had reasons for why they wanted to stay away. What should our response be? Are we willing to own those hurts, even though we were not the ones at fault? Are we willing to apologize for those Christians who were judgmental and hypocritical? This is challenging!

It is hard to overcome a bad first impression. Research shows that it takes, on average, five positive interactions to make up for just one negative experience.[5] That takes time and effort! It means if someone has a poor experience at another church, they're going to need several great ones at your church to change their mind about Christians.

---

5   Research by Dr. John Gottman and Robert Levenson, cited by Kyle Benson, "The Magic Relationship Ratio, According to Science," The Gottman Institute, *https://www. gottman.com/blog/the-magic-relationship-ratio-according-science*.

Not only is this hard, it might seem unfair. After all, you were not personally at fault. Your church didn't misrepresent Christ. Yet we are one body. Christ calls us to love one another in the same way we love ourselves (Matthew 22:39).

We have a lot of grace for ourselves. We know we have good intentions and are doing our best. But when others mess up, we can be quick to blame and criticize. We distance ourselves so others won't think badly of us too.

We naturally assume the best of ourselves and too often assume the worst of others. I remember feeling offended when my wife and I changed to a different church and nobody followed up with us from our old congregation. Nobody asked why we left or checked in to see if we were okay. It felt like no one really knew us, even though we had felt very connected when we attended every Sunday.

After reflecting on the situation, I felt convicted realizing that I also had not followed up with anyone else in the church or checked in on anyone who went missing. I had been upset that no one called us, but realized I hadn't given my phone number to anyone or asked for theirs. It was as much my fault as anyone's.

It can be all too easy to avoid responsibility by blaming others. Sometimes, we might not even realize we are doing it. When I was upset at the church, I used words like "they," "them," and "their" fault. Just like that, I had created division with my words. I separated myself from my fellow believers and put them at a distance. I grouped them together, faceless and nameless, so I could put my hurt on them and walk away. This is just a small example of the disunity we can experience and create every day.

Disunity happens because we are human, and human relationships can be frustrating. You might feel disappointed by other people, but they might not even know you had expectations of them. Or you might be the person letting someone else down without being aware of it. That is why we need to take seriously Jesus's command to love one another.

Loving others means having grace-filled assumptions towards them, just like we have towards ourselves. It means believing the best about others and being quick to forgive even when they make mistakes. But this is only possible if we are loving God first.

Truly loving God with all our heart, mind, and soul is what puts everything into proper order. It is what enables us to lay down our rights, even our right to feel hurt and offended, and be able to respond in love and forgiveness instead. We won't always do this perfectly, but if we are allowing God to work in our lives, we at least have common ground to start from. As you and I actively strive to love God with our whole selves, it can't help but draw us closer together in relationship as we do so.

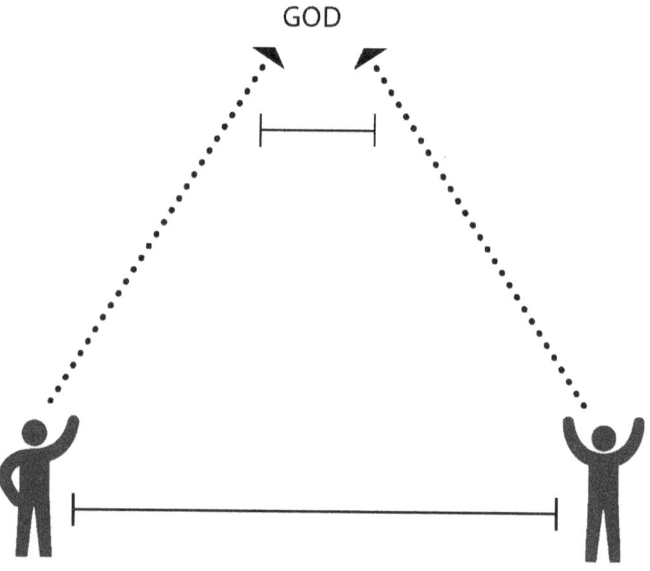

Loving others as we love ourselves also means not walking away from them. After all, you never give up on yourself, right? Even when you fail, you hope that next time you'll get it right. You need others to give you a second chance and support you in trying again. Believing in others is a critical piece of partnering well across God's kingdom. Oftentimes we know how to do this personally, but not so well organizationally.

Sometimes I ask my innovation students if they have ever experienced poor collaboration within the Church. Almost everyone has an example to share. Partnerships can start out with the best of intentions and great potential, but somewhere along the way they go horribly wrong. The process may be filled with disagreement, miscommunication, conflict in vision, and ultimately disappointment. The project doesn't turn out great, and no one wants to repeat the experience.

These kinds of situations may make us want to retreat and work alone. It is easier not to deal with other people and their messiness. But is walking away what Christ would want from us? Quitting on each other is not loving like Jesus says to love.

If you or your ministry find partnership difficult, I encourage you to reflect on why that is. What are the barriers that keep you from working with other ministries? Ask the Lord to reveal any pride, unforgiveness, feelings of fear, or competitive thinking.

Consider whether your posture and actions align with the Bible's picture of love. Even the Psalmist David had to honestly ask, "Search me, O God, and know my heart! Try me and know my thoughts!" (Psalm 139:23). Searching our hearts is not a one-time activity. We need the Holy Spirit to work in us daily because apart from Christ we do not have the ability to love one another the way God commands.

Ministry innovation thrives on collaboration because that is how God designed us. If you are not working as a unified part of the whole, you are depriving yourself of connections and resources God intends you to have. Similarly, you are withholding your own contributions from the kingdom. It is a loss in both directions.

We have access to so many skills, perspectives, and insights in the Body of Christ. You are part of the diversity required to come up with incredible solutions. What you bring to the Body is special and necessary. There are partners who need exactly what you have to offer to catapult their Gospel work forward. Similarly, others may have what you need to overcome a challenge or problem you face.

Love God's kingdom by bringing your whole self and your ministry to the Church. Reach out your hand in partnership. Be willing to serve and be served by others. Take your rightful place as part of Christ's Body. If you are an eye, help us to see. If you are an ear, help us to hear.

Above all, let us love one another and show a watching world that we are truly Christ's followers.

> *"A new commandment I give to you, that you love one another: just as I have loved you, you also are to love one another. By this all people will know that you are my disciples, if you have love for one another"*
>
> *John 13:34–35*

THE MAN WITH A VISION FOR THE SEA

A Poem

There was a man who dreamed of the sea.
He could swim farther than any could see
He loved the water like birds love the air
He swam like a fish, pulled kelp from his hair.
He stayed out from sunrise to golden sunset
Returning at dusk, dripping and wet.
But it was not the sea that drove him so far,
A dream of the other side pushed him so hard.
He was driven by purpose and wanted to cross
So he trained his body and grew strong as an ox
He was always forced to switch back and return,
He had no idea what he needed to learn.

He spoke to the Woodsman, his dearest old friend
Who traveled the forests from hillside to glen.
His church was the groves, his cathedrals of oak
He prayed and he walked and rarely he spoke.
"Far shores I must reach, to spread His Word,"
He studied his friend to see if he'd heard.
Nine words to share the dream that he sought,
Needing wisdom more precious than what can be bought.
Inspired, the Woodsman started to say
On top of the water, wood will stay.
Buoyant enough he could go all the way
Without straining his arms, swimming for days.
Dreamer tried—holding a log to help him swim
But it started to sink as the water soaked in.

Dreamer's brother, a Maker, a worker with wood,
He would do anything for Dreamer he could.
In his shop, he slept on his bench where he ate
His creations sprang forth, both simple and great.
Dreamer poured out his trials, now spoken anew,
Brothers have closeness shared only by few.
He told how he swam farther than ever before
But even with the log, he was forced back to shore.
Wood afloat was a new idea to Maker;
He thought he could work to make it greater.
The Maker and Woodsman started to plan
They might find a way to float far from the land.
They wanted Dreamer to find the far shore
They longed to learn if there could be more.
They worked out a plan to build him a boat
A vessel that Dreamer could sit in and float.

They chose all the wood, worked to make it all fit;
He wept in joy seeing where he would sit.
It carried him into the water it craved
It swam on its own, breaking the waves.
Dreamer set out in the new morning's dawn
Rowing much faster than ever he'd gone.
Double the distance was covered with haste,
But his thirst grew strong, sweat stung his face.
He was circled in saltwater with nothing to drink
His tired aching arms began now to sink
He steered back to shore; both a day and a night
Had passed since starting his passionate flight.

Once in sight of the shore, on the beach
Maker and Woodsman waited in reach.
They asked what he found, he said nothing yet;
The ocean kept going, past where the sun set.
The distance traveled grew longer and wider

His hopes flew high and his heart felt lighter
His failure was not a disheartening blow;
He knew his progress would continue to grow.
He needed water to go out to sea,
And he needed to carry a great quantity.

Solutions were lost, none could think what to say;
But a Child ran by with a pot made of clay.
The Child knew little of lost dreams that go cold
Old dreams that pile up as long years unfold
Dreamer bent down, a clay pot he now sought.
Can you take me to where one can be bought?
They ran to the Potter, a master with clay;
Child skipped and jumped each step of the way
The Potter was joyful and clay caked his hands
He was bold and imagined great faraway lands
Dreamer told Potter of his quest and his boat,
The long night rowing and his dry parched throat.

Potter's kiln glowed with fire and art
The Potter a craftsman, creative of heart.
The vessels were many, their tops open wide
The Potter knew they'd never keep water inside.
As the boat must rock on the distant tide
The water would spill whatever they tried.
Dreamer discouraged, was feeling unsure
The Maker arose, the dream must endure.
He spoke up and pulled out a box with a lid
Could they make a pot with the water all hid?
The splashing and spilling would then surely stop.
The Woodsman examined the jug and spoke up
Soon they were talking, hopes again running free,
A way to send Dreamer's water to sea.

After working all night, the man with the dream
Carried pots sealed tight, a gift from the team.
Pulling with all of his strength and then more
His friends gathered joyfully watching from shore
At night he grew thirsty, but water was sure;
At dawn he rowed on and drank water still pure
But his stomach cried out, it required much more
He turned back around returning to shore
After two days away, he was hungry and weak
His heart like a stone, his dream looking bleak.

Maker knew Farmer, whose heart was the best
The team went to see him to eat and to rest
Farmer used fables and sprinkled in stories
To keep them from sadness and wash away worries
Dreamer then told him his pain and woe,
How he worked and learned but still didn't go.
Farmer listened to all of Dreamer's sad tales
Hoping that he'd hear something of whales.

The Farmer piled food on a long wooden table
They ate as they planned and soon they felt able
The farmer was willing to send them with food
The joy and bright day brought a light mood.
But the meal was long, a great time it had run
And while talking the food had spoiled in the sun.
Exposed to the weather and harsh saltwater
They knew the food would need to last longer

Farmer was sure the food would stay
He was certain they could find a way
Whenever trouble had visited him
Always he had found a way to win
Potter stood up and said "I'm a fool!
I know exactly how to keep the food cool."

A strong box will keep the food dry
A straw lid for shade we can also try
A cool clay interior and strong woven lid
The food stuffed inside was protected and hid
From wind and rain on the long ocean run,
From salt and heat and the sting of the sun.

There on the beach, his five dear friends
Now all shared in his aspirations.
The Child came running, a kind little boy
Who had led them to Potter and filled them with joy
The mission that now so inspired them all
Together they'd overcome every pitfall.

After four days at sea, still nothing in sight
A tremendous storm blocked out all of the light
His boat carried high then pushed down low
He couldn't imagine how ever he'd row.
Dreamer's ship was torn, crushed under waves,
Wind blowing saltwater made land all he craved
Bedraggled and worn, swept up on the shore,
His weary muscles were exhausted and sore.
He wept aloud for the dream he had carried
His friends saw his dream now nearly buried.

A Girl then approached and said she could see
Clear his vision and his dreams of the sea.
She wore long garments of blue like the sky,
She seemed lifted by wind, as if she could fly
She too dreamed of something, not of the sea,
But flying and catching the wind and the breeze.
She studied the weather and knew all the clouds
And how to make use of the wind all around
Her vision soon lifted their spirits anew
She showed them her kites, how well they flew

Together the seven, their dreams soaring high,
Began building the dream that could fly.
They would glide on the water, pulled by wind,
Dreamer could see in his heart the far shore again.

She stitched them a sail she'd long waited to try;
Woodsman and Maker built a mast to the sky.
The Girl told of her father, an old Mason with stone,
He would look at the boat and let them all know
The Girl and the Mason didn't need to be told
They all dreamed the dream Dreamer did hold.
The story had traveled, twice heard and more,
Their hearts all longing for that distant shore.
Mason studied their boat and took Dreamer aside
I will line the center with stone inside
Your boat is too light it sits high in the water
You are in danger when you get in bad weather
The dream of the sea that had to be crossed
There could be no chance that the dream be lost.

A ninth man arrived, little boy's grandfather,
He heard from the Child, loved the endeavor.
He was a Wise man, soft-spoken and deep,
He knew the stars and the path they must keep
Wise grandfather's son, Child's own father,
Had scoffed at the dream, "Why would anyone bother?"
The Child sought his grandfather, "What do you know?"
The Wise grandfather said, "I wish I too could go."
Wise man and Child went down to the shore
They hoped they could help, do something more.

A tenth man joined, a joyous Musician
His lyrics and music flowed out as his mission
He sang and encouraged and jostled them all
With laughter as sweet as the honey in fall.

The vast sea he said is the best you can find
To inspire a poet from God's own mind
He'd go to encourage the man with the dream,
To bear him aloft on his songs like wings.
Bathed in music as the sail did whip,
They had built a vast and a tall sailing ship.

The vessel was stout and as tight as a jar
Now she was strong and could carry them far.
The Wise man said he would join the crew
To navigate routes and keep their course true.
He couldn't manage a sail or lift a great weight,
But his Wisdom would keep them all sailing straight.

Challenges had amounted to a great sum,
But every new trouble had been overcome.
Each new trade brought ideas they could see
Ways to cross the vast sea effortlessly
Their boat was complete, majestic, and strong
Using only the winds to push her along.
Three set sail to see the vision through
To find a far shore of wonder anew
Dreamer, Musician, and the Wise old man
Could surely unite to reach the far land.

After weeks away, farther than anyone knew,
The ship held fast and the wind pulled them true.
They followed the starlight, their spirits held high
'Til their food ran out and their water went dry.
Disappointed they turned once again for home
No hope remained now of continuing on
What else could they try, they had done all they could,
The sails, and the food, and the boat made of wood.
They had music and charts, weight, and a sail,

Yet obstacles always arose to make sure they'd fail.
Surely this was the end, with no way to prevail,
What was left now of the long-cherished tale?

But there on the shore they saw something new
A great many people instead of the few
Working together to accomplish much more
New workers, new skills, all worked on the shore.
Old troubles aside, problems being solved,
New teams working, new ships had evolved.
Dreamer never imagined this new undertaking
And wasn't involved in this vast wide making.
The Maker, Woodsman, the Potter, and Child,
The songs they had sung now rose in the crowd.

The Musician and the Wise man and Dreamer heard
Songs lifted high from the lines of God's Word.
A vast choir of voices, their hearts now on fire
The dream now their own and not feeling tired.
Working, they dreamed of the shore far away,
They carried their faith so the dream would stay.
Dreamer leaped to the shore his sorrow now past
He knew it was possible finally at last
They could reach the dream with so much help
He ran past every face with a shout and yelp
As each worker labored, their voices in song
They sang of the dream dreamt now for so long.

His dream was now theirs, their tasks not his.
His long-tired arms now lifted in bliss
Borne up by those whose faces shone
He no longer reached for his dream all alone.
Not all who heard the story had cared

Not all who heard the dream now shared
But those who could see had come to the shore.
Two faces now made Dreamer's heart soar.

The Child whose help had led to the Potter,
And the Girl who used wind to carry them farther.
The dream now ran faster than any oar's bend
The next generation would lead to the end
His Spirit, the wind. Our bodies, the clay.
The dream is the same as the disciples' way.

We carry the Gospel to each one's hands,
But only with many can we reach distant lands.
Swimming and dreaming, just one, all alone,
Can be like the weight of a cumbersome stone.
A vision you see, a dream you can share,
We can all join in and together get there.

• • •

> # Kingdom Builders look for ways to create connections to leverage the strength and diversity within the Body of Christ.

WHY WE MUST BE KINGDOM BUILDERS

» God established the Church to represent Christ to the world and has called each of us to His mission.

» As believers, we are united in our purpose and empowered by the Holy Spirit to collaborate in love.

» Innovation is not individual genius but the result of diversity focused on a shared goal.

» We have access to all the skills, resources, and people we need through our partnerships within the Global Church.

» Innovation is unlocked through the supernatural love and grace we reflect to others as we first embrace the Gospel in our own lives.

PRACTICE THE PERSPECTIVE

Reflect on a major success in your ministry and who was involved in accomplishing it. What were the critical skills, knowledge, or attitudes of the team? Now consider a current challenging project. What building blocks from your past success are present or missing? Whose perspective might help you overcome the barriers you face? Invite diverse opinions in a spirit of humble collaboration.

BROADEN YOUR PERSPECTIVE

Liam's book recommendations:

Cascades: How to Create a Movement that Drives Transformational Change. Greg Satell. New York: McGraw Hill, 2019.

Change Your World: How Anyone, Anywhere Can Make a Difference. John Maxwell and Rob Hoskins. New York: HaperCollins Leadership, 2021.

Mission Drift: The Unspoken Crisis Facing Leaders, Charities, and Churches. Peter Greer and Chris Horst. Bloomington, MN: Bethany House Publishers, 2014.

The Philosopher's Perspective

UNCOVER THE UNSEEN REALITIES
THAT AFFECT INNOVATION

THE SEED AND THE SHELL

A Parable

The great city stood atop a hill, a symbol of prosperity and safety with shining white walls visible for miles. People came from far and wide to buy and sell at its famous Grand Market, where it was said that everything in the world was available. You just needed to find it and have the right trade—for not all deals could be made with money.

Some things were very plentiful and some very rare, and others were simply one-of-a-kind. But everyone knew the market Master set the prices. The Master sat on an elevated platform in the center of the market. Each summer, one item would be declared one-of-a-kind and placed on a pedestal just in front of her seat.

People would come from all over to see and offer trades. The merchant to whom it belonged was kept secret so they could not be threatened or manipulated. They watched from the crowd as offers were placed in front of the Master to consider on the seller's behalf.

On the last day of summer an amber-colored wooden seed the size of a man's two fists clenched together was laid on the pedestal. The Master's clear voice called out:

"There was a tragic fire that destroyed an entire woodland. By pure chance, this is the only seed remaining of the Colossal Trees unique to those once ancient groves. It has value for two reasons: First, it is the key to regrowing those colossal trees, which may provide shade while living, lumber when cut down, and warmth when burnt.

Second, these seeds, legends say, are the most beautiful wood grain in all the world, supposedly radiant and glowing like a gem. Though all pieces have been lost, carvings and jewelry made from this could be worth more than you could spend in a dozen lifetimes! I call it the Heart of the Forest! Come and offer your trades!"

The first came forward, an ancient-looking man with the gnarled hands of a craftsman. He laid down a signed piece of paper. He spoke up to the Master, looking into her stern and impassive eyes, then around to the watching crowd.

"This is the deed to my shop and all my wares. I have mastered my trade. You all know me, everything I make is highly sought after. I have long dreamed of making a piece to be my legacy. I have more experience than any other here. I will offer everything I have ever made if I may have this chance to leave my unique mark on the world. It will be proof that I was here. I will write my name in history with this Heart of the Forest." The man stepped back to the crowd of watchers to see what else might be offered and to await the Master's decision.

The Master examined the deed, "A fine offer. Well received."

A second man stepped up with a confident step, strong and charismatic. He too placed a signed piece of paper before the master. He turned to face the crowd and said:

"This is a contract to provide 50 percent of the profits gained from my business. I grew up among the trees. I am a woodsman and I tend many acres of land to provide lumber for this city and many others. I will grow this seed and nurture a great forest that can again provide more of these wooden gems for us to reap the benefits in the future. I don't want my children to grow up in a world without its greatest trees growing upon it. This contract will provide wealth to you and future generations of your family, as well as to mine." He bowed theatrically before stepping down to return to the crowd.

The master reviewed the contract, "All is in order. A good offering."

Many others in the crowd offered fine treasures from across the land. Everything from vibrant silk cloth to rare perfumes, jewels, gold, and livestock were put forward as people sought the Heart of the Forest.

Finally, a small boy walked up to the platform with empty hands and sat down in front of the seed admiring it for à few moments. He looked up at the Master. "What caused the fire?" he asked.

The Master looked down at the boy, eyes narrowing slightly. "I do not know," she said.

"Do big trees burn that easily?" the boy asked. "What if someone used fire on purpose to make this seed more special? That would be mean…"

The crowd murmured unhappily at the idea of foul play. The Master replied, "I don't think we can know at this point."

The boy thought for a time before speaking again, "I guess not, but it seems important…" After another pause he asked, "How long does it take a seed to grow into a tree that produces more seeds?"

The Master replied again, "I do not know."

The boy turned to the woodsman. "Do you know? Have you ever grown one of these before?" he inquired.

The woodsman looked around, "Not that exact kind of tree…"

The boy innocently looked the woodsman in the eye, "How do you know you will be able to be wealthy by growing this into a forest? What if it takes fifty years before you get another seed to plant a second tree?"

The woodsman didn't have an answer and shifted from foot to foot uneasily. "I would hope it would go faster than that," he said.

The boy made a thoughtful *hmmm* noise and turned back to the Master, "Are we sure this is the last one? You said this was valuable for carving, what if some carver has a bunch in a bag somewhere that he hasn't carved yet?"

The Master smirked, "So far as we know, there isn't a 'bunch in a bag somewhere.'"

The boy looked over at the craftsman, "Have you ever carved something out of this stuff before?"

The craftsman stammered, "Well of course not. It's too rare. So . . . uh . . . I've never had the chance."

"You're willing to give up all you own? How do you know you can?" asked the boy. "Will your normal tools work? Master said this stuff was special, but what if you can't work it and accidentally destroy it?"

The old craftsman seemed at a loss for words. "I . . . I mean, I've worked all kinds of things! I'm the best there is. I wouldn't *mess it up*," he said, sneering.

"If you say so," the boy replied cheerily. The crowd murmured anxiously behind him, wondering at all his questions.

The boy went back to gazing at the seed and finally said, "It sure is pretty though. I don't know as much as you all do about a lot of things, but..." he gestured to the luxurious offerings that had been laid before the Master. "I don't know if it's worth all this."

He reached into his bag and pulled out a large mother-of-pearl shell with curves that glistened a multitude of rainbow colors. It gleamed in the light, but it was far from one-of-a-kind.

"I'd trade this shell I love for it; it's the prettiest thing I've got," the boy said. "I've carried it around for years, but it's not much good except for staring at."

A few people laughed as he set the worthless shell next to the other things and started to head back to the crowd.

Just before he reached the edge, the master's voice called out, "Deal!" and everyone gasped. A few people started to shout and talk amongst themselves, until the Master's commanding voice rang out above the noise.

Quietly, she directed her words to the boy, though everyone could hear as they listened intently. "Your questions are those of one who thinks before acting. None of us know the answers to your questions, but none of us thought to ask them besides you," she said gravely.

"With this spirit, you are my choice. I believe you have a better chance to make full use of the seed than those who moved blindly on past experience. You at least understand its beauty and will not destroy it or bury it in haste or greed. Perhaps you may decide to plant it someday or to become a crafts-man and make something of it. You are still young. Whether you try and fail, I believe you would undertake it with more care and would learn more from that failure than anyone else here who might have tried. And I pray someday your wisdom will lead us."

Raising her voice aloud she stated officiously, "To this boy, who more truly understood the value of this than the rest of us and has offered a fair trade, neither too high nor too low, the deal is made. Boy, come and collect your prize. Your offer is accepted."

The boy beamed as he picked up the seed that might not be workable to even the most expert craftsman. The seed that might not be growable or profitable to an able woodsman. The seed that might not even have been the last of its kind. Those unanswered questions added nothing to its value, but it was unquestionably beautiful to look at.

He placed it gently in his bag where the shell had once been and was glad he always asked questions about things he didn't know very much about.

. . .

THE PHILOSOPHER'S PERSPECTIVE

*"Judge a man by his questions
rather than his answers."*

—Voltaire, French philosopher

I took a career assessment in high school to understand what potential jobs would be a good fit for my personality and aptitudes. One of the top recommendations was "philosopher."

I was mystified. Who hires philosophers? What do they do? How do they get paid? To this day, I have still never seen a job listing for "Philosopher" or "recommended experience: five years in philosophy or a related field." Turns out, any one of us can be a philosopher wherever we are and whatever we are doing. A philosopher is someone who studies the world and asks questions in pursuit of knowledge.

The word *philosophy* comes from the Greek words *philo* (love) and *sophos* (wisdom). The definition is simple: someone who loves wisdom. Because of this, philosophers look at the world differently. They don't just accept something because it has always been that way. They want to make sense of the world, find truth, and discover connections and patterns. They want to think rightly and understand how things really work underneath the surface. They want to be wise.

Sometimes philosophers are seen as lofty and maybe a little useless. But I believe having a philosopher's perspective is really about being curious and humble. As we work to be ministry innovators, we need to be curious. We need to run after truth and be willing to ask questions even if we don't like the answers.

What worked for us yesterday might not work the same way tomorrow. We need to humbly explore the new and be willing to discard the old if it is not working well. Our innovation work should always stay faithful to the mission of our organizations, but there is a constant need to update our methods. Asking the right questions is key to this process.

When I first started on the Innovation Team at OneHope, I had a desire to solve all of the organization's problems. I wanted to make everything I touched better. So I tackled every project I was given and even sought to understand problems I was not assigned to think about. I worked hard to improve things, and that was useful in its own way.

But over the years, I've come to understand that one person working alone towards solutions does not change an entire organization. Many of the things I was problem-solving were results of problems I could not see.

Sometimes I was frustrated when solutions I proposed were not adopted. I often did not understand how they might affect other teams or other parts of the ministry. I didn't realize I was operating within a system with its own design and constraints. I was one small piece of a much larger organization, and my efforts did not always touch or change the whole. Now my goal is to make the organization itself better at solving problems. I don't want to be the only one thinking about innovation; I hope everyone becomes more innovative within their area of responsibility.

There is always more to a problem than the problem itself. Many factors shape our organizations. There is a whole structure and history behind our ministries that make them function the way they do. That history and those structures affect what we will be able to do today and into the future.

Systems thinking is the discipline that helps us understand those structures. It unlocks a new set of tools for us as ministry innovators, helping us see beyond the immediate problems we face to solutions that will solve those *types* of problems before they happen.

There is always more to a problem than the problem itself.

Remember the definition of philosophy: the love of wisdom. Wisdom is typically associated with the old and innovation with the new. The truth is that we need both.

We need to be wise innovators who learn from the old and respond to the new. We need to throw ourselves into doing the work that is in front of us today as well as step back to consider and improve *how* we work. Why are we focused on these problems and solving them in these ways? How did we get here and where are we going? Seeing in both directions is difficult and can create tension in our work. But the philosopher embraces these challenges.

I want to encourage you that even as the world changes, the Gospel's truths are timeless. We have the hope the world needs to hear, and the most important thing we can do is love God and one another with all our hearts and love the wisdom of His Word. He will provide what we need, and He will water the seeds of innovation that we plant in His perfect timing.

> *"If any of you lacks wisdom, let him ask God, who gives generously to all without reproach, and it will be given him."*
>
> *James 1:5*

UNSEEN PROBLEMS

Questions are powerful. They spark curiosity and discovery. They are the foundation of conversations that deepen our understanding and relationships. Children ask questions constantly. I saw this one day between my friend and his six-year-old son Cason. Cason is at the age where he loves anything mechanical. That Saturday we were at a local park near an airport. Cason pointed excitedly towards the runway and said:

"Look dad! That plane is going to take off!"

"Yeah, that looks like a military plane, doesn't it?" his dad replied.

"What's a military plane?" Cason asked.

"A plane that has guns on it," his dad said automatically.

"Why does it have guns on it?" Cason inquired.

"Sometimes planes need to shoot down other planes," his dad said.

"Why would a plane need to shoot down another plane?" asked Cason.

"Like if we were at war," said his dad patiently.

"What's war?"

I had to try hard not to laugh. The conversation that started out so innocently had devolved so quickly. How do you explain war to a six-year-old? With just a few questions, Cason had taken us from airplanes to the heart of human conflict.

"We'll talk about it later," his dad said helplessly in an effort to end the conversation. With any luck, Cason would forget about the unanswered question, distracted by all the other things he would want to know later.

Asking questions is an effective way to learn. Children do this naturally. They're curious and have fewer boundaries than we do as adults. They'll ask as many questions as we'll answer! But as we get older, we tend to question less. There are still many things we don't know about the world, but we lose the practice of questioning as freely as when we were children. This has been studied and documented. At thirteen years of age, we ask half the number of questions we asked at age four. By the age of eighteen, we are down to a quarter of the number.[6] There are many reasons for this.

CHILDREN ASKING QUESTIONS

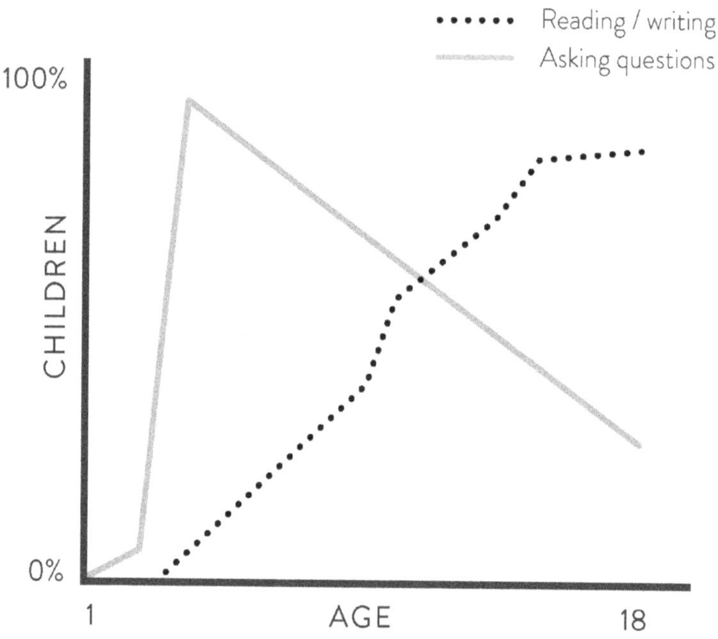

Educational systems tend to focus on teaching facts and formulas in preparation for taking standardized tests. Children are asked to memorize, not ask questions. Asking their teacher "Why?" or "How do you know?" can be seen as disrespectful behavior. We quickly start to self-regulate and hold back our questions. We

---

6 This fact came from Warren Berger, *A More Beautiful Question: The Power of Inquiry to Spark Breakthrough Ideas* (New York: Bloomsbury, 2014), 44.

stop asking because we don't want to be seen as stupid or uninformed. I'm sure you can think of a time when you didn't know something but pretended that you did. It's easier to nod along than to admit you have no idea what someone is talking about. It takes humility to ask questions.

It also takes effort and awareness to question. We tend to accept things the way they are without examining how they came to be that way. We work within systems every day and we even create them for ourselves and others. But rarely, if ever, do we stop to evaluate the systems we are in and whether or not they are well designed to suit the problems we face. Even more rarely do we examine how those systems came about in the first place, how they have evolved and changed, or remained static despite the changes in the world around us.

Inventor Albert Einstein wisely said: "The significant problems we face cannot be solved with the same level of thinking we were at when we created them."[7] In other words, if we are to improve the world, we first need to improve the way we think.

So how do we typically think? We ask ourselves and our teams, "What is important to do today?" In response, we make lists, we schedule meetings, and we do all the countless activities that help us move our work forward.

We imagine that to make things better we need to work as fast and as hard as we can every day in our predetermined directions. This is how we naturally operate, and it is not necessarily wrong. It is just incomplete. This way of thinking helps us solve immediate problems in the short-term, but it does not point us towards the complex problems that need long-term solutions. In other words, we can be constantly putting out fires without realizing we keep handing out matches.

---

7 Albert Einstein, quoted by David Peter Stroh, *Systems Thinking for Social Change: A Practical Guide to Solving Complex Problems, Avoiding Unintended Consequences, and Achieving Lasting Results* (White River Junction, VT: Chelsea Green, 2015), 4.

In order to truly solve a problem, we need to identify all the related aspects that are contributing to it. We need to examine the causes and effects at work in the systems around it.

Systems thinking is a way of understanding the world as deeply interconnected and taking time to analyze the relationships, rules, and processes in play that we might otherwise not see. Systems thinking helps us see past the urgent, everyday problems to the issues that lie at the heart of our work.

This way of thinking is uniquely suited to addressing chronic, complex social problems.[8] It is always more effective to cure the disease rather than keep treating the symptoms. This is the different level of thinking Einstein was referring to. Understanding systems can be transformational in the way we view the world and our ministry.

Let's look at a few examples. Consider homelessness, which is one of the case studies in the book *Systems Thinking for Social Change* by David Peter Stroh. There are many homeless people in cities all across the globe, and there are many organizations and government programs dedicated to helping homeless people. But the problem seems to persist. Homeless shelters provide a safe, warm place for people to sleep at night, and city governments help fund these shelters. However, the funds are often sent in response to the number of beds filled. This is intuitive on one level. Expenses increase along with the number of people who need shelter.

However, there is an unintended consequence to this system's design. It rewards shelters for filling beds, rather than focusing on helping people break the cycle of homelessness. These shelters meet the urgent need for a night's sleep, but they do not address the root causes of homelessness. The underlying issues are complex and difficult: lack of available employment; affordable education

---

8 Stroh, *Systems Thinking for Social Change*, 15.

or job training; assistance for mental health issues; and more. The needs go far beyond housing. Being homeless is often the symptom of some other problem. Despite everyone's best intentions and efforts, the cycle continues. City governments fund homeless shelters run by men and women who work tirelessly, yet people remain on the streets because the conditions creating homelessness remain untouched.

Ending homelessness requires a different kind of thinking and a different kind of work. Many of those who are involved may already be too overwhelmed by their existing work. Complex problems, such as the homeless crisis, require many organizations working together to transform the larger system.

It is the same in ministry. We can get so focused on the problem in front of us that we fail to see how other issues are impacting the situation. If we don't understand the systems at work, it's possible we are doing things ultimately counterproductive to our goals.

Since you will likely never experience homelessness, let's look at an example we probably all face—traffic. As with homelessness, slow traffic is both a problem itself and a symptom of the system designed around transportation. There are too many people on the road at the same time and not enough space to move them from one place to another as fast as we would like. Traffic wouldn't exist if so many people didn't have cars and motorbikes. Yet being able to produce vehicles affordably enough that so many people can have one was a huge innovation.

Henry Ford was the American inventor of the first mass-produced car. The Model-T was entirely new, taking people from the most common mode of transportation—a horse—to something totally foreign—a personal driving machine. Cars don't need to be fed and cared for in the same way as horses, and they are better suited to big cities where there is not enough space for pastures and stables. It took significant resources to engineer a way to mass-produce cars. But Ford showed that if you are willing to invest in long-term solutions, you might come up with the next big thing. It would have been far easier to start with the current solution of the day—horses—and try to improve those in the short-term. Perhaps Ford could have made more comfortable saddles, expanded ranches to breed more horses, or built bigger stables in cities. Instead he invented something that made horses no longer necessary for transportation.

Ford saw the challenge of transportation as an opportunity, and we are still benefiting from his innovation today. But now we are facing new challenges created by cars such as traffic delays, pollution, and accidents. Ford could never have anticipated the systemic problems that would arise because his solution became so popular. Traffic became a problem as a result of cars being a solution. The problems we faced yesterday will not be the problems we will face tomorrow. Systems that worked in the past will not work in the same way in the future.

The philosopher's perspective teaches us to ask the right questions. We must question the systems we are a part of. Don't assume it is someone else's job to ask these questions. As ministry innovators, it is our responsibility to understand the world around us and how our solutions fit into that world. The systems we work within or design for others may turn out to be deeply flawed or have unintended consequences. We should be willing to change those systems if needed. We need to look past the immediate problems and do the harder work of discerning how those problems arose in the first place. Fixing root causes is more difficult than treating symptoms, but ultimately it is much more effective.

> # Fixing root causes is more difficult than treating symptoms, but ultimately it is more effective.

Managing short-term priorities and long-term goals creates tension for most ministries. There are many pressures to perform and show results. There is work to do and goals to meet.

But if we only think about getting today's work done, we may miss out on accomplishing our mission in the long-term. This is why systems thinking is so important. Remember, systems thinking helps us address long-term, complex, social problems. That is the work of every ministry everywhere. We're addressing complex situations involving people faced with the chronic problem of sin.

The ultimate answer lies in the Gospel and what Christ has accomplished for us on the cross. God's system for redemption is the greatest truth we can ever communicate, and we need to ensure we are communicating it in the best possible way.

So next time you don't understand something, be willing to ask a question. How did we come to this decision? Why are we doing this? What are the consequences if we're wrong? Practice being a philosopher and you might be surprised by how much you will discover to help you innovate.

THE SYSTEMS WE INHABIT

I remember my mom giving me advice about how to succeed in school when I was young. She told me to give my teachers the answers they wanted to hear, rather than what I thought was the right answer. She was essentially telling me I had to play along with the system. This turned out to be good advice that helped me navigate many years in school systems. Systems thinking might be a new concept to you, but systems themselves certainly are not. We operate within them every day and have since we were children.

Systems tend to fade into the background of our lives. We often don't stop to examine them closely unless there is a problem that makes them visible, like an economic system collapsing, or a revolution overthrowing a government. But it is a good idea to understand the systems we live and work within because they directly impact what we are able to do. Some businesses and ministries lead incredible innovation while others struggle to even implement small changes. What makes the difference? Many aspects contribute to innovation's success or failure. One element we often overlook is the system we are in. Every new idea enters an existing system with factors that either help it thrive, or slow and even kill its growth.

Every new idea enters an existing system.

I am not a mechanic, but for some reason every time I have a problem with my car, I open the hood and look at the engine as if I might be able to figure out what's wrong. My wife then tells me just to take the car to the repair shop because I am a ministry innovator, not a mechanic.

Engines are a great metaphor for our organizations. Like with engines, ministries are intricate and complex. We have many interconnected people, projects, and activities that must all work together smoothly. A slowdown or breakdown in one area may significantly affect the rest of the machine.

Engines are built with a specific purpose. Car engines provide torque to turn the wheels, keeping the vehicle moving forward. To lift the car in the air would require a different kind of engine. "Systems are perfectly designed to achieve the results they are currently achieving," writes David Peter Stroh.[9] If you are unhappy with the results you are achieving as a ministry, it's time to look under the hood and see what the problem might be. You need to carefully examine your system and how the people, projects,

---

9 Stroh, *Systems Thinking for Social Change*, 5.

and activities in it all fit together. We are going to examine four elements of your organizational system to consider and adjust if needed.

Size: Can you fit everyone at the table?

Think back to the early days of your ministry. How many people were on your team? Was it just you and a few others? Maybe it was just you for a long time until God brought someone else to share your vision. Any organization or business typically starts small. No real structure is possible when there are not enough people to form teams, departments, etc. The founder and their team do everything.

I experienced this when I helped plant a church one summer during college. I was one of two interns and, together with the head pastor, we were the construction crew, A/V team, social media specialists, web developers, greeters, kitchen staff, janitors, and every other position.

As we prepared for opening weekend, the pastor's wife scrubbed the bathrooms and restocked the toilet paper. No one was too important for even the smallest of tasks. We all worked hard to get the job done. In a startup environment like this roles are more general, rather than highly specialized. Everyone is involved in everything.

Being small can have advantages. For example, when I started teaching an online course on innovation, I personally led every cohort for the first two years. I was the content designer, teacher, web developer, and champion. Any problems that came up, I heard about directly and fixed quickly. If the course had been run by a larger team, this reality would have looked very different. We would have needed time meeting to discuss the problem, the right people with the appropriate skills to help, and approvals to spend time and money to make changes. The larger the team, the more friction—things that slow our ability to take action.

With fewer people, you can move faster. Decisions can be made and acted on quickly. Communication is easier because everyone knows everyone. In a small team, like my team of one, everyone is usually highly engaged because they are close to the work, directly interacting with the audience.

Innovation tends to thrive in these sorts of environments because there are few constraints. If you want to try a new idea, no one is standing in your way. If there is a problem, you can fix it in whatever way you choose. This energy and momentum are part of what make startups exciting. There is freedom to experiment.

However, being small also has disadvantages. You don't have many people to share the work, so capacity is limited. You might lack time or funding to carry out your vision. Startups are uncertain. You don't have a guarantee your ministry will be around tomorrow. Established organizations offer real benefits. They have money, people, and processes to carry out the work. They have a history of success, along with the connections and reputation that come with success. They have economies of scale, where things become less expensive as they grow.

Large organizations can do more, but they also move slower. They are not able to adapt to change as quickly as a smaller team. Because large organizations have more departments, regional divisions, team leaders, etc., decision-making is complex and takes more time. Rather than everyone being on the front lines, some are further from direct ministry work. It is similar to a restaurant where the cook in the back doesn't get to see the smile on the customer's face when they eat. As a result of distance like this, people may have difficulty seeing the significance of their personal contributions.

This is not to say large organizations are bad and small ones are good. They are just very different. It is important to be aware of your ministry's size and the impact that has on your culture and work. There is a shift within an organization as soon as your team gets so large that you can no longer fit around one table. Sitting at one table means everyone is involved in the same conversation. You can talk, share opinions, and figure out what needs to happen together as one group. Everyone at the table is empowered to go out and do the work because there is no one else to do it.

When you can no longer fit your team at one table, the dynamics of your system change. There are now insiders and outsiders—those who are at the table (decision-makers) and those who carry out the work once decisions have been made. More meetings are needed because information has to be repeated and relayed throughout the team. It can take a while to get everyone headed in the same direction. But once you do, you benefit from the tremendous weight of the organization. It is difficult to stop a heavy object once it gets moving. The momentum becomes nearly unstoppable as large organizations direct their resources and people to accomplish their goals.

When you can no longer fit your team at one table, the dynamics change.

Growth in an organization typically happens slowly over time, so we don't always notice its effects right away. But if you really look and listen, you can see and hear the changes that have occurred.

Business consultants James Allen and Chris Zook studied the way businesses start and grow, along with what is gained and lost on the way. Their book, *The Founder's Mentality*, calls small organizations "insurgent" because they have high ownership and engagement. The founder of the organization is usually directly involved in the work and leading the team personally. In contrast, the book calls large organizations "incumbent"—a term usually referring to an established leader.[10] Incumbent organizations have grown to the point where people must work through complex processes, rules, and bureaucracy. While those things slow them down, they also allow the organization to specialize and be efficient at what they do. Your organization is probably incumbent if it feels like a victory simply to get alignment about what needs to be done.

Both insurgent and incumbent organizations have strengths and weaknesses. But there is a trend that happens as organizations grow: they tend to lose a way of thinking they had in the beginning. A founder's mentality carries with it the original inspiration and passion from the organization's start. It drives the creativity and initiative of being close to the work.

The good news is that organizations can learn to reclaim their founder's mentality through intentional system design and culture building. Organizations that can maintain this mindset while still achieving benefits of scale are set up well for success.[11]

Pace: How fast do you want to go?

Growth sometimes happens slowly and silently. Other times, it is something you deliberately pursue. Pace is another variable to consider within your system. Pace does not mean how fast everyone works, but rather it describes the kind of growth you seek. How quickly do you want your organization to expand?

You might hear the word "scale" being used to describe ministry: "We want to scale that program," or, "Our church has really scaled up our children's ministry." People tend to use the word *scale* in the same way they use the word *grow*. But it is important

---

10   Chris Zook and James Allen, *The Founder's Mentality: How to Overcome the Predictable Crises of Growth* (Boston: Harvard Business Review Press, 2016).

11   There is no simple, how-to guide to reclaim the founder's mentality, because every organization is different. However, the concepts in this chapter as well as "The Culture Maker's Perspective" should help.

to define these terms separately and use them distinctly because they are not the same.

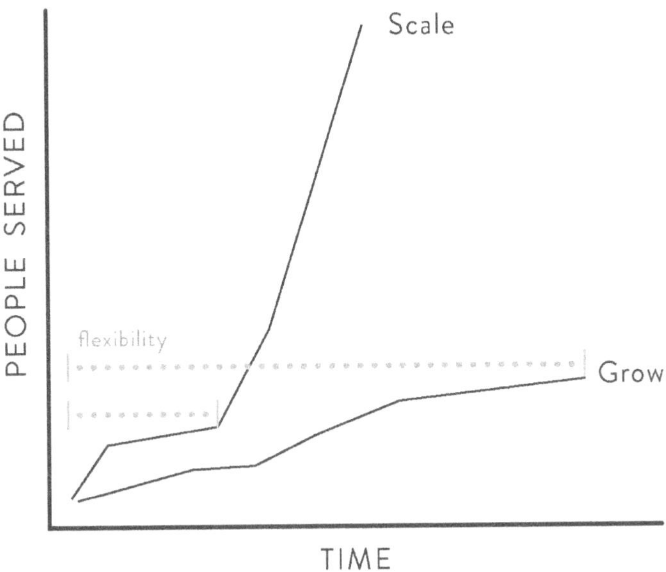

Let's look at the example of a bakery to illustrate how growth and scale are different. You might open a bakery because you love baking. You want to try new recipes and share them with the world. The bakery makes enough money to support you and the small team that helps run the business.

You focus on doing a good job and things continue to grow naturally. Growth is the more general term that describes gradually improving the reach of your organization. It is usually the natural result of ethical people working hard. You can expect a well-run business, church, or ministry to grow as it serves people well.

On the other hand, scale would be aiming to create the next Starbucks, but for bread. Your goal is to be the number one bread provider in every city globally. You need to optimize your bakeries, secure supply lines, train large teams, and ensure quality control.

Scale is a specific kind of growth where the primary goal is to reach the maximum number of people as quickly as possible. As ministries, it is obvious why we would want to scale: we desire to reach as many people with the Gospel as we can! Scale is a pace you can adopt that is aggressive and strategic. But scaling also has tradeoffs. It requires different ways of thinking.

"There is only one valid strategy for a startup: *stop being one*," writes author Les McKeown in his book *Do/Scale*.[12] In other words, A startup's goal is to stop being a startup as quickly as possible. Being small and nimble is great, but startups are usually dependent on outside resources and haven't found a profitable business model yet. They have promising ideas but are still unproven and can go out of business very quickly.

We tend to glorify startups because of companies like Google and Facebook with humble origin stories of starting in someone's garage. But in reality, 90 percent of startups fail.[13]

Businesses aiming to scale often look for a new CEO to replace their original founder. The person who started the business is usually not the right kind of person to pursue scale. Founders tend to be creative, big-picture visionaries who love new endeavors and are willing to take big risks.

In contrast, CEOs who scale businesses are the kinds of leaders who create great systems and processes. They are excellent at finding and fixing inefficiencies to produce faster, more consistent results. Founders may quickly become bored at an organization that is pursuing scale, while scaling leaders will struggle in a business that is always changing directions and trying new things.

---

12 Les McKeown, *Do/Scale: A Road Map to Growing a Remarkable Company* (London: The Do Book Company, 2019), 49.

13 There is no one authoritative source for this statistic, but you can Google it for yourself and find it is an agreed-upon estimate based on the available data on business failure rates.

Pace both affects leadership and places constraints on innovation. A growth-minded organization is typically strong in the area of creativity. It harnesses new ideas and ways of doing things as it seeks new people to reach. Innovation in this context is usually called "blue sky" because it describes brainstorming with no limitations.

Blue sky innovation focuses on possibilities rather than constraints. Teams might try new products or strategies simply to find out if they work. The organization might experiment without a clear goal or return on investment before finding a successful idea. This is often the kind of work we associate with innovation. We picture boundless creativity and inventing things the world has not yet seen. However, that is not the only type of innovation.

Scaling organizations also embrace innovation, but for a different purpose. Innovation at these organizations is focused on solving the problems that slow down work. This is sometimes called "process innovation." Scaling organizations look for solutions that make them more efficient. Anything that helps them go faster or save time and money is welcomed. "Blue sky" innovation—ideas without a clear purpose—don't tend to thrive in this environment. Instead, this kind of thinking is seen as a distraction.

To scale successfully, organizations must maintain a single-minded focus on reaching their goals and avoid straying off the path they have set. Innovation in this environment must be action-oriented and produce visible results.

Considering your system's pace clarifies what innovation can and cannot do for your ministry. We often want to have it all. We want to try creative new things *and* we want to scale them to reach millions of people. We want the energy and freedom of a startup, but we also want the people and resources of a larger organization. These goals pull us in different directions and can bring real tension to our work. It is difficult to do both because they are fundamentally different.

As a ministry innovator you may find you are more comfortable in one environment over the other. If you find yourself feeling frustrated in your work, consider your organization's pace and how that affects your ability to innovate. It is possible that your organization might not have clarity and unity about its pace. This can result in growing pains and frustration as teams pursue different strategies for accomplishing their goals.

Pace is a helpful term to introduce to organizational conversations. Size and pace are critical aspects of our system's design that we can be aware of and change. They are conscious choices for our ministries that both open opportunities and place limitations on what we can do.

Span of Control: Do you want to be flat or tall?

When I first started working at OneHope, I had much to learn. One thing people kept telling me was that we were a "flat" organization. For a long time I had no idea what that meant.

"Flatness" is an aspect of an organization's design. It is a way of describing *span of control*—another term I had to learn. Now I know it refers to how many levels are between me and the president of our ministry. Because we are flat, there are only a few people in the hierarchy between the president and anyone in our ministry. We call this being flat, but others refer to it as being wide.[14]

In contrast, an organization with lots of hierarchy might be called "tall." Tall organizations have lots of middle managers. Everyone has a boss, and that boss has a boss, who has a boss, and there are many steps between the top and the bottom. Both are valid ways of structuring your ministry, they are just very different and offer different benefits and drawbacks.

---

14 This definition is taken from the book *Loonshots* by Safi Bahcall. It is a great read with lots of interesting and memorable stories of innovation in practice. Safi Bahcall, *Loonshots: How to Nurture the Crazy Ideas That Win Wars, Cure Diseases, and Transform Industries* (New York: St. Martin's Press, 2019).

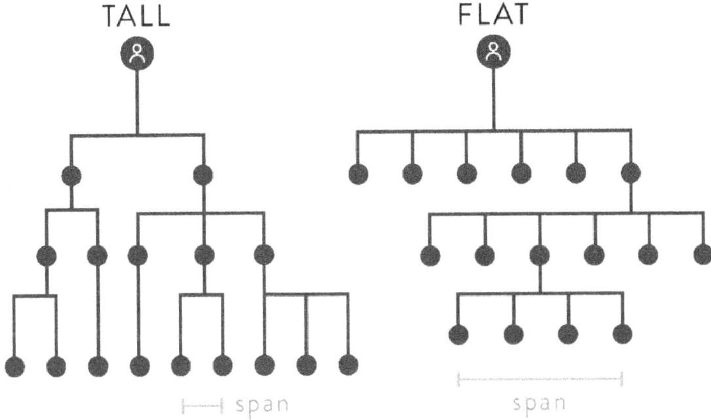

To see how flat or tall your organization is, think about the average number of team members who report to the same leader. Wide organizations have a lot of workers who report to just a few leaders. Tall organizations have more leaders and managers with fewer direct reports for each.

Your organization's span of control is another aspect you can fine-tune about your system. It impacts many things including communication, team member engagement, efficiency, and of course, innovation.

In a flat organization, ideas and requests can reach the top quickly. Communication is more direct, rather than being passed through many messengers. Because more people are equals, they tend to feel more comfortable talking to one another and seeking help or ideas. This has a significant effect on encouraging creative innovation. Anyone can have an idea and rally people around it. Team members have the freedom to try things more quickly without needing to go through a lengthy approval process.

Innovations can hatch informally and be nurtured to see if there is value before taking them further. People are closer to the work and to the audiences they are trying to serve, which can help them take a high level of ownership over their tasks.

A flat organization in essence is like a sports team. Imagine your favorite sports team coming together on the field. The coach is the leader of the team, and there might be a team captain, but all of the players on the field are equal with one another. Some may have been on the team longer, but for the most part, everyone is on the same level. The team works together to score points, nobody pauses to ask what to do because everyone knows the rules and is empowered to take action when they get the ball.

It might seem like wide organizations have everything going for them. But the truth is that it can become increasingly complex and confusing to be flat as your organization grows. Structure is beneficial for organizing large numbers of people and their work.

Tall organizations have a high level of control, particularly when it comes to decision making. People are empowered to make decisions over their area of responsibility at each level of management. This helps clarify communication and avoids contradicting messages. There is a clear path up and down the hierarchy, not only for information but for people.

Many people find they thrive working within clearly defined boundaries. In addition, tall organizations offer the possibility for promotion, increased leadership, and responsibility. This can be a very motivating incentive for people and help them want to stay and grow within your organization over many years.

Tall organizations are more like a factory than a sports team—people are specialized and do specific tasks efficiently. Imagine an assembly line that puts together cars. There are teams of designers and engineers who design the vehicles, fabricators who produce specialized parts, welders who join large components, and mechanics who assemble the engine. The focus on efficiency and specialization allows the factory to produce hundreds of vehicles a day. An unstructured sports team would find this task impossible.

New ideas move differently through a flat sports team versus a tall factory. If a welder wanted to make a design change to the car, it would probably be a long process to get the engineers and designers to consider his suggestion. But if it were approved, the change could be incorporated into thousands of cars to improve each one. In a sports team, when someone has an idea for a creative play, they just mention it to their teammates and try it the next time they have an opportunity. But too much freedom can easily lead to confusion and miscommunication on the field.

Span of control is an aspect of system design with powerful effects. Consider the right fit for the mission and culture of your organization. Fine-tune the balance to give people the right blend of autonomy, empowerment, and incentives.

Structure: Are you the right shape for your goals?

It is possible you have never really thought about your organization's structure, but it has significant effects on the work you are able to do. Remember our example about engines. Engines come in many different configurations. They are designed differently depending on whether they are powering a rocket ship or a scooter and everything in between.

It is the same way with our ministries. You have some kind of organizing structure for your people and projects and your method may look very different from another ministry's.

Organizational structure is often something we take for granted because it's just there in the background. We don't think about how it came to be or how it may need to change. I didn't consider it at all until OneHope went through a significant restructure two years after I started working there.

Our leadership team thoughtfully redesigned the way work would flow through our teams and shuffled people and leaders into new positions that were a better fit. This was necessary because of how our ministry and work had grown over the years. We needed different structures to move us forward in new ways to tackle new problems.

An easy way to figure out your structure is to pull out your ministry's organizational chart. Or if you don't have one—make one! That simple diagram will help you see how people and processes are organized. It is the blueprint of your engine that reveals how you are spending your collective time and energy to reach your goals. If your system isn't achieving the results you want, it might be time to change your structure.

In many practical ways, organizations simply become less innovative as they grow. There is less space for creativity in larger, taller organizations pursuing scale. When something is working well, it makes the organization successful—which makes an organization focus on that thing even more. This creates a reinforcing loop that can deprioritize innovation. Why look for something new when you have something winning? However, it is possible to reclaim some of that creative space and recover the founder's mentality of startups even within large ministries.

The book *Reinventing the Organization* takes a detailed look at some of the world's most innovative companies such as Google, Amazon, and Tencent. Authors Arthur Yeung and Dave Ulrich found that these businesses have similar underlying structures that preserve many of the critical strengths of startups, even though the companies themselves are now quite large.

The organizations they analyzed are intentional about their system design. They pursue a structure that leverages the strengths of being small and minimizes the weaknesses of large organizations. The book calls this new approach a *market-oriented ecosystem*.[15]

---

15 Yeung and Dave Ulrich, *Reinventing the Organization: How Companies Can Deliver Radically Greater Value in Fast-Changing Markets* (Boston: Harvard Business Review Press, 2019), 12.

In a market-oriented ecosystem, teams form who resemble independent organizations. Project leaders function more like founders. The organization provides administrative support in the form of human resources, finances, etc., but the teams themselves are free to experiment and collaborate. If projects end up failing, people are reassigned to other teams, allowing them to learn from the failure and try again.

Reinventing the Organization describes how Amazon at one point adopted a system of self-management called Holacracy—a radical structure without constraints.[16] Employees were free to choose the work they thought most important to the company. They could be part of multiple departments and projects simultaneously. People moved around frequently depending on project needs and their own personal interests. There was an internal hiring board where teams posted their own job listings to internally recruit more people to join them.

I found this example inspiring because it shows the possibility of nurturing innovation while avoiding the non-innovative tendencies of larger organizations. Thoughtful system design can accomplish this. However, there is no one best structure.

Every organization is unique and should be structured in the way that best suits its mission and culture. Structures evolve in response to growth and opportunities. Just know that over time they can become reactionary and outdated. They may no longer match current needs and future demands. We can and should design our structure as carefully as we design anything else in our ministry and be open to changing it if it is no longer serving us well.

---

16 If you're interested in learning more about this, refer to Brian Robertson's book *Holacracy: The New Management System for a Rapidly Changing World* (New York: Henry Holt, 2015).

But I'm not the CEO...

At this point, you might be thinking, "This all sounds really great, but I'm not the one in charge. I can't really make decisions to change our organization's system. So why are we talking about this?" The work of thinking about your system and improving it is not just for the leader of your ministry. Systems affect all of us and the work we are able to do.

Quite simply, we are all in it together. Everyone in your ministry is bound by the system and structure of your organization. Everyone needs to understand its opportunities and limitations. We as ministry innovators especially need to be aware of the system and navigate it well as we propose changes. We need to understand the causes and effects that will be triggered.

Systems affect all of us and the work we are able to do.

Systems thinking is transformational because it helps you see factors that impact innovation and yet were previously invisible. It has often been a mystery to me why obviously great ideas would fail to catch the attention of others and be advanced. I imagined that by climbing higher in authority and responsibility, I would be able to more easily make changes and champion good ideas.

However, I have come to realize that even leaders at the highest levels cannot snap their fingers and make everything more innovative overnight. Everyone has someone they report to. Even my ministry president is accountable to the board of directors, and the board is in turn accountable to our ministry partners who fund the work. Every individual, team, and department is responsible for something and accountable to someone for those results.

Picture a chain of interconnected links. The chain bears the weight of your ministry's mission, and it is strong enough to carry that load. However, it is difficult to rearrange individual links without disrupting the whole. This is why our structures sometimes resist innovation. Change threatens the stability of the chain. Even though it is possible to find a stronger configuration, it takes time and the results are uncertain. A chain is extremely strong but inflexible.

Remember, innovation enters into existing structures. We are not like artists who start with a blank canvas. We already have a picture we are adding to. For some of us, there are many years of history behind the ministry structures we have, and those will not change quickly. Our engines are already built, and there isn't time to stop the work we're doing to reconfigure and rebuild.

What a gift it would be to pause everything our teams are doing for a short season to have time and energy to look at the big picture together. How might we operate differently if we had the chance to start over knowing what we know today?

Of course, stopping everything is impractical. I suggested it once in a meeting with some of our leaders and was literally laughed at. I knew they were right, but I was still saddened. Tinkering with our systems is like trying to rebuild our engine while still driving the car—sometimes at high speeds. It is not an ideal situation.

But you can make some adjustments as you go. In addition, you can ask good questions that help others understand the system too and think about what changes might strengthen their areas of responsibility.

Authority is not what primarily shapes our systems. We shape it by asking good questions and looking below the surface to the causes and effects at work around us. We shape the systems we work within by understanding the goals we are working towards and how our activities are advancing or distancing us from those goals.

We all have a responsibility to be thoughtful about the system we are in and open to change things when they are not working.

THE SYSTEMS WE CREATE

It's late and I'm sitting in the dark in my bed, but my face is lit by the glow of my cell phone screen. I'm watching YouTube and my wife is asleep, so I keep the volume muted. Thanks to captioning, I can still easily watch hours of soundless video content. I just have to be careful not to laugh out loud at the funny ones.

I'm amazed by how my YouTube feed is customized to reflect my interests and preferences. It knows which videos I linger on and which I scroll quickly past. The content mix is always updating, and it is seamless to go from video to video. I could spend a lifetime and never see all that is available on the platform. This is just one of the systems I interact with daily that in turn shapes me as well.

Before YouTube was available, I didn't have any way to watch funny videos when I was bored or get step-by-step visual instructions on how to do something I had never done before. YouTube offers access to a global community of content creators, experts, scammers, and entertainers alike. I have even uploaded videos to the platform, feeding my own ideas and thoughts into this vast machine.

We interact with systems every day, especially through the digital technologies that have become so central to our lives. Our phones and computers can connect us to almost any piece of information and give us countless options for how to spend our time. Our seemingly endless appetite for content and digital experiences has created huge industries aimed at putting things in our hands for us to use and enjoy. The Internet, and everything it makes possible, has profoundly shaped the world in just the few decades since it was introduced.

In many ways, digital technologies have shaped and forever changed us as individuals and as societies. Yet behind every app, website, video game, or virtual reality experience are just people creating things. Coders, software engineers, tech company CEO's, and most importantly, designers.

Everything that is created has some kind of design. That design might be well thought-out, resulting in an excellent product, or it might be hasty, resulting in a poor experience. You can see this reflected in the countless number of new apps that fail to become popular and the handful that rise to the top.

The fields of UI and UX design are specific to technology development, but it can be helpful for anyone to understand them at a basic level. UI stands for User Interface and focuses on how easy an app or website is to use. Are users able to find their way around? Do they know the purpose of the app and how to get the intended benefits from it?

The Google Maps app on my phone apparently has a camera feature that can identify the buildings around me and help me navigate by foot if I get lost in an unfamiliar place. It sounds like a helpful feature, but I've never actually used it. I don't even know where to go in the app to find it. That's an issue of user interface design. UI designers are focused on overcoming that kind of problem to create seamless experiences for users.

UX stands for User Experience. This field of design focuses on what it feels like to use an app or website. What makes it enjoyable for someone? This often involves good graphic design, but it also takes other things into account.

I was at a conference where the lead UX Designer for the online shoe company Zappos talked about their shopping app. The process of shopping for shoes can be boring, and lots of apps and websites look the same. His team wanted to create a memorable and unique experience. They tried to think of what people enjoy.

They came up with cats! "The Internet loves cats," he said. There are countless cat videos and cat memes. Cats can become Internet celebrities with huge social media followings. The Zappos team decided to fill their app with cats. When a user added something to their cart, it rained down celebrating cats. When they started to input their credit card information, a cat popped up to scan the card with laser eyes. Most buttons in the app were designed to make some sort of cat noise.

The Zappos app is no longer filled with cats, but this version helped me see UX in a new light. Cats have nothing to do with shoes, but they created an experience. They made the app fun, comical, and surprising. They helped achieve the goal of making users smile, leaving them with positive memories of shopping there. Hopefully, people will remember the app's fun cats and want to come back to buy more shoes.

UI and UX design are extremely important because they are the key to creating excellent digital products and experiences. If something is easy and enjoyable to use, you are more likely to return to it and recommend it to others. When something is not intuitive or beautiful, you will probably quickly uninstall it.

Apps such as Facebook, Twitter, Instagram, and YouTube have excellent UI and UX and are used daily by millions of people. These are hugely influential platforms. But some of the big tech companies behind these apps have been criticized for the design choices they have made. They are so good at making people come back to their content that they can create addictive tendencies.

Sometimes the tools we use end up using us.

For example, most apps use a feature called "bottomless scrolling" where there is no limit to how far you can scroll. Content keeps being shown even if you keep scrolling for hours. YouTube has an algorithm that suggests videos for you to watch next and even queues and plays those videos automatically, keeping users engaged long past when they might have otherwise stopped.

Instagram's design encourages people to get as many likes on their photos as possible. So users put a lot of effort into getting the perfect picture, pairing it with the right filter, and using as many hashtags as possible to get it in front of people.

Many people obsess over their social media feeds and the life they are portraying to the world through their careful choices of content and images. It's not just social media that has become addictive, it's our devices themselves.

Research has shown that people swipe, tap, and click on their phones between 2,500 and 5,400 times a day and that hearing the notification sounds our phones make causes our body to release dopamine—the pleasure chemical—like some drugs do. These systems that other people have designed for us are having real, physical consequences in our daily lives.

We cannot always predict the cause-and-effect relationships of the things we create. We cannot always account for human behavior and what will be beneficial or problematic. It seems innocent enough to include a "like" button so people can acknowledge each other's pictures. But it can become harmful when we get caught up in comparing how many likes we get versus someone else and then feeling depressed when we are not as popular. I know some people quickly delete photos that don't get enough likes right away because under-performing content doesn't look good on their feed.

Sometimes the tools we use end up using us, even though this was not the intention. Social media apps and the companies who create them are profit-focused, and this motivation can lead them to make design decisions that ultimately end up having negative effects. They will do whatever they can to maximize their profits by increasing the number of users and the time people spend on their apps—they think of it as just good business.

One of the great things about digital technologies is that they can be changed. In response to the critiques of their platform, Instagram tested an option to hide "likes" on photos. I immediately enabled this feature as soon as it was available. I appreciate that it helps me focus on the content and not become distracted by likes that can turn browsing into a popularity contest.

Instagram also inserted a "stopping cue" so that once I had scrolled through my entire feed, it said, "You're all caught up for today!" That was a signal to close the app and move on to other things rather than keep endlessly scrolling through content. Design changes like this can be simple solutions with impactful long-term effects. Only time will tell if they succeed in helping people have healthier social media habits, but they are positive indicators that some tech companies are listening and adjusting for the good of their users.

As ministry innovators, it's important that we assess the systems we design and their effects on people. We have a responsibility to create systems that shape people for Gospel purposes. Kingdom-focused motivations should guide our decisions and lead to positive results in the lives of our audience. In anything we create, we are giving someone an experience and driving them towards action.

Our ultimate goal is to point them towards the greatest action of accepting Christ into their lives. I am not saying what we make has to be boring and plain. Quite the opposite! We should use the tools of UI and UX well and learn from the very best apps and websites. We should do anything and everything we can to create excellent digital products because we have a greater goal than selling shoes or helping people share photos. We have the Gospel to share—an eternal purpose that changes everything.

Introduction to Gamification

One of the fields I have found really helpful in informing the design of digital experiences is *gamification*. This is often thought of as simply the use of games. But gamification is really the study of human motivation. What causes people to take action? It has the word *game* at the beginning because games are something we do voluntarily. We don't have to be paid to play. We do it because it's fun.

I love games of all kinds: board games, video games, phone games, games I have made up. I can get lost in them for hours working really hard to achieve the goal set out for me. What makes games inherently fun? There are mechanics at work within them that cause us to want to participate. Gamification is a part of many of the systems you use every day. The principles behind how games work and how they motivate us can be studied and leveraged in our own projects.

A friend of mine and fellow believer, Yu-Kai Chou, is a pioneer in this field. His book *Actionable Gamification* presents the framework he created, called Octalysis, which helps people understand and apply gamification principles. When I read the book, I was filled with new ideas for how to design ministry products. I was also able to see why innovations I had worked on in the past had fallen short or were even problematic because of their design choices. I want to introduce you to the eight core drivers of human motivation that the Octalysis framework describes, and then we will look at how these apply to ministry work and products.[17]

---

17 This is a very brief overview of these concepts, so if gamification interests you I encourage you to read Yu-Kai Chou's book *Actionable Gamification: Beyond Points, Badges and Leaderboards* (Milpitas, CA: Octalysis Media, 2014). Or check out his website *yukaichou.com* to learn more.

1. **Epic Meaning:** Meaning is powerful. A sense of epic meaning is created in situations where people believe they are doing something bigger than themselves. People want to leave a legacy and be remembered. An example of meaning used well is the website Wikipedia. It is the world's largest encyclopedia, and it is created and maintained by ordinary people all over the world. Millions of people have contributed information to this website, and there are over 1,000 administrators who check every edit to ensure accuracy. None of these people get paid. Everyone volunteers their time and effort to build this repository. There are many reasons they do this, but the biggest one is that they feel a strong sense of meaning in helping contribute to this cause and protect knowledge for the world. Wikipedia has done an excellent job of using epic meaning to motivate people to action.

2. **Accomplishment:** We need both goals to aim for and challenges to overcome on the way. It's not fun to be too good at something. If a game is easy to win, you're not likely to keep coming back to play it. You need a sense of accomplishment to keep moving forward. The tasks you complete and the trials you overcome are success markers on your journey. Success isn't possible without the chance for failure. The more challenging the task, the more meaningful and significant victory is. Milestone moments become vivid memories. Graduations are a tradition for celebrating academic accomplishment when completing high school or university. Promotions at work, completing a difficult project, or helping someone accept Christ—these are accomplishments that are motivating to achieve and drive us to action.

> ## Success isn't possible without the chance for failure.

3. **Empowerment:** Making opportunities to do something in your own way is a powerful motivator. Experiences with infinite possibilities create spaces to flourish and represent our individuality. People are creative, so games that give you opportunities to exercise creativity are fun. Just think about children. They love playing with the simplest things like a big cardboard box, playing in the dirt, painting, or drawing. These things are inherently rewarding because there is no right or wrong way to play with them. You can do anything as long as you have imagination. Digital experiences that do this well are games like Minecraft, which is popular because it's a "sandbox" environment where people can explore, build, and share their creations. Anything where people can play and experiment freely will create motivation. Empowerment helps people come alive and want to participate to create their own unique journey.

4. **Ownership:** Collecting activates the core drive of ownership. People feel attached to things that belong to them and naturally want to gather more. The harder you have to work to obtain an item, the more valuable it will probably be to you. Many people have a goal of owning their own home, and this motivates them to save money and look for the perfect house to buy. Once you have a house, you may spend even more time and money making it look just the way you want. When my wife and I got married, I knew she had a habit of collecting things. If she had two of any similar items, it was the start of a collection. For years, I refused to put up any shelves in our house because I knew she would fill those shelves with knick-knacks. But I've also realized that I have a tendency to collect things too. People are often motivated to collect items in a category that matters to them, like stamps, seashells, or marbles. Similarly, we tend to like to complete sets of things. Ownership is a powerful motivator that causes us to take action.

White Hat vs. Black Hat: In his book, Yu-Kai uses these two terms: *white hat* and *black hat*. These are categories that describe how something motivates you. White hat motivators have intrinsic appeal. They are more internally-focused and positive motivators. They play to the four you've read about so far—epic meaning, accomplishment, empowerment, and ownership. These are all white hat motivators. White is a color that represents purity. You want to take the action for its own sake.

In contrast, black hat motivators tend to be extrinsic—they come from outside yourself. They may add urgency to a situation to motivate you to take action. There may be consequences for not acting or not taking the right action. Black hat motivators are extremely effective at getting us to act. But they should not be used alone. Extrinsic motivators can create obsessive behavior and ultimately an experience that is empty or meaningless. They drive you towards action but may leave you without that essential sense of purpose or accomplishment.

White hat motivators are not naturally good, just as black hat motivators are not naturally evil. They are just different from each other in the way they activate us to take action and are suited to different situations. Let's learn about the black hat motivators and then we will discuss why both are valuable and needed in our ministry work.

• • •

5. **Social Influence:** Human beings are naturally social creatures. We want to know what others are doing and how our actions fit or don't fit in with the crowd. This is largely why social media has become so wildly successful. Humans have always been curious about each other's lives, and these digital platforms give us access to each other and as much of our

daily experiences as we want to share. These platforms have also enabled people to become influencers—users whose choices and tastes others want to imitate. Social connections, whether in-person or online, motivate us to take action.

However, social influence can also be used in black hat ways. For example, social media challenges drive people to take action simply because everyone is doing it and we long to be connected. Sometimes those actions are foolish or even dangerous, but people do them because they don't want to be left out. Social influence may also be black hat if people feel they cannot leave a group because of social pressure. They may feel they must stay to preserve status or relationships. As with any of the core drivers, the application of the motivator to the situation makes the difference in whether it is beneficial or potentially harmful.

My wife was invited by a few friends to participate in a women's Bible study. She agreed with no idea what the commitment level would be. When she went to the first meeting, she was shocked to find the study was not going to last a few weeks but was actually nine months long. She was intimidated, but returned the next week because her friends were also attending. The friends dropped out of the study after a few months, but three years later my wife is not only still attending but now leading one of the groups. The social connections she made with her group leader and new friends at the Bible study kept her going back and even moving up in responsibility and influence. Mentorship, leadership, and acceptance into a group are meaningful to us. Social influence can be a powerful positive motivator.

6. **Scarcity:** *Scarce* means to be in short supply. People often want things just because they are rare or prestigious. Think about the Olympics and how hard athletes work to compete for the gold medal. The medal itself isn't that valuable (it's not even solid

gold!), but what it represents is nearly priceless. There is only one first place, and it can only be achieved once every four years. Restaurants use scarcity when they have special menu items you can only get for a limited time. Collectible cards come at differing levels of rarity, and the ones that have the fewest copies can be sold for a high price. The same is true of almost any item.

People value things that are hard to get because it's human nature to want to distinguish yourself from others. Some social media networks operate on an invitation-only basis, which only seems to make them more popular. Holidays are also an example of scarcity. People who never go to church show up a couple days out of the year—Christmas and Easter—because it is that one special opportunity. If they miss it, they will not get another chance for a year. Scarcity drives us to action.

7. **Unpredictability:** One day I was late and stuck in heavy traffic. Cars were stopped and we only moved forward in inches. It took a long time to get up to the source of the problem. I was surprised to find that the car accident wasn't even on my side of the freeway. It had happened on the other side, but drivers all around had slowed down to look at what had happened. Natural human curiosity is a powerful motivator. When we don't know what's going to happen, our brain engages to try to predict and figure it out. Our brains love puzzles and surprises. It's stimulating on a biological level.

Yu-Kai shares an example in his book about a researcher studying rats. The researcher set up a lever that released a pellet of food every time the rat pulled on it. The rat quickly learned that the lever dispensed snacks. But it wasn't long until the rat got bored because pulling the lever always resulted in the same snack. From then on, he only activated the lever when he wanted food to eat. So the researcher changed the conditions of the experiment. The lever was set up to dispense a variety of snacks and sometimes wouldn't give the rat anything at all. After that change, the rat would sit in front of the lever constantly and obsessively pull it just to see what would come out next. The researcher discovered that the element of unpredictability was highly motivating.

It's easy to see parallels to human behavior. Just think about gambling. People sit in front of slot machines and pull levers to try to get matching pictures, not knowing what will happen with every spin. Sometimes they spend hours and lots of money doing this. This is a sad example of how unpredictability has been used to encourage addictive behaviors. But remember, black hat motivators are not bad in and of themselves. It is only in their application that they can become problematic.

8. **Avoidance:** Avoiding pain or loss is a powerful motivator. I relate to this one because I am a peacekeeper by nature. I avoid conflict at all costs. I will say whatever I think my wife wants to hear if it will get me out of an argument. We avoid what we dislike and work hard to protect what we have. You see this in games or sports when people play defensively. In chess, for example, you might play carefully to avoid losing pieces but fail to attack aggressively enough to win the game. In soccer (football), playing defensively helps you keep the other team from scoring points on your goal, but it doesn't advance you towards their goal.

People don't like to risk losing what they have and will take action to avoid that outcome. We see this at work in advertising as well. A store or website might offer an opportunity to save money if you buy now! You want to avoid losing your chance at the better price and the deal is quickly running out of time. Only one item left and the clock is counting down! Avoiding the loss of that deal motivates buyers to go ahead and make the purchase decision.

Applying Gamification to Ministry

When I teach gamification to people in ministry, there is always at least one person who has a real problem with these concepts. "Isn't this manipulative?" they ask. "As Christians, there's no way we should use gamification to force people to take action." I'm always glad for the person who is brave enough to raise this challenge because it's a good question.

Is gamification manipulative? Would God want us to use these principles in our ministry programs and products? You might ask, "Why should we do this?" In response I would ask, "Why not?"

The eight core human drivers is not something Yu-Kai created, it is something he discovered about human nature. God created us with these aspects of motivation. Why wouldn't we use this knowledge to make outreach and evangelism as effective as possible?

Gamification is not the ultimate solution. It is simply another tool we can use to innovate ministry. The world is already using this knowledge to sell their products and apps and motivate people to take action. As Christians, we should not overlook any tool that might be helpful to advance the Gospel and fulfill the Great Commission.

The Church is uniquely positioned to offer eternal value in response to the eight core drivers. We have the ultimate *meaning* to offer humanity in the epic story of Christ's redemption of sinful humanity. The Bible says that the *accomplishment* of leading someone to Christ causes the angels in heaven to rejoice (Luke 15:10). God *empowers* us to take His Gospel to the ends of the earth. The call is clear, but He does not tell us exactly how to do this and leaves room for infinite creativity.

We are called to *ownership,* not of rare things in this life, but to take actions that will store up for us treasure in heaven. Churches are full of opportunities for leveraging *social influence* in how we build relationships with one another and welcome others. The *scarcity* of hope in the world makes the Gospel truly Good News. Everyone can enter God's kingdom if they have faith. What an incredible message! God's plan to send His Son to earth to die for our sins was unbelievably *unpredictable.*

We do nothing to accomplish salvation. We are instead the recipients of unexpected and undeserved grace that enables us to show grace and love to others. We can offer people the chance to *avoid* the consequences of sin that result in death and put their hope in Christ for eternal life.

Every single motivator is accounted for. If we are presenting the Gospel clearly, choosing faith should be the easiest decision a person ever has to make.

Interestingly, the person who initially opposed gamification as manipulative and forceful ended up changing his mind after discussing these concepts with the rest of our group. By the end of our conversation, he was enthusiastic about using these principles well to make the Gospel as accessible and compelling as possible. He ultimately agreed that we should do whatever we can to help people encounter God and experience the life transformation that inevitably follows.

What you are doing in ministry matters so much! Think about how you can design in response to these natural human motivators. Don't stop with gamification. Take the best thinking from every industry you can find and apply it to what you are doing because nothing could be more important than God's mission.

We have a much bigger weight of responsibility than the creators of even the world's most popular apps. We are ambassadors for Christ in this world, entrusted with the ministry of reconciliation. God's mission is our ultimate white hat motivator as Christians, and the limited time we have on earth before Jesus returns again is our ultimate black hat motivator.

ASKING THE RIGHT QUESTIONS

I once spoke with a leader at a ministry whose goal is to reach college students with the Gospel. They were founded on a model of in-person evangelism and that continues to be their primary focus today.

I asked a hypothetical question, "What if you could prove by every measurement that engaging people online was more effective at leading people to Jesus than your traditional method? Would your ministry ever abandon the in-person model and commit your resources and people to focus on digital?"

He replied that they never would. Although they were actively working to grow digital teams and programs, their primary evangelism approach would likely never change. I was not that surprised. Change is hard, and we all like to continue doing what is familiar and seems to work. But it was an important question we should at least be willing to ask.

Consider the question for yourself and your own ministry. Is there anything you would be unwilling to change even if it could be proven that by changing it, more people could be reached for Christ?

We must be alert to anything that may have grown more important to us than the Great Commission. If our ministry models become more precious to us than the Gospel, it is time for some serious evaluation of our priorities. I don't know if that leader ever thought about my question again or if anything will happen because of it.

But as a ministry innovator with a philosopher's perspective, it was a good question to ask. The answer revealed that digital innovations would only go so far at that organization because of their mindset.

If our ministry models become more precious to us than the Gospel, we must evaluate our priorities.

The practical work of applying systems thinking is truly the work of being a philosopher. As you are invited into conversations, do not be too quick to offer your opinion. Seek to understand first. Take time to ask questions that help you uncover the context. Come alongside people and think with them. Hear what they are trying to accomplish and empathize with the problems they are experiencing. Sometimes all people really need is someone to talk to. You may discover people already have good ideas but just need some help clarifying them. Be a caring conversation partner.

It is much more effective to work with people to help them shape their ideas than offer them an outside solution. Author Adam Grant describes this principle in action when he writes about motivational interviews in his book *Think Again*.[18]

Motivational interviews focus on how to help someone make progress through asking open-ended questions and simply letting them talk. You can help by being a reflective listener and repeating back the main ideas they are sharing. Grant says there is usually a point in the conversation where people move into "change talk." This is when people start discussing ways they wish to make progress. This is the thread to pick up and build upon. Affirm the person's desire and ability to change and help them continue to clarify and add detail to their view of the future. By summarizing the new understanding they are gaining, you can

---

18 Adam Grant, *Think Again: The Power of Knowing What You Don't Know* (New York: Viking Press, 2021), 146.

help them solidify their plans and conviction to move forward. This sounds a lot like what a counselor does, but Grant successfully applies this method to business and other areas. He describes several powerful stories in his book from how a CEO changed his company to a politician who negotiated peace talks with an African warlord.

Motivational interviews are a powerful tool to help people embrace change because the desire comes from within. People are much more likely to act on something that is their own idea. You must resist the temptation to simply tell them what to do, even if the solution seems clear to you. This robs people of being able to own the change for themselves. It puts them in the position of depending on you to help them.

Change is not won by telling people what they need to do but by asking people what they want to accomplish. Help them state their goals and barriers clearly and then ask them what they think needs to happen. Do this in a spirit of humility and sincerity, not as one who already knows the answer and is withholding it. You are on a journey together. They should be able to feel that you care about them and want to see the best happen.

> # Change is not won by telling people what to do but by asking them what they want to accomplish.

One of the most valuable things you can learn to do as a ministry innovator is to guide conversations so that people can discover solutions for themselves. This principle has helped me no matter what setting I find myself in or what level of authority I have in the conversation.

On Monday, I might be facilitating a group of people to work on ministry problems together. On Tuesday, I am meeting with my boss and receiving his directions and feedback on my projects. On Thursday, I am teaching a course on innovation, and I am the leader giving directions and feedback to my students. Authority can vary widely from day to day, but I have found that my approach can remain the same as I diffuse innovation to those around me.

I have seen better results as I focus more on asking questions and less on providing answers. I can ask questions of the people I lead as well as the people who lead me, but the questions are often very similar.

One place to start is with a question that brings everyone back to the core mission: "Why are we doing this?" or, "How does this align with our ultimate goals?" You might need to phrase it a few different ways and ask it a few times until you get to the true answer.

Don't assume everyone has thought deeply about the *why*. Challenge people to answer the question "Why must we do this?" because that purpose will guide every decision you make going forward. Document that answer so anyone can come back and refer to it later. It is most natural to answer this question at the start of the process, but you can come back and have a conversation around the *why* at any time.

It can be clarifying to frequently revisit your purpose. I have often asked my leaders "why?" and the question has never been poorly received when asked sincerely. Allowing my leadership to explain the *why* to me ensures I have a similar understanding of our shared goals so I can better focus my work in those directions.

Once we know our *why*, we can dig into the specifics—the *what* and the *how*. In his book *The Goal,* business consultant Eliyahu Goldratt teaches three key questions to ask as we seek to bring about any change:

1. What must we change?

2. What must we change to?

3. How do we bring about that change?[19]

These questions seem basic, but you would be surprised how often we fail to answer them clearly. Correctly identifying the problem is the first step because the right solution applied to the wrong problem does not move you forward. The second question reveals the desired end goal. What are we aiming for? How will we know if we have succeeded?

"If you don't know where you're going, you'll probably never get there," a wise old saying reminds us. Finally, we look at the *how*. What do we need to do? Consider the people who will be involved, their roles, and how you will communicate with them about the change that needs to happen. You might not be the person directly responsible for the work, but you can set them up for success.

These questions provide needed perspective and refocus you and your team on what is important before you jump straight into accomplishing work. You can use these questions for any change you might be involved in. Project managers can ask them as they seek to improve a specific process to better accomplish work. Ministry presidents can ask them as they examine their organization and think big-picture about whether their team is headed in the right direction.

We should have question askers at every level of our ministries and involved in every project. Strategic questions help us step back from what we are doing and think bigger. How did we get here? Where are we going? Why are these the problems we are trying to solve today? How should we solve them in light of the

---

19 Eliyahu Goldratt, *The Goal: A Process of Ongoing Improvement,* 4th rev. ed. (Great Barrington, MA: North River Press, 2014).

future where we are headed? It is worth slowing down to check your course and ensure you are going in the right direction.

I once consulted with a ministry who had an app that was not accomplishing its purpose very well. The app was hard to navigate and find what you were looking for. But it did a good job of showing off how many languages the app had available. This was something the team wanted to celebrate with their ministry donors to show they had been successful in meeting their translation goals. But as more and more languages were added, the app's design ended up being too complicated for the end user.

Changes were proposed to simplify the user experience, but the development team encountered unexpected resistance from others within the organization. For example, the training team had already developed and translated training for how to use the app with its current design. It was inefficient and expensive for them to redo all that work, and they had already moved on to other needed projects.

The organization had to make a tough decision. If they improved the app, they would lose time and money they had already spent and sacrifice progress currently being made on other projects. But if they made the change, the app could be more useful to people and help them do better ministry. Perhaps in the long-term, the training they had created would no longer be needed because the app could be so intuitive no one would need additional explanations.

You can see the benefits and drawbacks on both sides. The decision that seemed right for one team seemed wrong for another. Ultimately, the ministry decided to move forward with the change so they could better fulfill their mission to spread the Gospel. The app's design was becoming a barrier to that, so it needed to be changed even though it was inefficient and expensive to do so. Knowing their end goal helped them make this practical decision to prioritize their mission over operating their teams and work efficiently.

Asking the right questions helps us identify places where we have accidentally drifted from caring about mission success to team success. It seems to make sense that if every team improves the way it operates, the organization will be more successful as a whole. However, that is not always true. Our goal is not for every team to operate at 100 percent efficiency to produce the most work possible. The goal is that the efforts of those teams would reach people with the Gospel and produce life transformation in the lost.

Overall organizational effectiveness is not the sum of all teams working efficiently in isolation. Rather, it is about working together towards our mission. Getting all the parts of an organization working best together is different from getting all the parts working best on their own. In fact, you may need to slow down a team by redistributing their people or budget to more critical areas to increase the effectiveness of the whole. This might seem counter intuitive, so let's consider a simplified example.

Suppose a marketing team is advertising to thousands of people on social media and connecting them to a team of online missionaries for spiritual conversations. However, the marketing campaigns are so successful that the online missionaries can't keep up. People are waiting a long time, and many conversation requests go unanswered. Although the marketing team is exceeding its goals, the organization's goals are suffering because their audience is not being well served and are forming a bad impression of the ministry.

It will be necessary to strengthen the online missionary team and even divert funds or staff from the marketing team to decrease the incoming flow. In the short-term, this will make the marketing team less effective. They didn't do anything wrong. The opposite in fact—their work was too excellent! There may be other solutions of course, but this is just an example. It is not always wise to keep strengthening teams who are succeeding if they are accidentally creating problems in other places of the organization.

In order to recognize that this is happening, we must step back and take a philosopher's larger view of ministry success. Internal efficiencies or goals should never become more important than the mission, and meeting them does not necessarily mean we are being successful to spread the Gospel.

Jesus showed us the power of asking questions many times during His earthly ministry. He used questions to show the Pharisees the flaws in their religious practices. He asked questions of those who came to Him for healing to allow them to express the depth of their faith. He asked His disciples questions to teach and challenge them.

Jesus Himself is a question that demands an answer. In Mark chapter 8, Jesus asks His disciples, "Who do people say that I am?" They gave Him a variety of answers, and then He asked them again, "'But who do you say that I am?' Peter answered him, 'You are the Christ'" (8:27, 29). Jesus's question allowed Peter to confess and confirm his faith. This is the central question we are also bringing to the world through our ministries.

Jesus Himself is a question that demands an answer.

We are reaching people with the Gospel so that they will come to believe in Christ as their Savior. Who we believe Christ to be is the only thing that matters. As we carry out our ministry, let's do everything we can to ensure people will be able to answer that question the way Peter did.

Philosophers uncover the unseen realities that affect innovation and problem-solve underlying causes to current challenges.

WHY WE MUST BE PHILOSOPHERS

» Many of the challenges we face are symptoms of deeper problem cycles that must be addressed.

» Our efforts to innovate will be governed by the systems at work within our ministries.

» We must understand our organization's current context and past journey in order to bring positive change for the future.

» Understanding how to motivate and engage people is a powerful skill an innovator can learn.

» The key to being a philosopher is having the curiosity and humility to ask good questions.

PRACTICE THE PERSPECTIVE

What is a challenge that keeps repeating itself in your ministry work? Try to identify what type of problem it is beneath the specifics of each situation. Examine and work to remove or change the conditions that seem to lead to the problem. If it happens again, you know there is something deeper going on. Invite others to help you reflect and problem-solve.

BROADEN YOUR PERSPECTIVE

Liam's book recommendations:

Systems Thinking for Social Change: A Practical Guide to Solving Complex Problems, Avoiding Unintended Consequences, and Achieving Lasting Results. David Peter Stroh. White River Junction, VT: Chelsea Green, 2015.

Loonshots: How to Nurture the Crazy Ideas That Win Wars, Cure Diseases, and Transform Industries. Safi Bahcall. New York: St. Martin's Press, 2019.

Do/Scale: A Road Map to Growing a Remarkable Company. Les McKeown. London: The Do Book Company, 2019.

Actionable Gamification: Beyond Points, Badges and Leaderboards. Yu-kai Chou. Milpitas, CA: Octalysis Media, 2014.

The Goal: A Process of Ongoing Improvement, 4th rev. ed. Eliyahu Goldratt. Great Barrington, MA: North River Press, 2014.

The Beginner's Perspective

GO BACK TO BEING A BEGINNER
TO DISCOVER THE TRUTH

THE CAVE

A Parable adapted from Plato's Allegory of the Cave in Republic

"Three right hands!" The man in front of me called out. There was a murmur of agreement, and he sat up straighter, proud of his call.

From behind, someone made a prediction confidently, "Next will be two arms crossed from the left."

We all waited to see if it was correct. A shape appeared on the right. This was one of my strongest ones; I always recognized it immediately. Before anyone else, I heard my own voice call out instinctively, "Sticks!" there was a groan from behind from the one who made the incorrect guess.

"Nice, I always lose that one to you," his gruff voice said.

I smiled. The trick was not to guess too much. I preferred to be quick on the calls, but I only specialized in a handful of shapes. The tactic I had developed helped me keep an edge. I had gotten to advance a few positions closer to the front of the line already in just a few short weeks since I took this new approach and was feeling confident I could keep up my progress.

The shape of the sticks made its way across our view, but before it had fully disappeared from the great wall, another shape appeared from the left this time. Nobody had predicted anything and the shape was unfamiliar. I waited an extra second to see if I could make it out more clearly, but the light was a little dimmer than it had been earlier.

I heard a man further back call out in desperation to be first, "It's a banner!" We watched, but it turned out to be a plank instead. The flickering light had made it look like something it was not. I cringed as I heard the thud of the man getting hit. He groaned and there was a rattling of chains as he was shoved and jostled back further away from the wall in front of us.

Punishment like that is rare unless you make a habit of wrong predictions and show no talent at all. But bad calls are unacceptable. It makes us all look bad to the other lines. A good prediction has huge rewards, but it's also rare. The wall is fickle like that. You think you've figured out the pattern when it suddenly changes or like today a plank shows up out of nowhere.

It had been a pretty good day for me with two correct calls. If I could just get one more tomorrow without a miss, I'd advance up the line again. The light was becoming too dim to see the shadowy shapes, so everyone adjusted their shackles and got comfortable for the night. I lay awake, thinking hard about the shapes we'd seen that day, the order, and which sides they had come from. I knew I was close to seeing how it all fit together. Maybe I'd make a big prediction after all that would really show them. I daydreamed for a while. It was important to be well-rested, but I felt restless. I stared up at the dark walls around us, or rather the walls I knew were there when we could see. Everything now was thick blackness.

Schff Schrsh...

A strange sound interrupted my thoughts and cut through the typical sounds of snoring and jangle of chains as people shifted in their sleep. I listened intently as it grew closer until it was right next to me. I heard a tinny jangle close by that startled me. It reminded me of chains but was lighter sounding. I waited, petrified. I had never in all these years experienced something so out of place like this. There was nothing for a long time; whatever it was, it was gone now.

I reached out and felt around for the source of the strange tinkling noise I had heard earlier, and my hand eventually landed on something cold and metallic. It had a peculiar shape, like the straight part of a chain, but not as thick. It was longer and had some sort of square edges at one end and a rounded flat part at the other, and it was attached to a thin perfectly round hoop. I played with it for a while, turning the strange thing over and over in the dark. It reminded me of something I had seen on my shackles, a hole that was small and round with a straight line coming off the bottom. I always stared at it dangling between my wrists when I was thinking hard about a call.

Out of curiosity I felt for the familiar shape of the hole and slipped the new object into it. It fit perfectly. Maybe it was part of a set or something I had been missing? I pressed it all the way in, but nothing happened. I sat there confused. Where had it come from? What was its purpose? Carefully, I felt around the thing as it sat snuggly in my shackle and turned it from side to side. I twisted that perfectly round loop in my hand, and it turned something, and then…

Cling! Tlang!

The chains and cuff on my wrists dropped to the floor. There were some muffled grunts from the disturbed sleepers nearby. I sat there stunned. I didn't know the chains could do that! I felt around for the shackle and the thing that had opened it, pulling it out in wonder. My wrists had never felt so light! I stood up and stretched my arms. I tried the thing on the shackle on my ankle, pushed it in, gave it a twist and it fell right off. I took a big step, careful not to step on anyone.

At the front of the cave, the big wall started to glow dimly again. This was how each day started. People would begin stirring soon and I didn't want to be seen up and around, not properly seated. But how could I put the shackles back on? They seemed fully broken in two. Starting to panic, I headed towards the one place no one wanted to be: the back of the cave, far away from the wall. Perhaps I could hide there with my head down until the day was over.

The line of people stopped but the cave kept going, further than I ever knew. I wanted a place to hide and wait, but nowhere seemed safe. I kept going. Eventually, I saw a dim light ahead. Perhaps it was another wall, or maybe whoever gave me this thing was up there. As I drew nearer, the light looked stranger and harsher. It was an opening to some vast chamber whose ceiling I couldn't see. I walked through hoping to get to the other side, but it seemed like it went on forever.

• • •

It was too bright to see. My eyes were open, but I was blinded entirely. The light was worse from above, so I looked only at the ground. Finally, I saw something. Familiar shapes from the wall: sticks, moving hands, folded arms. Gratefully, I hurried towards them. The air seemed a bit cooler, almost like being back in the cave. My eyes ached and sweat dripped down my forehead. I wanted to go back, but how would I find my way?

I heard a voice close by. "Sir, are you alright? You are huddled in the shade of that tree as if you are unwell."

I searched the ground and saw the shape of a man. Was it talking to me? "A tree?" I said. "I'm resting on this shape of sticks."

"Call it what you will," the voice said. ". . . uh, well, you seem well enough. Good day to you!" The shape withdrew to the left.

I sat there puzzled. It was like being in the front of the wall again, but why did the shapes now talk? What was a tree? I wished desperately for the harsh light to go away, and as the hours passed it did seem to dim. Was it only my imagination? No, it was becoming more comfortably dark, and I could see more and more. I lifted my head to a great many unfamiliar sights. Towering things, objects with strange shapes, figures moving to and fro. But I couldn't keep my eyes open from exhaustion.

I awoke to the familiar glow of the cave. It had all been a terrible dream, I thought relieved. But something was different. I didn't hear the sound of my sleeping companions and my hands and feet felt strangely light. My eyes flew open with the memory of my chains falling to the ground and stumbling out of the cave into a too-bright place. Where was I?

I was still outside, and the world around me was a strange color. Everything was strange compared to the darkness of the cave. My eyes still hurt, but the light was less painful than before. I could look up instead of just at the ground. There was movement and life everywhere I looked. Even the air seemed to move in a strange way. The only thing I recognized was the shape of sticks, now opposite where I sat.

"Are you alright, dear?" the voice of a woman came from behind me and I quickly turned to look.

"I . . . I'm not sure. I'm lost. I don't know where to go. But I recognize this," I said pointing to the shape of sticks.

"The ground? . . . Or do you mean the shadow?" She asked pleasantly.

"What is a shadow?" I asked, confused. It was obviously sticks.

It was her turn to look confused. "A shadow is cast by light. You see the sun cannot shine on the ground there because the tree is blocking it, so it makes a tree-shaped dark . . . uh . . . shadow."

A tree again. What could it mean? I didn't know what to say as I thought about her words. Finally, she said, "Well, good luck to you!" before hurrying off.

I stared at the shape on the ground and looked at the . . . tree? I struggled to comprehend the relationship between the towering thing above me and the familiar shape on the ground. I looked at my own feet and saw a dark shape . . . shadow? . . . extending away from them. I raised my hands and the shape on the ground matched my gesture inch for inch, turn for turn. But where my hand and the tree were solid and whole, the "shadow" on the ground was flat and crisp. They didn't look the same. They also didn't look like the blurred shapes I was used to seeing on the great wall.

Desperately I looked up, hoping the woman was still close by. There was so much I needed to know.

"Wait!" I called out, scrambling to my feet. I could just see her a little ways off and hurried in that direction. The woman seemed a bit disappointed that she hadn't managed to escape more questions as she turned to smile hesitantly at me.

"Why is it so sharp?" I asked. "Normally, are these more…" I waved my hands back and forth in a little wobbly gesture in front of me, "like this?"

She looked at me thoughtfully, "Well, shadows would look like that if lit by a fire or torch, but the sun is bright and its light is steady."

"Ah, right." It seemed I was asking questions that she thought everyone ought to know the answers to. I wanted to seem like I was familiar with it after all, so I said, "Of course! Right! I forgot about fire. Thank you!"

She seemed about to say something more, but she just nodded and started hurrying away. I wandered down the road, still transfixed by my own shadow. The shape of hands was there, but it was my hands. The shape of sticks fell regularly across the road, but now I knew I could look up and see trees instead. The shadow was dark and lifeless compared to the color and vivid detail of what formed it.

I walked for a long time.

It was dark before I stopped; too dark to see clearly, but my eyes were drawn to light up ahead. Not light from the sun, but from little fires on the top of sticks. They formed a line leading towards something. Shapes larger than trees behind a great wall much bigger than the wall in the cave. I heard the warm sound of voices and drew closer to watch.

People passed by, like the man and woman I had spoken to earlier. Some carried things on their head, others pushed strange shapes in front of them. They headed towards an opening in the wall, disappearing into it, and others came out heading in the opposite direction. Each one cast a shadow on the wall that shifted and changed in the flickering firelight. The shapes were totally different from the people I could see. The patterns of coming and going were not as we had thought in the cave. We had misunderstood everything.

I thought about my brothers and companions who were still trapped in that dark place staring at the wall. They were unable to move freely, and I wanted to go to them. To show them the truth. Surely they would rejoice to see this bright world and the source of the shapes we had looked at for so long.

I resolved to return the very next day.

• • •

"Look who it is!" a jeering voice called out.

"He'll have to start in the back. Where did you go anyway?" it was a kindly older man's voice.

I fumbled along the right wall of the passage I had used to escape only two nights prior and tripped, just barely catching myself. "I was outside!" I said excitedly. "I must te—"

"Rock pile!" someone ahead of me in the darkness called out.

"Nice!" Someone affirmed.

I blurted out, "You have to listen to me. These shadows aren't what you think they are! That was a basket of fruit, not rocks. It's from—"

"Shhh! We're in the middle of calling right now!" someone shouted from behind me. "Sit down, and in the back of the line!"

The kindly sounding old voice spoke up again, "Uh . . . Maybe you should just sit down." I sat down in the back, perplexed. I tapped on the shoulder of the man in front of me, now no longer in the very back.

I whispered, "Hey, this wall is not actually all that important because . . . Well, you see there's a fire and there are people over there who are probably just..."

"Sticks!" Someone shouted up ahead.

Thud.

There were stars in my vision. "Would you *shut up*! I could have had that if you hadn't been yapping at me. Listen, maybe you're okay being in the back, but I want to move up, and you don't get ahead by talking."

I sat dazed for a moment; he had turned around and hit me square in the jaw. I was trying to help him! I tried to think. Several people made calls, one shifted position forward. I could barely make out the shapes on the wall. It was very dim in here, not like the bright sunlight outside. The air was still and oppressive.

This is ridiculous, I thought. If I can just show them. I pulled the strange metal thing out of my pocket and stood up. Felt my way past the person who had hit me and went to a large man a few places in front of him. I started feeling for his shackles to unlock them.

"Hey . . . HEY! What are you doing!" He kicked out towards me and I struggled with him for a minute. "He's mad! He's gone crazy being outside!" I felt chained hands come up from around the man I was trying to free. They pulled me off of him roughly and shoved me to the ground. Angry voices called out from all sides.

"He's trying to ruin my work! Do you know how hard I worked to get this far ahead?"

"Look at him, he's not even looking at the wall, he doesn't even care."

"He's unchained too. What if we catch his crazy?"

"We should kill him! What was he trying to do?"

THUNK! . . . *whiff* . . . *ta cla ta.*

A thrown rock hit my knee, and another flew past my head bouncing off the floor behind. Then the kind older voice said above the noise, "That's enough. Listen, if you can sit down and be quiet, we won't have to hurt you. But no more disturbances. We don't have the time for this."

I limped my way back to the end of the line and sat down. I was confused and sad sitting in the darkness. I couldn't see much on the wall and I didn't want to make calls anyway. I knew it was pointless.

The line started to rattle as people turned to sleep for the night. The same jeering voice from before called out. "Did you see? That crazy unchained man didn't make a single call today, he can't see at all."

"Ha ha, at least we'll never have to be in the back again!"

I could never unsee the outside world, or unknow the truth of the objects behind the shadows. How could I help them understand? They were blind, but it wasn't their fault. Every day, they worked hard to make sense of the darkness and move up in the world. But this wasn't the real world at all.

I wanted desperately to lead them out that very moment. But it is not leading if nobody is following. First, I would need to become more than the crazy unchained one. If I were to have any hope of changing their mind, they would need to see me differently. Based on how it went today, I knew it would be slow work by their rules to build trust.

But I could imagine it. The whole lot of them, dazzled by the light, seeing the tree for what it really is rather than the shadowy sticks they used to believe. A tree of life and color. I will wait and work, I told myself.

Loving them through their scorn and rejection, working towards the hope of seeing the truth of that beautiful tree, as I did. I will wait. I will work. I will lead them out of this cave into the truth, gently, slowly. Eventually, we will go together into the light.

• • •

THE BEGINNER'S PERSPECTIVE

"In the beginner's mind there are many possibilities; in the expert's mind there are few."

—*Shunryu Suzuki, Japanese Zen teacher*

What was the last new thing you learned or tried for the first time? Recently, my wife and I got inspired to do some projects around the house. We ended up with a couple of walls that needed drywall repairs. I am not skilled in construction work and have never dealt with drywall before. But I felt certain I could do it if I tried. However, it was intimidating to realize how much I didn't know.

I had no idea what to do first. I had to buy specific tools and materials I had no clue how to use. I had to learn new terms and watch YouTube tutorials of people demonstrating the process. These people were experts, though, so their work looked much better than my clumsy first attempts. I was really slow at doing the work because the motions were unfamiliar. I had to repeat some things and fix problems I accidentally created. I had lots of questions and had to look at several different resources for instructions. The walls turned out pretty well, by my standards, but the entire experience was valuable in that it made me a beginner again.

We don't always make time in our lives to do new things, and when we do it can feel pretty uncomfortable. When we approach something new and try it for the first time, we're forced to really look and listen. We have to slow down to navigate the situation. It takes time to figure out what works. We don't have any habitual ways of doing this new thing or methods that will ensure success. We might not have any past experience to draw on that will help us. This might feel frustrating, but it is in reality a great thing. It puts us in the position of being a beginner and gives us the opportunity to start fresh as we learn something new.

We have spent our lives naturally building up expertise in various areas. While that is valuable and needed, it can also get in the way of innovation. We often don't realize the extent to which our past experiences color our expectations. We bring our knowledge and assumptions with us wherever we go. We have developed ways of seeing, thinking, and acting based on what we know of the world. When we face a new problem, we instinctively apply solutions that have worked in the past. But that isn't always the best approach.

We must see the world as it is, not the way we imagine it to be.

A beginner's perspective is vital to innovation because it helps us look at the world without the lens we have developed over a lifetime. It allows us to operate in truth and reality.

We must see the world as it is, not the way we imagine it to be. We need to see clearly without the filters of our past experiences. Most importantly, we must be aware of how our experiences and expertise shape how we think and act. Otherwise, we are essentially blind—just like the people in The Cave parable.

There was order and accomplishment in the society within the cave. People were able to make progress, as they understood it, but it was all painfully misguided because their entire foundation of understanding was wrong. The world they thought they were seeing was completely different from their interpretation. Although they watched carefully and tried to understand, they were trapped in darkness and operated blindly.

The beginner's perspective is a powerful tool to help us avoid making this mistake. Operating in the beginner's perspective helps us become aware of our assumptions and intentionally choose to set those aside for a time to approach a situation from a new vantage point.

Putting ourselves in the position of a beginner is challenging. It takes humility and courage to set aside our hard-earned expertise and let go of what we think we know. This posture requires that we change the way we do things—even change the way we think—to see with fresh eyes. It will feel unnatural at first. But this work is worth doing so we can live in the light of the truth.

SEE THE WORLD AS YOU DO

You are unique in all the world. Just think about it this way: nobody could take your place for the day and pass themselves off as you. A stranger in your body could not hope to replicate your behavior and mannerisms, knowledge and skills, even your voice and way of speaking. Everyone would see the difference immediately.

Your personality and way of thinking along with your past experiences and choices all combine to make you . . . you! Nobody else can see the world the way you do, because nobody has lived the life you have lived. The calling on your life is also unique. The Bible tells us this in Ephesians 2:10, "For we are God's handiwork, created in Christ Jesus to do good works, which God prepared in advance for us to do" (NIV).

You are God's special creation and He has special things in mind for you to do. You are uniquely suited to carry out a specific part of God's mission. He has given you perspectives and experiences that shape the way you see the world. You carry unique burdens and passions. We don't always know what living out our vision will look like. But as we dream about the future, we can also look back on our lives and see how God has used both our challenges and our opportunities in His story. I want to briefly share my testimony so you can get a glimpse of the experiences that have shaped my view of the world.

In my own life, I have clearly seen how God has worked even when I had no idea how things were going to turn out. I was born into a family of entrepreneurs and creatives, raised by an incredibly hard-working mom who started multiple businesses while I was growing up. Almost every sentence around my house would start with the excited phrase, "I have an idea!" Just saying that to each other seemed to fill the air with energy and enthusiasm.

My mom found time to nurture both me and her innovative ideas. Everything from teaching classes on embroidery, to doing costume design for TV, all the while working full-time and even making space to homeschool me for a year in second grade. All this contributed to giving me a strong sense that anything is possible if you work hard and make it happen.

I had lots of ideas for what I wanted to be when I grew up. My mom tells me that once I even said, "I want to be the king of the world." When she asked why, I replied, "Because I could do things better." I no longer have the goal of being a king, but I still carry the sense that the world could be better and have a longing to help bring positive change.

When I was a teenager, I realized how different my values were as a Christian from the rest of the world. Most of my friends were not believers, and they were already losing their way to sex, drugs, and alcohol. I cared about them deeply because they were my friends, but I didn't know how to help them make better choices or how to talk about Jesus with them. After one of my close friends moved to another school and we gradually stopped talking or seeing each other, I realized that the people around me were my friends almost by accident. Had I been born somewhere else, I would have different friends who I would care about and who would need Jesus just as much. I could go anywhere in the world and the people around me would need the Gospel. It was the start of a missional calling on my life.

This burden for all the potential friends I could have in the world made me feel completely inadequate to the task. I wanted to be able to share the Gospel well, and so I needed to better understand it myself. I enrolled in Biola University in Los Angeles and pursued an undergraduate degree in Biblical Studies and Theology. I worked multiple jobs to cover the cost of tuition. Some of those jobs gave me the opportunity to refine skills in the areas of graphic design, film production, and web development.

I didn't know what to do for my career, and my brilliant plan was to buy a one-way ticket to Latin America because I spoke Spanish. I planned to start walking south and share my faith with people I met along the way. I imagined myself in a coat and boots dusty from travel, guitar over my shoulder, a faithful dog at my side, on a mission to share the Gospel. My girlfriend, who later became my wife, didn't hesitate to tell me what a terrible idea that was and that I'd likely die before I made it through Mexico.

Turns out we did buy one-way plane tickets, not to South America but to South Florida. I made a connection through my university to a seminary that offered me a scholarship. It was God's perfect next step for me. The only challenge was that I needed to propose, get married, move, and find a new job in a state I had never even visited in just three short months. But when God opens a door, the details fall into place.

We found a place to live through a student at the seminary. One day I got a phone call from a complete stranger asking if I was looking for a job. A professor I had never met had given my resume to someone at OneHope, a ministry I had never heard of. They hired not only me but my wife as well! It has turned out to be a dream job for both of us that leverages and has expanded our gifts, passions, and missional calling. OneHope's mission is to bring God's Word to every child, and it is a privilege to be able to work towards that goal every day. I feel incredibly blessed to have found vocational work—a job I both love and feel called to.

I am telling you my testimony not because I am a model for what an innovator should look like. Quite the opposite. My story is my own, and you have a story that is uniquely yours. I could have never imagined how God would take my diverse life experiences and use them for His glory. But God works through every person's story to bring them into His kingdom and equip them to fulfill the Great Commission. He has created you for work that only you can do. You will be able to better accomplish your work by developing the perspectives described in this book.

Your past experiences and your testimony play a big role in shaping your perspective, but so does your personality. I don't have children, but parents tell me that their sons and daughters had their own personalities even in the womb. We are seemingly born into this world with a specific way of seeing and reacting that goes even deeper than how we are raised.

I have learned a lot about myself through taking personality assessments. One of my favorite frameworks is the Enneagram. It has helped me see some of my blind spots and helped shed light on potential trouble spots with others. After my wife and I took the assessment, we had the obvious, but still surprising, revelation that we don't see the world exactly the same way. Things that are completely reasonable to her make no sense to me, and the opposite is true too. We have to work every day to navigate our differences.

For some reason, it is easy to think that the way you see the world is the only possible way it can be understood. In reality, my wife and I often have the same experience and interpret it completely differently because of the unique lens we have. I encourage you to take the Enneagram and learn more about yourself and those around you. Most people can identify themselves just by reading the descriptions of the different types, but there are free tests you can take online as well.

The personality types are identified by a number and a name: 1. Reformer, 2. Helper, 3. Achiever, 4. Individualist, 5. Investigator, 6. Loyalist, 7. Enthusiast, 8. Challenger, and 9. Peacemaker (that's me!).

ENNEAGRAM

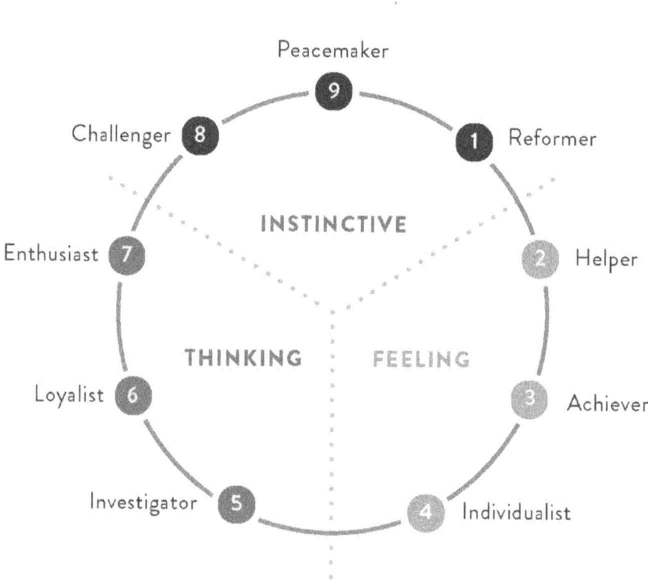

The Enneagram helps put words to some of your fears and desires. You will learn what motivates you and stresses you. Your inborn personality is a big part of the way you see the world. Each person is different, but there are patterns we can learn about each other that help us build relationships and communicate better.

No two innovators will ever make the same thing. You could stand beside another person today looking at the same problem and come up with vastly different solutions. Both may be good, and both may be needed.

What you create will be informed by how you see. Your unique perspective creates strength that others do not have. But your assumptions can also carry weaknesses. It is important to know yourself and what shapes the way you see so that you can respond well to the needs and opportunities God puts in front of you. He has prepared good things for you to do, and He has also prepared you well to do them.

What you create will be
informed by how you see.

SEE THE WORLD AS OTHERS DO

We all have the lens of our experiences and personality that forms our view of the world. But knowing this is only half of the work we need to do as ministry innovators. We also need to learn to observe the world through other people's eyes. You have probably heard the saying "Before you judge a man, walk a mile in his shoes." It is easy to see what someone does, but it is much harder to understand why they do so. This requires us to dig in, to understand their story, to develop empathy, and to extend grace.

We can observe someone's actions but we might only be able to guess at their motivations. Sometimes, we don't even try to guess at all. This is a critical failure in ministry innovation. If we don't understand why people do what they do, how can we share the Gospel with them in a way that is relevant and personal? The beginner's perspective helps us set aside our assumptions and our own way of seeing the world to glimpse how the world looks from someone else's viewpoint.

I used to teach the Sunday School class of six-year-olds at my church. Seeing the world from their perspective meant literally getting down to their level. At six, you're not very tall, so most of what you see are people's legs. Imagine getting dropped off by your parents and left in a strange room with strange adults towering above you. Are your parents ever going to come back? Maybe they are abandoning you forever.

Looking at it from the child's point of view, it was easy to see why some were afraid or sad. They had no control over the situation, and some didn't even want to be there. The way they expressed that fear though was through uncontrollable crying or temper tantrums. Children aren't very good at controlling their emotions, so it was easy to become frustrated by their external behaviors.

But it was also an opportunity to develop empathy that allowed me to respond better to what was really going on. Eventually, I became known for having a very orderly Sunday School classroom. It wasn't because I was strict with the children. Instead, it was because I had empathy for them, which made it possible to create a setting where they could feel comfortable and engage with the lesson.

Empathy is powerful because people cannot always easily describe the problems they feel. Many times, we can be trapped in believing "this is just the way things have always been" without realizing it could be better. The people in The Cave parable had no complaints about their chains. They didn't know it was possible to live outside the darkness of the cave. People may accept a broken reality as the way the world is supposed to be.

But we bring the Gospel's powerful message of freedom and light. It is our job to do everything we possibly can to help people receive and accept that Good News. We must look at the world and its challenges from their perspective.

To see through someone else's eyes, we need to stop and be intentional in our focus. We must spend time building the relationship, listening attentively, and coming alongside to share in both their burdens and their joys. You do this naturally with the people you care about in your life. You know how to be a good friend and how to develop new friendships. But sometimes we forget to apply those same practices to our ministry work and to all those we are hoping to reach with the Gospel.

As ministry innovators, we must thoughtfully adopt ways of doing things that build our empathy and understanding of those we are trying to serve. One method that does this well is called Human-Centered Design (HCD), developed by Stanford University's Design School, and popularized by the organization IDEO.[20]

HUMAN-CENTERED DESIGN

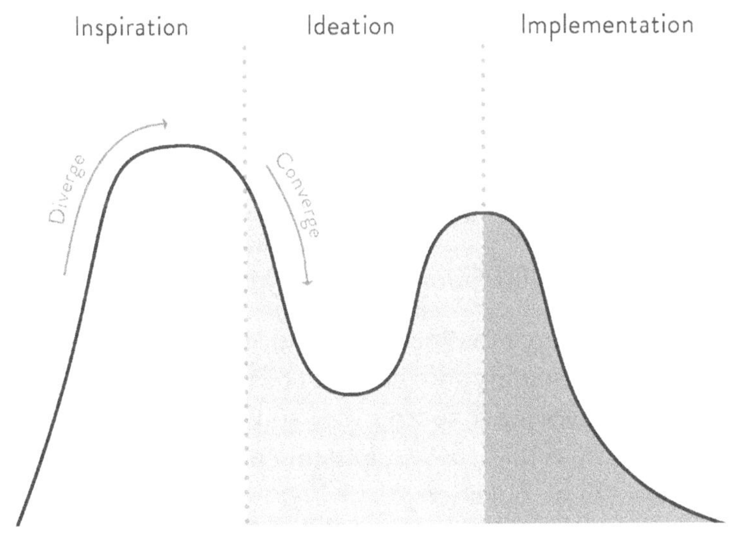

---

20 IDEO offers many free online resources sharing human-centered design principles and tools. Start exploring at *https://www.designkit.org/*.

The first phase of Human-Centered Design (HCD) is called *Inspiration,* and it focuses on discovering more about who you are trying to reach. There are many ideas for how to do this. For example, you could do some research to find data on the target audience; or ask questions in a one-on-one interview to find out more about their life, goals, and challenges. You could spend time with the person to observe a day in their life. One idea I loved was to give people cameras to take photos of things that are important, interesting, or represent key moments in their day. This idea literally lets you see the world from their perspective.

The key to HCD's approach is immersing yourself in another person's reality. Empathy is difficult at a distance. The closer you can be to the people you are trying to serve, the more you can feel what they feel. You don't just want to imagine their lives, you need to get as close as you can to their experiences and thoughts. You should be overflowing with stories and real examples from the lives of those you are trying to reach. It is like the difference between a photo in black and white or a movie in full color. The more you see through their eyes, the easier it will be to design something they will really want.

I had an opportunity to see this in action when I visited Holy Trinity Brompton Church in London in 2016. This church has worked hard to understand the non-Christian's perspective of church, and they discovered several critical things. First, they found out that many people felt lonely and isolated but did not see church as a solution for community in their lives.

They also discovered that people outside the church don't really understand Christianity and that churches were not offering ways for interested people to learn more and ask questions. Finally, they determined that the Sunday morning experience didn't make sense for an outsider.

Just think about it for a minute. You are a non-Christian with only a vague idea what Christianity is about. You show up to a church on Sunday, not sure what to wear or how to act. Everyone seems friendly enough, but pretty soon it gets weird. Everyone is singing songs out loud and raising their hands in the air. They all seem to know the words and melody, but you just feel awkward. You stand up for a while, then sit down because everyone else is and seems to know when they should.

Some random guy talks for an hour about some stuff that happened a long time ago, using a really old book that is hard to understand. Everyone takes notes and seems to get it, but you are completely lost. Then they ask you for money, sing some more songs, and everyone socializes for a while afterwards. You don't know anyone, and no one talks to you, so you quickly leave and never go back.

This is an oversimplification, of course, but you can see how a Sunday morning church service might not be the best first experience for a non-believer. Holy Trinity Brompton responded by starting a program called Alpha. It is specifically designed for seekers and invites anyone in the local community to come to the church for a free dinner and to meet new people. After dinner, they share a message specifically designed for non-Christians that explains Christianity simply and easily for someone hearing about Jesus for the first time.

After the message, people are invited to talk about it in small groups with a trained facilitator. There's no debating and no right or wrong answers, just friendly conversation without judgment. The facilitator encourages everyone to share their questions and experiences with the goal of exploring what Christianity really means. Week after week, people can come back to eat more, learn more, and eventually to pray for themselves and experience the power of the Holy Spirit.

Alpha has spread from the UK around the world, and many people have found Jesus through this incredible initiative. Alpha shows the impact of designing with empathy for the person unfamiliar with Christianity. Alpha's model also demonstrates what can happen when you set aside your assumptions and create environments where everyone can approach faith as a beginner again.

Seeing the world as others do can lead us to unexpected solutions we would never have created otherwise. IDEO shares an example of a healthcare organization that invested millions of dollars to build local health centers in some of the most remote parts of Africa. The centers were built, furnished, and staffed. Everything was ready. There was just one problem—nobody from the community came. The centers remained mostly empty.

The company was confused and concerned. Should they build more centers to make them more accessible? Perhaps transport was needed to help people get there? They had some ideas but didn't really understand the problem. So they invited a human-centered design team to help.

Seeing the world as others do can lead us to unexpected solutions.

The team discovered that the challenge was not location or transport or anything the company had guessed. Rather, people were afraid to come to the centers because they didn't know how much it would cost. They worried treatment would be too expensive and they would have to leave embarrassed. The solution was not another multi-million dollar investment, but something much cheaper: a sign outside each center displaying the services offered and their cost. They made the signs in large print so they could easily be read from the road as people were passing by. The solution was much easier than anyone had imagined, but it was only discovered because the team spent time with the people they were trying to reach. They asked questions, listened to them, and observed their daily lives and needs. They encouraged people to share about their past experiences with doctors and mapped out the whole patient experience from beginning to end. Eventually, they were able to identify the barrier that was keeping the community from coming to the health care centers. Having the beginner's perspective allowed the team to consider all possibilities and find the problem no one had thought of.

It is critical that we learn to do the same in our work as ministry innovators. We may be very different from the people we are trying to serve, so we cannot assume that what is obvious to us or motivating to us will be the same for someone else. We must take the time to see the world as others do.

HOW CULTURE SHAPES YOUR WORLD

Before I joined OneHope, I had never traveled outside the United States. But working for a global ministry quickly changed this. Just a few months into the job, I had the opportunity to go to Chile to meet with our regional team there. I was the only bilingual American on the trip, so I ended up helping with translation.

The days were full. We started early in the morning with presentations and training. There was so much new information we wanted to share with them. We talked about research and design and how to make the best Scripture engagement products for their context. We dreamed about the future and problem-solved their current challenges. We didn't waste a minute of the valuable time, knowing it was short. At the end of each day, we went back to our hotel rooms exhausted, but pleased with what we were accomplishing. At the end of the second day, however, one of the local team members approached me looking sad.

"These past few days weren't what we were expecting," he told me in Spanish. "We thought we would get to know you guys. Spend time together and hear about your lives and families. Instead, we spend all day in business meetings."

It was my first experience of cross-cultural miscommunication. Each side had a different expectation of our time together and what was important to accomplish. We Americans were there to get things done. But the regional team was less interested in the information we brought and more interested in who we were as people. We didn't realize it, but when we went back to our hotel rooms early every night we signaled that we didn't care about getting to know them or letting them get to know us.

I didn't know it at the time, but later I learned that every culture has different ways of building trust. In the United States, trust is highly task-based. You prove you are trustworthy by doing what you say you will do. Relationships are secondary to accomplishing work. But in Latin America, trust is relational. You earn trust by building a relationship with someone, and this should be done first before you try to work together.

As Americans, we treated the meeting time as the most important aspect of our trip. But the Latin team perceived our work-focused approach as rude and needed time to get to know us. We were able to adjust our agenda for the rest of the trip to make more time for relationships, and we learned something very important about how everyone sees the world differently.

How we build **trust** is just one aspect of many that make cultures and the people in them so different from one another. I learned this from the book *The Culture Map* by Erin Meyer. I didn't find this book until several years after that trip to Chile, and I now recommend it to everyone working in an international ministry. It would have saved me confusion on other trips and prepared me to enter unfamiliar cultures and navigate them better.

We all have a different perspective on the world that is profoundly shaped by the culture we are a part of. We have expectations of how others should behave, and we interpret their actions through our cultural lens. We might not even know we have these expectations until they conflict with someone else's, like I experienced in Chile.

In her book, Meyer describes eight dimensions of culture and how they differ in countries around the world. Knowing these dimensions and the spectrum of possible responses is valuable as you interact with people from different cultures through your work. In addition to Trust, which we already examined, there is Communicating, Evaluating, Leading, Deciding, Disagreeing, Scheduling, and Persuading.[21] Let's look briefly at each of these concepts and how they shape people's perspectives and responses.

COMMUNICATION

Communicating would seem simple enough, however it is more complex than you might suspect. On one end of the cultural spectrum is low context communication and on the other end is high context communication.

In high context cultures, a lot of meaning is communicated "between the lines." The way something is said and a person's body language is just as important, or even more important, than the words they use. Things may be hinted at indirectly without being verbalized, but you are expected to pick up on these hidden meanings. Low context cultures are much more direct and emphasize the words that are spoken. It is the attitude that

---

21 Erin Meyer, *The Culture Map: Breaking Through the Invisible Boundaries of Global Business* (New York: Public Affairs, 2014). These sections give a very brief introduction to each of Meyer's concepts, but are illustrated with some of my own examples.

"what you see is what you get." The United States has a low context culture. Americans traveling overseas can have a reputation for being rude and oblivious because we are very direct in what we say and have trouble recognizing hidden meanings.

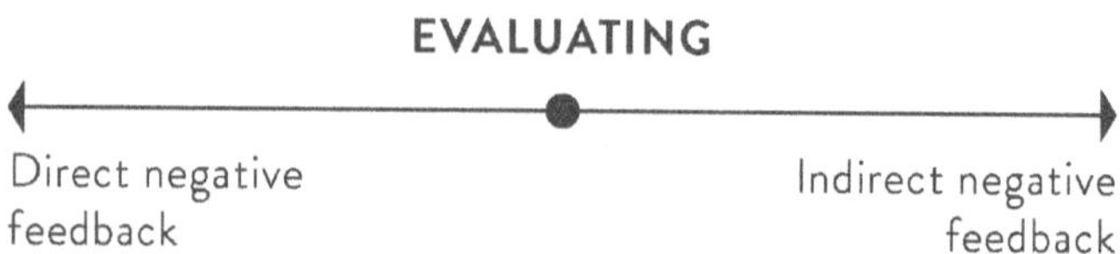

Evaluating has to do with how feedback is given. The two ends of the spectrum are direct negative feedback versus indirect negative feedback. Even though Americans generally say what we mean, we tend to be very indirect when correcting someone.

My friend Aaron from New Zealand experienced this when he first came to the United States to work in ministry. He was in a meeting and one of his colleagues suggested an idea. Aaron immediately shot back, "That's the worst idea I've ever heard in my life!" and went on to explain why it would never work. Aaron is from a culture where negative feedback is given directly. He treats criticism as a gift to be given freely to help everyone improve and believes it should be given quickly to avoid wasting time. His American co-workers, however, did not see it this way and were offended by his direct approach.

I have definitely been in meetings where I've heard ideas proposed that I think are terrible. But I am not from New Zealand, so instead I say things like, "That's so good! I like the direction this is going. Maybe we should just consider adjusting (*insert better and completely different idea*) to make this even stronger." Sometimes, the negative feedback I give or receive is phrased so gently you might think it is positive feedback! That is what it means to be indirect, depending on what kind of culture you are from, this either makes total sense or feels completely ridiculous.

LEADING

Leading is another area where there are huge cultural differences. Some countries are very egalitarian, meaning everyone is treated equally, even the boss. The opposite is hierarchical, where there are clear lines of authority and leaders are expected to be set apart and respected. Most of Africa, Asia, and Latin America tend to be hierarchical, whereas the United States and Europe tend to be egalitarian. One of my co-workers in Nigeria always calls me "boss" as a sign of respect, and it always sounds strange to me. As an American, I treat others casually, even my boss. I don't worry too much about titles or addressing people in a particular way. I have not yet traveled to Africa, but I know that when I do it will be important for me to be aware of the power dynamics and show respect and deference to those in authority.

Knowing how different cultures expect to be led will be critical for you as a ministry innovator working with people around the world. Meyer points out that a leader in China would never ride his bike to work or dress casually in the office. But in Holland, a suit and chauffeur would be out of place. If you're leading cross culturally, it may require you to behave in ways that feel unnatural in order to lead your team well. You will need to exercise humility, laying aside your personal preferences to be a servant leader.

DECIDING

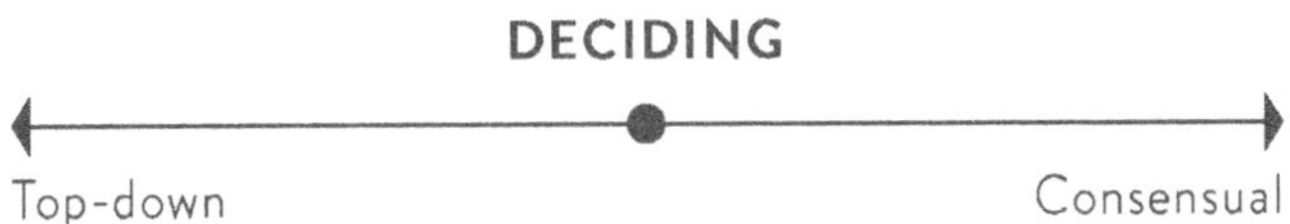

Deciding is something you might expect would match up with a culture's leadership style. It would make sense for hierarchical cultures to make decisions at the top that are then handed down and obeyed. Conversely, in an egalitarian culture it makes sense that decisions would be made by consensus, with everyone having a chance to give input. Sometimes these do match up this way, but not always. The United States is oddly inverted, preferring top-down decision making even though we are not hierarchical. In Japan, it is the opposite. Japanese culture is very hierarchical but decisions are consensual. Some businesses have an entire process around gathering feedback and input on a decision before it is proposed up to the next level of the hierarchy. By the time it reaches the CEO, all the details have been worked out and everyone is in agreement so there is no possibility for conflict when the leader signs off.

You can probably determine whether your culture is top-down or consensual simply by thinking about your own experience. Are you often asked for your opinion by your leadership, or are you expected to wait for a decision to be made and then follow it? Both are valid ways of reaching decisions, they are just very different, and leading a diverse team that represents a mix of decision-making backgrounds requires sensitivity to how each person wants to be engaged.

DISAGREEING

Disagreeing is something you probably do every day, without thinking about exactly how you do it. Disagreement deals both with information at hand and with the relationships at stake.

Some cultures are confrontational while others avoid confrontation. A confrontational approach puts the focus on the subject rather than the individual and separates information from relationships. Some cultures, such as the French, are famous for arguing passionately when they disagree, but they can laugh together a few moments later with no hurt feelings. Disagreeing with an idea is separate from disapproving of the person behind the idea.

Cultures that avoid confrontation are more sensitive to criticism and take it more personally. Disagreement is carefully worded to avoid sounding negative. In extreme cases, even asking what someone thinks could be seen as confrontational. It is important to be able to foster good discussion in a multicultural room, but you also want to be considerate of those who may be uncomfortable with disagreeing or might feel attacked by direct feedback.

SCHEDULING

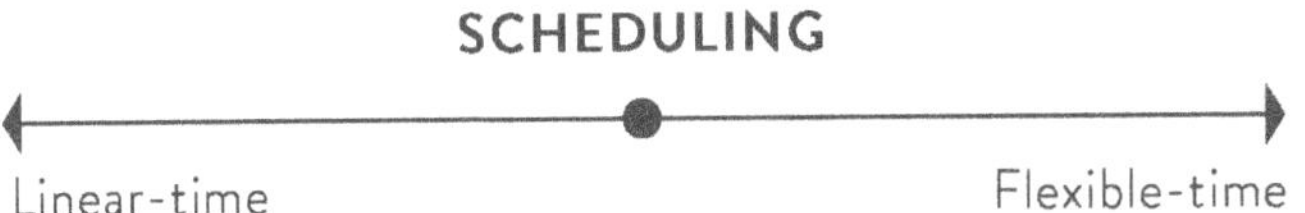

Scheduling is another area where cultures see the world very differently and people behave in ways that are sometimes mysterious to others. The two ends of the spectrum are linear time versus flexible time. In linear time cultures, time is seen as limited and valuable. In the United States we have the saying "time is money," because we think about time as a resource we spend. Everyone is expected to be in place for a meeting at the exact time it is scheduled to start, and if someone is late it costs everyone else precious time. We are very strict about schedules. I remember even as a child synchronizing my watch with the school's bells so I would be on time to classes.

In contrast, you might have heard people say, "Oh, we're on Latin time," or "We're on island time," as an excuse when they are late. They may indeed be in a different time zone, but what they are really saying is that they have a flexible view of time. Flexible time cultures see time as an almost endless resource. There will always be more tomorrow, so it is okay if something doesn't get done today.

Schedules are secondary to relationships, so you wouldn't cut a great conversation short just because you might be late to the next thing. It can be almost disorienting to realize that people can see something as fundamental as time very differently based on their culture.

PERSUADING

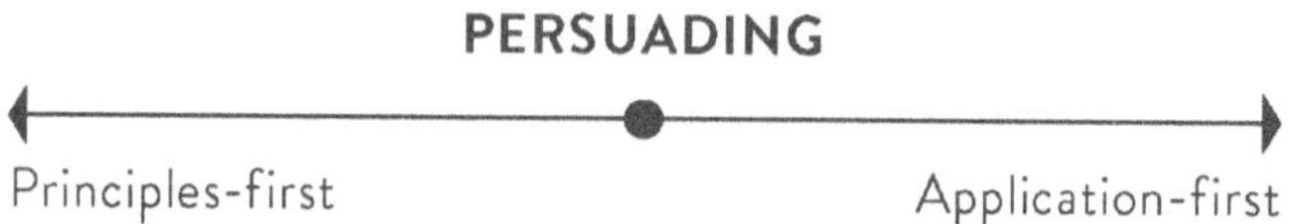

Persuading is the final aspect of culture mapping, and it is a critical one. As we think about the work of ministry innovation, we need to be able to present information and champion our ideas persuasively. But what people will find convincing depends a lot on the culture they are from.

The two approaches are principles first or applications first. The United States is application first, so we always start with our "so what." We begin by telling others why our idea matters and how it will affect them. Only after we have convinced our audience that they should care do we explain the details. In a principles-first culture it is the opposite. Your audience won't be convinced of anything until you show the process that led to your results. The conclusion is less important than the way you arrived at that conclusion. You must show the evidence that supports your idea.

I personally found this fascinating because I had never even questioned what was natural to me. All my life, I have heard application-first argumentation and learned that this is the way to present information. I believed this was the only way. This was a powerful lesson in seeing the world as others do and learning to adjust the way I behave to better fit my intended audience. The next time you are preparing a presentation, make sure you check the culture of your audience to find out if you should focus on the "so what?" or take the approach, "Here was my process."

These eight dimensions help us understand cultural diversity in simple and practical ways. Across all of these dimensions, you should look at where your country falls relative to the culture you are interacting with.[22] Even if you are on the same end of the spectrum, there will still be differences that matter. Scheduling is a good example. The United States, Germany, and Switzerland are all on the linear-time end of the spectrum, but in slightly different spots. So to Germans, Americans seem perpetually late; but to the Swiss, both Germans and Americans always run late. None of us are flexible-time cultures, yet the differences are still felt between us.

Cultural intelligence and the ability to understand people are critical to the work of ministry innovation. Innovation requires patience and empathy to lead others into a new way of seeing the world. Like the prisoners in The Cave parable, some of the people we work with and minister to may find it difficult to accept a truth that conflicts with what they believe. Having the beginner's perspective helps us put our own experiences to the side and approach people with a willingness to see the world as they do. Only then are we equipped to help people take the first steps out of the darkness and towards the light.

SEE THE WORLD AS IT IS

There is a woman living in my neighborhood who is 106 years old! Just think about how much the world has changed in her one lifetime. She has lived through the invention of movies, microwave ovens, electric guitars, and nuclear bombs. Transportation evolved from having your own horse to having your own car and then being able to fly around the world on airplanes. Think about the impact of the Internet, GPS, mobile phones, and solar power. Everyday things like touch screens, bar codes, refrigerators, and

---

22 In addition to her book, Meyer offers helpful resources online including a culture mapping tool that can be used for a small fee. You can look up any culture and the way it interacts with others. *https://erinmeyer.com/tools/culture-map-premium/*.

smart light bulbs would have been unimaginable. In contrast to whatever she did as a child, kids today learn about the world on YouTube. Her grandkids are playing video games and uploading content to social media.

The speed of information and the access we have to it is overwhelming compared to 100 years ago. We know the world is changing quickly, but I don't think we fully realize the impact of those changes on society and ministry. Having a beginner's perspective means we take time to examine the world and see it as it truly is. You might be surprised at how different it is from the last time you looked!

We tend to assume that things will generally stay the same, but that is not the case. We must continually check our assumptions against reality. We must think deeply about what new things mean and how they might change our lives. Pick any item from the list above and think about the impact it has had on the world.

It might be easy to think of the obvious ones like the Internet or smartphones, but consider electric guitars. This instrument birthed entirely new genres of music that have shaped culture and generations around the world. What about airplanes? Not only do they give us access to places faster than before, but this new industry has given entire nations the opportunity to shape their economy around tourism and foreign travel. These countries have developed in unexpected directions because of this one invention.

It is impossible to predict the full impact of any change. But it is critical for ministry innovators to be alert to changes and their potential effects. Peter Drucker, often referred to as the father of modern business management, says that we must identify the "future that has already happened."[23] In other words, the new realities that are here but no one has responded to yet. The world

---

23 Peter F. Drucker, *The Daily Drucker* (New York: HarperCollins, 2004), 4.

is changing even when we are not paying attention. Innovators have eyes to see those changes and recognize what is needed because of them. This starts with the humility to admit that we don't know everything and constantly need to update our views and understanding. If we don't, we put ourselves and our ministries in danger of becoming irrelevant. This happens more quickly than we might expect.

Reality does not wait for us to catch up.

A clear example of this comes from the business world. Every year, *Fortune Magazine* publishes their list of the 500 most profitable U.S. corporations. Making the Fortune 500 list means you are a business success. But here's the interesting thing about the list. Only around 50 companies that appeared on the first list in 1955 are still in business today. That's just 10 percent who have managed to survive. Businesses open and shut down every day with increasing frequency. The average lifespan of businesses on the list is going down, and you will outlive most major companies.

What does that tell us? It points to how much the world around us is constantly changing. Competition is fierce, and there is always another business ready to take your place. The thing that made you successful originally may not be enough to sustain you into the future.

In business, as well as in ministry, we must constantly pursue an accurate view of the world and be willing to learn and change in response to what we discover. Reality does not wait for us to catch up. The Fortune 500 list is a cutting reminder of that. There are a lot of very successful people in the world who have everything going their way today but will eventually lose it all overnight or over time. Recognizing how the world is changing around us can help our ministries avoid the same outcome.

Take a moment to think: What cultural shifts are taking place in your local area? What demographic shifts are happening within your audience or community? What realities are different today than when you first started in ministry? Regularly asking questions like this opens us to seeing the world as it really is. It puts us on the leading edge. You will have the ability to see things others do not because they are not looking.

People see what they expect to see. In research, this is called confirmation bias. You might have an idea of how you think the world works, so you carry that assumption into your research. You are more likely to find things that confirm your existing belief and discount things that contradict it. This is very natural and very human. Seeing what we expect to see can have an even deeper influence on our lives than we know. Our experiences shape what we know and our knowledge shapes our beliefs.

Beliefs can become core to our identity. Suddenly, we find ourselves unwilling to change our beliefs based on new experiences because it threatens our understanding of ourselves and the world. Again, this is natural and human, which is why we have to be intentional as ministry innovators to fight this tendency. We have to remember to go outside our caves.

Not every belief becomes core to your identity, of course. There are plenty of things we are wrong about all the time, and we are happy to correct ourselves when we discover them. I regularly mix up days of the week. When I find out it is Wednesday instead of Tuesday, I quickly embrace this new reality. It's great news after all—I am one day closer to the weekend than I thought! Mistaking the day of the week is not reality-shattering for me.

But the closer to my core a belief has become, the less likely I am to let go of it. For example, it would be extremely difficult for someone to convince me I should no longer have faith in God, since that belief is central to how I interpret the events of my life.

As kingdom innovators, I want you to be very aware of your natural disposition to resist change. We too often assume we already know how something works and dismiss new information and evidence of change. To effectively spread the Gospel, we must constantly re-examine and re-learn the things we hold to be true. We must look to see the world as it really is so we know how to properly respond.

We must constantly re-examine and re-learn the things we hold to be true.

We are only human, so we cannot predict the full impact of changes. Unexpected events surprise us and leave us scrambling to catch up. What did you think would happen in 2020? Many ministries had ambitious goals and Vision 2020 statements of things they intended to accomplish. No one could have foreseen that we would instead be dealing with a global pandemic that challenged every part of the way we lived and did ministry. It took time for the implications of our new reality to settle in and for us to adjust our lives in response.

Events like COVID push us to innovate out of necessity. Prior to COVID-19, the Church had access to digital platforms and live-streaming, but few had incorporated these technologies into their programming because they saw no need to. The typical Sunday morning experience at most churches was working well. Who could have imagined that something would happen to prevent people from gathering in person? It was not until COVID made gathering in groups dangerous that churches began to leverage digital as an alternative way to gather. But it was difficult to figure out at first, and many ministries struggled to make it through the pandemic. The churches and individuals who were thinking ahead in that space were better prepared to adapt and transition to being fully online. They were able to lead and thrive amidst this massive change that proved to be the downfall for others.

The interesting thing is that digital was not new. These tools already existed. We could have been live-streaming Sunday services and using Zoom to convene Bible studies at any time. Digital was a present reality, but we failed to respond to it until a time of crisis demanded that we must.

This is an extreme and obvious example, but this pattern happens all the time in our ministries. There are new possibilities we have not yet responded to that could bear much fruit for our ministry.

Why do we so often choose to ignore the way the world is changing and carry on doing things as we have always done? We all do it, so we can all answer. Think about what it might be for you.

Maybe you lack time or resources. It may be inconvenient, or you don't see the immediate benefit of making a change. Perhaps you are satisfied with the way your ministry is going and see no need to do things in new ways. Each of these mindsets is fatal to ministry innovation.

Apathy, pride, or fear will not set us up to see the world as it really is and make the changes we must to navigate the future well. Understanding change and responding well takes time. But it is something we need to do if we hope to remain relevant. There is no reason the Church should have to lag behind instead of leading the way in innovation. We can learn to observe and be open to new connections, ideas, and inspiration.

We have resources that Fortune 500 companies will never have. We have the voice of the Holy Spirit guiding us into all truth. God can give us eyes to see both the physical and spiritual realities at work. Ask Him for wisdom and He is glad to give it.

MAKING SENSE OF IT ALL

I know almost nothing about keeping bees. Here is the sum of all my knowledge in this area:

Beekeepers use a smoke can (mysteriously) to calm the bees. Beekeepers wear mesh clothes to protect themselves. Bees produce honey from flower nectar, and the honey is harvested (maybe using the smoke can?) and sold. Finally, the entire process of what bees do is a vital part of pollinating crops that produce the food to keep humans alive. Apparently bees are dying off and in high demand.

My knowledge in this area was acquired accidentally from random people I have talked to or from TV documentaries. If I were to begin beekeeping tomorrow, I would need to learn. I don't know where to acquire the tools and the bees, how to harvest honey, identify the queen, or keep myself safe if the bees should get mad at me. I don't know what makes bees get mad at you. I know nothing.

My success would depend on how well I can learn, practice, and apply new information and skills. But I'm not ashamed of my lack of knowledge in this area. I am a beginner and I know it. If I truly wanted to succeed, I would attempt to fill myself with as much knowledge as I could find. I would happily submit myself to any teaching, new experiences, advice, correction, or opportunities to grow. This is the beginner's perspective at work.

It can be easy to have the beginner's perspective for a subject we know close to nothing about (like beekeeping). However, we also need to embrace the beginner's perspective in areas where it is not easy: the areas where we are already highly skilled and we no longer consider ourselves beginners.

The world changes constantly, so even what we know may not be useful anymore. The areas where we desire to have the greatest impact are the same areas in which we must continue to explore and grow. When you are full of knowledge, you believe there is nothing else to be gained, nothing else you need to improve, and nothing anyone else can teach you. That is when you are most likely to become obsolete and ineffective. When you feel that you are the expert, you are tempted to stop learning, and that makes you vulnerable.

God knows this about us, and He gives us kingdom values to pursue. God values humility and elevates the humble. God hates the proud and opposes them (Proverbs 3:34, NIV). Being willing to defer to others, to learn, to relearn, and to continually empty ourselves so we can be refilled is a practice that helps remove pridefulness—a major stumbling block in our work as innovators.

We must always leave room for God to be the one who opens our minds and helps us to see. One startling example of this in the Bible was on the road to Emmaus after Jesus's death and resurrection. Luke chapter 24 describes how some of the disciples met and walked with the resurrected Jesus but did not even recognize Him. They were talking about Him while He was right there with them! Afterwards, they asked each other, "Were not our hearts burning within us while he talked with us on the road and opened the Scriptures to us?" (Luke 24:32, NIV).

Their hearts were burning, but it was as if their eyes were closed. They were sure that Jesus was dead. They had seen Him on the cross. Their minds were closed to new information, full of the knowledge and experiences of the past few days. They were unable to consider the possibility that Jesus was alive until He opened their eyes to recognize the new reality.

It can be the same for us in our ministries. There are new realities we have yet to see and understand. The world is changing all around us. How do we make sense of it? There is a lot of information to process, but don't be overwhelmed. The beginner's perspective is the place to start. It puts us in a posture of humility. The best way I have found to practice the beginner's perspective is to not try too hard. Go into exploring mode. Seek out new knowledge. Don't worry if you don't understand it all or know the implications right away. Your brain is incredibly talented at categorizing and identifying patterns. Simply set aside time to interact with new information and let your brain do what it does best. Look for trends, patterns, and connections. If something is interesting to you, learn more about it. Be willing to take detours and go deep.

Opportunities for innovation depend on how well we are able to recognize and respond to change.

Peter Drucker describes seven sources of innovation.[24] We will look at each one a little closer as part of our journey towards the beginner's perspective.

The Unexpected: When something unexpected happens, whether good or bad, it is an excellent indication that there is a new or unexplored opportunity in front of you. Growing up, my mom taught a Sunday School class at our church. She is an artist and incorporated many creative ideas into teaching the Bible lessons.

At the end of the year, children didn't want to graduate to the next teacher's class because they loved her so much. This was unexpected! Kids normally move from one teacher to the next without too much complaint. Instead, children were crying on Sunday and trying to go back to her class. This was a perfect opportunity for the children's pastor to find out what my mom was doing differently. She was invited to lead a workshop for the other Sunday School teachers, sharing her innovative ideas so they could also make their classes creative and enjoyable. Things that are unexpected point to opportunities for innovation.

---

24 Peter F. Drucker, *Innovation and Entrepreneurship* (1993; repr. New York: HarperBusiness, 2009).

Incongruity: This is a big word, but it simply means "something that doesn't make sense." Anything that seems illogical. The word literally means "does not follow." Imagine a line of baby ducks following a mother duck, except one of the baby ducks is actually a kitten. That is an incongruity, and it should make us pay attention. In ministry, an incongruity could be when something is growing that we did not expect to. Or perhaps when something is failing that should have been a success.

When I first joined OneHope, there was a huge innovation project to create a virtual world Bible game for churches. It was a large investment of time and resources, and it seemed like such a good idea. Children love games, and churches need a way to stay connected to families throughout the week. We believed in the project, and it seemed to have everything going for it. We expected it to be an incredible success to help us reach millions of children. Instead, it was a major failure. The team was confused and disappointed. But there were things to learn from this too. We realized we had made some incorrect assumptions about what churches wanted and needed. We had also invested in a technology that didn't allow us to make quick changes in response to feedback.

However, there was an opportunity for innovation in this painful incongruity. Later, we made the *Bible App for Kids*, which has been a huge success worldwide. The app accomplished a similar purpose as our original project: to engage kids with Scripture in a fun gamified way. But instead of going through churches to do this, we went straight to parents, and they loved it. The incongruity of our first failure pointed us towards the real opportunity for innovation.

Process Need: The moment you think, "There must be a better way!" is an indication of a process need. For example, think about the way tithes are collected in churches. There was a time not that long ago when you could only give through cash or check. Physical money was required to put in the offering plate as it passed by. But many people don't carry cash, so they couldn't give even if they wanted to. Some entrepreneurial people thought, "There must be a better way!" So they developed the idea of a text-to-give system. People always have their phones! Now you can simply send a text message to the church's number with the dollar amount you want to tithe. Your bank processes the request, and the money is transferred. You can give right away while you are thinking about it. This was a significant innovation in response to a process need. Many people had probably encountered this barrier, but finally someone took action.

Market Structure: Many factors, such as new or growing businesses, can change demand for products in related areas. For example, consider Uber. This mobile app allows individuals to use their personal vehicle as a taxi service. Airbnb is another example. This online platform allows people to use their home or spare bedroom as a hotel alternative for travelers. These apps changed the market structure in their industries. Uber dramatically shifted the need for taxis, rental cars, buses, trains, and other transportation services. Airbnb similarly disrupted the hotel industry including not only traditional lodging, but travel agencies, tour companies, and more. Uber and Airbnb as businesses are innovative themselves, but they also create new opportunities for innovation because of the way they restructure the market. The balance of supply and demand is now different, which changes people's needs in a ripple effect. For example, if more people are driving their own cars as taxis, then the demand for car maintenance might rise. Similarly, if people are renting out their homes, cleaning services will probably become more popular. Pay attention to how the market is changing, and you will find many ways to innovate in response.

Demographics: Opportunities for innovation also arise because people themselves are changing in some way. The continent of Africa currently has the world's youngest population, is rapidly growing, and also has the highest percentage of Christians. By 2060,

Africa is predicted to become the global center of Christianity. Six of the ten countries with the largest Christian populations will be located in Africa.[25] OneHope's regional leaders in Africa recognize that this moment in history is an innovative opportunity. They intend to work between now and the year 2060 to prepare the African Church to respond well to this new reality.

One of the things they want to change is to transform the mindset from a receiving Church to a generous, sending Church. They are also working to invest in the next generation, because today's children are tomorrow's leaders. Imagine a world where culture is led by committed Christians and missionaries are going from Africa to every nation to spread the Gospel. I love their vision! Our team is demonstrating wisdom in reading the times and responding to them.

Changes in Meaning: When the way people think about something changes, that is an opportunity. We saw this happen during the COVID-19 pandemic. Almost overnight, we found ourselves living in a very different world. In many of our countries, it would have been unusual to see someone wearing a face mask. It might have been unsettling to see someone with their face covered. But during the pandemic, face masks were preferred for protection. It was unsettling to see someone without one. The meaning around social gatherings changed too. Meeting in person shifted from normal to something to be feared. The world and the Church witnessed many changes in behaviors and choices as we reassigned meaning around in-person interactions. But opportunities for innovation abounded in the digital space. People still need other people; they just need a different way to connect to them. Organizations and businesses that were able

---

25 According to "The Changing Global Religious Landscape" study by Pew Research Center, 42 percent of the global Christian population will live in Africa by 2060. Tanzania, Uganda, and Kenya are projected to displace Russia, China, and Germany as countries with large Christian populations. They will join Nigeria, Democratic Republic of Congo, and Ethiopia on the top 10 list.

to recognize the changes in meaning and adapt to them found the greatest success.

New Knowledge: Remember, the world is always changing. Discoveries are being made daily, and humanity has access to more information than ever before. Are we paying attention to this new knowledge? Innovation is not invention. You don't have to create something entirely new that the world has never seen before. Instead, you can build on what already exists or respond in new ways. Innovation creates value through new combinations of existing knowledge or solutions. Apple is praised as innovative in its design of the iPhone, and this is a good example. Apple didn't invent phones, palm-sized computers, cameras, touch screens, or Internet browsers, but it did innovate by putting them all together in one device. We all have access to new knowledge, but we don't always do something about it.

These are Drucker's sources of innovation, but they are certainly not the only ones. The beginner's perspective helps us recognize these opportunities and respond to them well. We must learn to slow down and really see. As you practice this, let experiences and input come to you without immediately trying to sort and evaluate them. It is okay if you don't understand everything perfectly right away. Someone who is a beginner is not highly skilled from the start. Everything is new and unfamiliar. We must be intentional to set aside our expertise and experiences to be a beginner once again.

We should even be a beginner when it comes to the Gospel. There is so much joy in rediscovering the incredible Good News of Christ as our Savior. Each day in our faith is a new beginning; a new chance to depend on God and experience His undeserved grace in our lives. "The steadfast love of the LORD never ceases; his mercies never come to an end; they are new every morning" (Lamentations 3:22–23). Never forget the wonder of the Gospel as you minister to others.

Beginners look at the world with fresh eyes to discover how to truly serve well.

WHY WE MUST BE BEGINNERS

» You are unique and your perspective is a valuable source of strength for your ministry. But you are fundamentally different from those you are trying to reach.

» We need to see life through the eyes of others to develop empathy and dismantle our assumptions.

» Culture is key to innovation as it shapes our understanding of ourselves and expectations of others.

» We tend to depend on the past to prepare us for the future. But the world is changing so quickly that our knowledge is soon out of date.

» New realities are opportunities for innovation if we can learn to recognize them.

PRACTICE THE PERSPECTIVE

Go explore an area of your ministry that is unfamiliar to you or spend time with a team you don't often interact with. Try to see the world as they do in their daily work. Be open to the new experience and note what surprises you.

BROADEN YOUR PERSPECTIVE

Liam's book recommendations:

The Culture Map: Breaking Through the Invisible Boundaries of Global Business. Erin Meyer. New York: Public Affairs, 2014.

Black Box Thinking: The Surprising Truth about Success. Matthew Syed. New York: Penguin Publishing Group, 2015.

Innovation and Entrepreneurship. Peter F. Drucker. New York: HarperBusiness, 2009.

The Storyteller's Perspective

CONNECT YOUR INNOVATIONS TO THOSE WHO NEED THEM MOST

THE HALF-CIRCLE WALL

A Parable

There was once a hill encircled by a stone wall. The purpose had long been forgotten. But it had been there for as long as anyone could remember. People often came to see it and would comment:

"What a well-made wall, and so old!"

"I wonder how it was made? It seems to have fallen apart in some areas, but it has stood the test of time in other places."

To some it was an ugly and inconvenient thing. To others, it was an ancient marvel worthy of attention.

One day, two women walked past each other along the wall. One tripped and said aloud, "Something must be done about this wall. It's falling apart!"

The other nodded along. "I agree, it's a danger to everyone who uses this road! It doesn't seem as if anyone is willing to do what it takes. It's only been getting worse for years."

"Why don't we take care of it once and for all?"

"Quite so! Many people come to look, but they never take action. It seems as if nobody truly cares!"

"Well, I care!"

"As do I!"

"I live not far away, just to the north. I can come back this very night. I simply won't stand for it any longer."

"And I live not far, just to the south. I will join you!"

So the two women resolved to do what must be done that very night. One woman approached from her home to the south. She picked up the broken pieces of the wall and refit them into place so the wall would be preserved and nobody would stumble again on scattered stones.

The other woman approached the hill from her home in the north. She pulled stones down from the wall. She threw them as far away as she could so the rocks would be far from the road and the wall would no longer be an eyesore in disrepair.

The two labored diligently for hours both working their way around, unable to see the other or their progress over the hill. They worked with conviction, united in purpose and glad to have a collaborator to share the burden.

As the sun began to rise, they both came to the point where the other had begun. The one who was tearing down the wall was surprised to see the wall in such good shape, perfectly mended and tall. The one who was repairing was shocked to find the wall completely gone, its rocks spread far off the road.

So it was that the following day the people from all around marveled at how the wall was now a perfect half-circle, completely repaired on one half, and completely missing on the other. Nobody knew who undertook such labor or why. The two women who worked so hard never told a soul.

The one who took down the wall chose the road by the side where it was gone, and the one who admired it took the road where it stood firm. They never crossed paths again.

• • •

THE STORYTELLER'S PERSPECTIVE

"The most powerful person in the world is the storyteller. The storyteller sets the vision, values and agenda of an entire generation that is to come."

—*Steve Jobs, former CEO of Apple*

If I could read my wife's mind, it would save me a lot of trouble. Most disagreements we have are the result of poor communication. We don't express ourselves clearly enough, even though we think we have. Or somehow the other person interprets a completely different meaning than what was intended. I am quite certain there have been times when my wife heard the exact opposite of what I am sure I said!

We spend so much of our lives engaged in some form of communication. Our days are filled with conversations, meetings, emails, texting, and engaging on social media. These activities are all about sharing and deciphering meaning.

With so much practice, you would think we would all be perfect communicators! Yet we still often experience confusion and miscommunication because we do not know what is in the mind and heart of another person. This happened to the women in our parable. They thought they were clearly and openly communicating with one another about something they both cared deeply about. But each listener brought assumptions that were not revealed in their conversation. Their resulting actions undermined each other. Because neither woman knew where the other was coming from, their shared connection was false.

This happens in our ministry work too. We have something we are trying to accomplish in the world, but our effectiveness often depends on how well we can communicate that goal to others. We must help others see our story, as well as see how they can be a part of it.

We must help others see our story, as well as see how they can be a part of it.

We all have stories that we believe about ourselves and about the world. We align our actions with those stories. But we cannot assume that the story we see tying everything together is the same story another person sees. You and I can experience the exact same event and take away something totally different about it depending on our perceptions, life experiences, and beliefs.

We must learn to be careful listeners. We need to get to know other people and the things that have shaped them. We need to realize what they care about and what they need. When we set aside our way of seeing things, we can more fully grasp what the world looks like to them.

All of this happens naturally when you spend time with others developing a friendship. If you have listened well, you unconsciously construct a framework for how others think and feel. You might be able to anticipate what will upset or excite them. You may guess their reactions and feelings. The more you know them, the more accurate your predictions become. Few things are more precious than being known and understood.

Ministry innovators must build genuine connections with people who will join us on our journey. Doing that with even one person can be difficult, let alone with the hundreds, thousands, or even millions of people you might be trying to reach. However, the principles of good communication apply regardless of your audience's size. Effectively communicating an idea requires understanding what you want to say, the audience you want to say it to, and how that audience will receive the message. The storyteller's perspective is a powerful tool to help us do this.

"No one would have followed Martin Luther King Jr. if he had said 'I have a plan,'" says author and business leader Simon Sinek. "They followed him because he said, 'I have a dream.'"[26] A dream is compelling. It is an opportunity to bring an imagined reality to life. It is a story that may or may not come true. It is a journey you choose to take one step at a time.

You have dreams for your ministry and for the lives of those you are seeking to reach with the Gospel. You dream of the life transformation that will occur when their eyes are opened to the truth. You long for this to happen and for God to work through you to shine light into the darkness and speak life to a broken and hurting world. Maybe, like Martin Luther King Jr., you can see what and no one else can see yet.

It all starts with the story you tell.

WRESTLE WITH YOUR WHY

Why is one of the most powerful words in the world, especially when it is used as a question: *why?* This simple word quickly cuts to the heart of a situation. It prompts us to seek truth. Knowing our *why* reveals both what we are and what we are not.

However, it can be a scary question to ask of ourselves and our ministries. I've asked pastors this before: "Why does your church exist?"

---

26 Simon Sinek, "How Great Leaders Inspire Action," September 2009, *https://www. ted.com/talks/simon_sinek_how_great_leaders_inspire_action.*

I was driving through an unfamiliar town one time when I saw two large churches directly across the street from one another. I asked myself "Why?" Why does this town need two churches on the same street corner? Why did someone decide to build a church when one was already there?

Pastors sometimes have difficulty answering this question. They quickly tell me *what* they do. They talk about the many programs they have and how many people attend each Sunday. Some churches focus on outreach and missions, while others have excellent children's programs to engage families, or incredible praise and worship. These are all good things, but these are not why the church exists. These are their activities, not their core purpose. So I simply ask it again: "Why?"

"People don't buy what you do, they buy why you do it." This is what author Simon Sinek says. In his TED talk "How Great Leaders Inspire Action," he shares that leaders do not inspire by discussing the *what* or the *how*, but rather the *why*. People don't follow leaders because they do great things but because they have great vision.[27]

I was so inspired the first time I heard OneHope's founder, Bob Hoskins, share the story of our ministry. Bob was called into public ministry at the age of seven and filled with the Holy Spirit, who enabled him to preach with the vocabulary and maturity of an adult. Many people were saved through his crusades around the world.

In 1986, at the age of fifty, Bob received a distressing vision from God showing the devil's plans to destroy an entire generation. Bob was shown how the children of the world would be attacked through all manner of evil such as human trafficking, abuse, AIDS, and being put into armies of child soldiers. The vision was

---

27 Simon Sinek, *Start with Why: How Great Leaders Inspire Everyone to Take Action* (New York: Penguin Publishing Group, 2009), 41.

so dark and terrible that he wept for days. He asked God why he was seeing this, and God answered.

God told Bob that the only thing that could save this generation was His Word and it should be delivered through leaders. So Bob immediately went to work. He reached out to world leaders requesting permission to bring Bibles for their nation's children. He assembled a team to produce Scripture engagement resources and partnered with churches to deliver those products around the world.

Today, OneHope continues with our mission to give God's Word to every child. That is our *why:* to affect destiny by providing God's eternal Word to all the children and youth of the world. That *why* is what drives us and what we lead with when sharing about our ministry with others. Hearing Bob's story of why we minister to children is far more powerful than hearing some statistics or facts about what OneHope does.

Facts give credibility, but stories drive memories and engagement.

Organizations that lead with their *why* are more successful than others because they offer people the chance to connect with what they do on an emotional level. Other ministries may do similar things or have similar programs, but the story behind your purpose is something that nobody else can copy. Your story is a unique part of God's story and what He is doing in the world. We are the branches connected to the vine, and Jesus reminds us that "apart from me you can do nothing" (John 15:5).

Facts give credibility, but stories drive memories and engagement. Interest will always outweigh information. Story creates emotion, loyalty, and commitment. Stories are memorable and meaningful. That is why being a storyteller is a critical part of your work as a ministry innovator. It should be a priority to communicate your story well, especially to those you encounter for the first time.

We tend to forget information we have learned, but stories we hear stick with us. There is a reason for this and it comes from biology. Lisa Cron, author of several books on this subject, explains why stories are so powerful. She presents research on how our brains function when interacting with narratives. Surprisingly, our brain reacts in the same way to an event in a story as it would to an event in real life. This is incredible! When you listen to a story, your brain lives it out and responds accordingly. You identify with the character, searching for ways to overcome the challenges they face.

"We don't turn to story to escape reality," Cron says. "We turn to stories to navigate reality."[28] It turns out that story is like a playground for our brain. We crave stories because they are how we learn about the world and how to live in it successfully. We can internalize the lessons characters learn without suffering the dangers they face.

I was taught in school that it is fairly easy to write a story. All you have to do is create a plot, or series of events, that follows this formula: context, rising action, climax, falling action, and resolution. But when I followed this pattern and made up people and events to fit into it, the stories I wrote were not amazing. Now I know why. Cron says that it is not the plot that drives your story. Reading about one event after another does not activate our brain.

The heart of a good story is not what happens. Rather, it is what those events mean to a specific person. A compelling story shows

---

28 Lisa Cron, *Story Genius: How to Use Brain Science to Go Beyond Outlining and Write a Riveting Novel* (Berkeley, CA: Ten Speed Press, 2016), 16.

us how the plot affects and eventually changes the main character. At the start of a good story, the character has a defining misbelief about themselves or the world. The events of the story help them discover this misbelief and overcome it to reach a goal that would have been impossible otherwise. Over the course of a good story the characters grow and evolve. It is the internal struggle of the characters and their ultimate victory over the struggle that holds the meaning of the story.

Let's look at the story of Noah from Genesis as an example. Here's the plot:

God tells an old man he needs to build a boat to save his family and a bunch of animals from a flood. The old man builds a boat, and God sends the animals. Then it rains for a long time and floods as God said it would. Everyone not on the boat dies. After many days at sea, the old man and his family find land, release the animals, and repopulate the earth. God sends a rainbow promising to never flood the world again.

A lot happens in this story! But this description is boring. Now let's look at it not from the plot perspective, but from the character's perspective:

Noah was an old man who loved his family. The world was dark and sinful, but he still hoped and believed in God. One day he heard God's voice speaking to him specifically out of all the humans on earth. God said there would be a flood, which Noah couldn't imagine. What would the whole world look like covered with water? His family's safety depended on his ability to build an impossibly large boat. He faced a choice to either believe God and obey Him or ignore Him like the rest of the world. Noah chose to believe God and followed His specific directions for how to build the boat. Sometimes he felt doubt as people around him called him crazy. The project was massive and he was old. Would he even finish the boat in time? Sometimes he secretly wondered if his family thought he was crazy too, even though he was doing this work for them.

Noah worked and strained for a long time, hoping his faith was the right choice. He hoped he had spent his time and effort on something that would matter. Trusting God, he finished the immense project, and miraculously, animals began to show up in pairs. He herded them onto the ship along with his family. In his heart, hope was rising that it really was the voice of God he had heard. Storm clouds began to rage in the sky and it began to rain. All the people who had said he was crazy for believing in God were suddenly desperate to get on the boat with them, but God had closed the door. The flooding lifted the ship and for forty days and nights they were set adrift in a vast, endless ocean like they had never seen before. When they finally made it back to dry ground, Noah kissed the earth, wept, and prayed aloud his thanks and love to God for sparing his family. He knew God to be real and saw that His justice and wrath were deserved. Yet in His mercy, God provided a means of escape from judgment. Noah's family would forever tell the story of God's personal loving care for them. God set a rainbow in the sky so that every time Noah saw it, he remembered God is a merciful Savior.

We all know what happened to Noah, which is exactly why I chose this as an example. I wanted you to see how different it is just to read the plot versus seeing how the events affected Noah. It becomes a compelling story when you see Noah's emotions, doubts, and ultimately trust in God that saved his life and ours too. After all, we would not be here if God had not called Noah to play this part in His story!

The most powerful way to draw someone into your ministry is to tell them your story. People commit to things they feel matter. Your story communicates that significance to them. Consider how you can invite people in to experience your story for themselves. How can they feel the emotions, urgency, and passion you feel?

Avoid the temptation to focus on facts, numbers, or even what you've accomplished. None of that matters if people don't know why you're doing it. Story is what creates connection and helps people look for ways to participate in God's mission.

Storytelling is not just the job for your ministry's founder or your church's pastor. You have probably heard them tell the story of your ministry through the lens of their own experience. Maybe it feels more powerful than your story because they lived through some incredible experience. Like Bob receiving a vision from God and starting OneHope with nothing but faith. But you have stories too. You have your own story of how God called you into His work and what He has done through you. You have stories of challenges that felt impossible to overcome and how God miraculously provided for you. Maybe you have a story you don't see the end of yet, but are still waiting and praying to see what God will do next. Own those stories and tell them to others.

Being a storyteller is important for the work of innovation because it is the key to drawing people into the journey with you. Story is what will make others care about the things you feel passionate about. Story shows where you've been, where you're trying to go, and what kind of help you need to get there. Trying to win people over to an innovative idea or ask them to take action without understanding your *why* is a losing battle.

Asking people to take action without understanding why is a losing battle.

At the end of the day, the Gospel's *why* is very clear: "For God so loved the world, that he gave his only Son, that whoever believes in him should not perish but have eternal life" (John 3:16). Jesus knew His *why* too and prayed it passionately: "Father, I want those you have given me to be with me where I am, and to see my glory, the glory you have given me because you loved me before the creation of the world" (John 17:24, NIV). Incredible, isn't it? Jesus's *why* is to be with us. He laid down His life so we could be reunited with God in the beautiful fellowship displayed by the Trinity.

Ultimately, that is the story we are telling and the *why* behind everything we do in ministry. We exist to communicate God's message of hope to a deeply broken world. God's *why* holds the answer to why we are here and what we should do with our lives every day. As you practice the storyteller's perspective, you will be surprised at how much easier it is to invite people to join the work you are doing and ultimately to join the kingdom you are a part of.

YOU CAN ONLY CHOOSE ONE

Once you've wrestled with your *why*, it's time to tell your story to the world. There's just one not-so-tiny problem: you can't talk to everyone at once. Hold on, you say, of course I can. The Internet and social media give me access to almost anyone. All I have to do is blast my story out into the world for everyone to hear. This is true, but practically speaking, it doesn't work. It would take more resources than any ministry has to reach everyone *effectively*.

Technology gives us access to more people than ever before, and that means we need to customize our message more than we ever have. People are flooded with information competing for their attention. Every day, they see advertisements targeted to them specifically by businesses hoping to capitalize on what they care about and search for online. To cut through the noise, we must show how our story is something our audience should care about deeply. We also have to find the right people who will care about our *why*.

As we think about who to reach with our story first, imagine the process of starting a fire. This is the analogy Greg Stielstra shares in his book *PyroMarketing*. To build a fire, you don't hold a small match to a great big log. It takes far more heat than the match can provide to light a log on fire. Instead, you start with something smaller. Dry grass and tiny twigs catch fire easily. Then you can slowly add larger sticks and small pieces of wood to build the blaze. You feed the fire until eventually it is strong enough to burn the large log.

Building a fire is a great picture for reaching people with our message. Stielstra says to look for your driest tinder.[29] These are the people who perfectly align with your mission and who will love your product or program. They are the evangelists who will convince others to believe in what you do.

Your driest tinder are your passionate champions who will bring people in who might not have been interested otherwise. Those people will then point you to others, and as momentum builds, eventually no log will be too large to withstand your fire. Your message will reach even people who were previously not interested in what you had to offer.

We don't need to reach everyone with our message, we just need to reach the right people first.

Stielstra offers us a valuable lesson in this example of building a fire. We don't need to reach everyone with our message, we just need to focus on reaching the right people first. This is great news because as ministries we don't have unlimited resources for promotion. We can be efficient and strategic by looking for our driest tinder—the people we have the best chance of winning.

---

29 Greg Stielstra, *PyroMarketing: The Four-Step Strategy to Ignite Customer Evangelists and Keep Them for Life* (New York: HarperBusiness, 2005), 75.

If we've done the work to make our *why* clear and powerful, it will be easy for those people to share our story with others and spread that fire far and wide.

So how do we find the people who will be our initial champions? This process is called *audience segmentation,* and it is critical work that cannot be skipped in our ministry innovation efforts. Segmenting your audience means looking at all the people you want to reach and dividing them into smaller and smaller groups until you have one very specific group to focus on.

I do this work with OneHope's teams around the world. It is always challenging because after all—the Gospel is for everyone. We want everyone to hear it. But I remind our teams that if your message is for everyone, it becomes too general to connect deeply with anyone. Your story has to be for someone specific to be understood.

The Apostle Paul gives us a good example of this in his ministry. God called him to share the Good News with everyone and fulfill the Great Commission Jesus left us. The Gospel is for the whole world and intended for every person to hear. But how did Paul go about spreading this message? He writes in 1 Corinthians 9:22, "I have become all things to all people, that by all means I might save some." Paul chose to become a lot of *specific* things to a lot of *specific* people so that they might hear and understand his message. Even though the Gospel is for everyone, he did not take a one-size-fits-all approach. He took time to think about the cultures and people he was trying to reach and looked for entry points to share the truth.

You must have absolute clarity on the person you are designing for and speaking to. You should know what they care about, what they fear, and what their challenges are. You should be so specific in your approach that when the person encounters your ministry or program, they breathe a sigh of relief. They think, "Yes! This is what I've been looking for all along!" When that happens, they will not only embrace your solution for their own lives but share it joyfully.

Our audiences—the people we are trying to reach—are multifaceted and diverse. Many times people tell me their target audience is pastors. But take a minute and think about how broad that really is. There are lead pastors, campus pastors, youth pastors, and children's pastors (to name just a few positions). Pastors come in all different ages and nationalities and serve a variety of denominations. They speak different languages and have different educational backgrounds and training. Pastors have different passions and focuses for their churches. Think about the difference between a young youth pastor in a big city versus a middle-aged church planter going to a remote village that has never heard the Gospel.

If you were to have a conversation with each of these people, it would sound completely different. You would recognize that each person has unique needs and challenges in their ministry work. The resources and help you might offer to each would be very different. We must get more specific and understand pastors in greater detail. You don't take an apple and swallow it whole. It's easier to bite if you cut it in half. It's even easier to consume if you cut it in smaller pieces. Like with an apple, you can slice your audience into segments of any size. Segments are based on shared attributes.

A helpful way to get started is to think about a room full of people you want to reach. If you were to walk into that room, how would you divide everyone into smaller groups you could talk to more easily? What characteristics do people share that would help you group them? You can think about who they are, where they are, what they believe, or how they act. You can be as specific as you like with your slices or combine attributes to form larger groups.

Audience segmentation helps us narrow and focus our efforts. Remember, you are not going after everyone. You are looking for the audience segment that will resonate with your story and what you have to offer. You are seeking your driest tinder that will most easily catch fire and spread that flame to others.

THE 3 W'S OF AUDIENCE SEGMENTATION

Who	What	Why
Age	What they do	Inner thoughts
Nationality	Choices they make	Preferences
Location	Behaviors you observe	Attitudes
Language	Barriers they face	Beliefs and worldview
Marital status		Goals and dreams
Education		

As you do the work of understanding and segmenting your audience, you will come to the inevitable and painful decision point: you can only choose one. You may have dozens of audiences you feel are important to reach. But you can only focus on one to go after first. It is challenging to tend many fires at once, so ultimately you cannot keep them all burning.

You must simplify and clarify your efforts. Who is the most important audience? Imagine yourself back in that room full of people. They are no longer one big group but are now nicely divided. You understand what each smaller group cares about, and now it's time to tell them what you care about. It's time to share your story and invite them into the journey with you. For a short time, you have the gift of their undivided attention. But you can only choose one group out of the entire room. You can only approach one and share your powerful message. Who will it be?

This is a difficult decision for most ministries, and it can feel counterproductive. We want to make our resources go as far as possible to reach the most people with our message. But to do our best work, we have to focus our efforts on our most important audience and let go of others. Too often, we jump straight to creating solutions without stopping to ask the foundational question: "Who is this for?" Who will care about what we are creating? The answer cannot be "everyone." It is tempting to make the mistake of going after too many audiences. Perhaps resources are limited and we want to maximize our project's impact. But if we are not designing with a specific person and their needs in mind, by the end of the process, we might find we've made something nobody cares about.

Focus on your most important audience and let go of the others.

Your ministry's *why* helps you prioritize what you work on and who it is for. This is a powerful tool for the ministry innovator. Let your *why* guide you. Let it define what you do and especially what you choose not to do.

In ministry we can easily go too many directions. We can have a hard time saying no to opportunities or cutting programs or products. Everything is needed. Everything is speaking to a broken world. But we can be easily overwhelmed trying to do everything and lose sight of our most important work. When we become distracted from our core purpose, it is called *mission drift*.[30]

What are the things God has called your ministry to do that only you can do? Pursue those things. As you start each new project, have absolute clarity on why you are doing it and who it is for. You may need to have the courage to let go of things that have a long legacy and history of success in your ministry. If they are not helping you reach the people you are called to reach in the future, then carefully consider if it is time to let go of some of those things. Knowing your audience and knowing your *why*

---

30 To read more about this important concept, I recommend Peter Greer and Chris Horst's book *Mission Drift: The Unspoken Crisis Facing Leaders, Charities, and Churches* (Bloomington, MN: Bethany House Publishers, 2014).

will guide you. We must avoid the temptation to just start working and figure it out later.

The time you invest in audience segmentation now will pay off later on. The more time we spend getting this right, the less time our audience will have to spend figuring out how they fit into your story. The opposite is true too. If our message is not clear, even to ourselves, how can we expect others to grasp it?

We can only communicate a clear message when we know who we are talking to. And we can only talk to one audience at a time. Who will you choose to share your message with?

MARKETING YOUR MINISTRY

I remember when I first noticed that my smartphone was listening in on my daily life. I would have a conversation about something and then later that day I would see an advertisement for that exact product on Instagram. Initially, it seemed like a coincidence. I assumed I had visited a website or searched for the product online before. But it became undeniable when something I had never even heard of before was advertised to me after having a conversation where it was mentioned.

It was a little scary to realize how easy it is for advertisers to reach me. However, it also shows we are in a new era of marketing. Businesses no longer have to guess what I care about. They can show me the exact product I might be interested in within moments. They can intersect with me at my point of need and show me potentially helpful solutions.

Marketing might seem like it doesn't apply to ministry. After all, we are not businesses trying to sell products. But advertising and selling is just one slice of marketing. Marketing is a much larger discipline, with communication and connection at its core. It is about helping people connect with what they need.

Marketing is helping the right people find you at the right time.

Think about what a market is. It is where people go to exchange things of value. Everything has a cost. Money is just one way of representing value. Even something that's free, like church, costs people time as well as physical and mental effort. People who value church are happy to exchange their time and effort for the benefits of being in that community. Sharing why they should do so is the work of marketing.

Branding and marketing are often closely associated. Branding is not just for businesses; it absolutely applies to ministry. Your brand isn't your logo. It is the perceptions, thoughts, and feelings people associate with you. Your brand lives in the mind of your customer. We all have a brand—whether we are being intentional to build it or not. Have you thought about what your brand communicates to people? What impressions do they have of you?

Building a brand means working to create positive thoughts and feelings in your audience when they encounter you or anything you create. We all exist in the global marketplace of ideas and resources. What will make people want to come straight to you and not to another brand? Hopefully it will be because of your reputation for excellence and the story people associate with you. These are what create trust and elevate the perceived value of your offerings.

Advertising catches people's attention. Branding is your reputation in people's minds. But both are part of the larger discipline of marketing—of making connections. Marketing is about helping the right people find you at the right time. It is connecting our story to those who want to hear it. Many ministries have suddenly found themselves in this new reality of digital marketing. It can be a confusing and strange place to be. There are many things to learn about advertising, algorithms, and analytics. You may need specialists to help you get started with some of the complex tools and programs available.

The scope and access digital platforms enable is incredible. Suddenly you can talk to almost anyone in the world and put your message directly in front of them (for a fee). In today's digital economy, ministries have the same opportunity and access to people as any big brand with millions of dollars to spend on advertising. This is both encouraging and intimidating. What do you say? How do you catch people's attention as they go about their busy lives?

Digital marketing, and any marketing really, is not hard if you have clarity on your story and on your audience. It is everything we have been talking about so far. Start with your *why* and let that *why* shape the story you share with those you are trying to reach. Then leverage online platforms to put you in touch with those people. Digital marketing helps us greatly because it is easier than ever to locate our audience segments and put our message in front of them. This is invaluable. But the opportunity is only as good as we make it. We must do our best to ensure the brief intersection people have with our ministry is a powerful one.

Sun Tzu wrote the following in his book *Art of War*:

> *If you know your enemies and know yourself,*
> *you will not be imperiled in a hundred battles.*

His writings in *The Art of War* were about military strategy, but his thinking is just as relevant to today's digital strategy conversations. Here is how I would update the saying:

> *If you know your audience and know yourself,*
> *you will not be misunderstood in a hundred interactions.*

Marketing is, after all, good communication. It is communicating what we have to offer to people who might want and need that in their lives. Digital platforms put us directly in our target audience's path. It puts us in their space and in their lives in ways we could never accomplish on our own. What is critical is what we do once we get there. Harry Beckwith, author of *Selling the Invisible* teaches that the best marketing for a service is the service itself.[31]

I want you to remember that marketing is much more than advertising. Promotion is one aspect. But once we have attracted people to us, the most important thing is how we serve them well.

Digital gives us access, but access does not guarantee relationship. Digital marketing makes initial connections, but it is up to us how we nurture and build on those connections. People take different approaches depending on their industry and goals.

Digital gives us access, but access does not guarantee relationship.

Companies who provide products focus on making their products the best they can be. Their goal is to take something from an idea to an item on a shelf for people to buy. Many product companies are masterful storytellers. Their advertisements cast a vision of the lifestyle you could have if you just buy their product. These companies use marketing to help create a pool of customers they can sell to and then come back to with their next great idea, and the next. But once the product is out in the world, the job is basically done. The customers either buy the item or not, but

---

31 Harry Beckwith, *Selling the Invisible: A Field Guide to Modern Marketing* (1997; repr. New York: Warner Books, 2012).

they don't interact with the people who made it. The customers and business don't really expect to have an ongoing relationship outside the point of sale.

In contrast, a company that provides a service depends entirely on relationships. No product is involved, just the interaction between the business and customer. Doctors, lawyers, and teachers are examples of service providers. The mindset is long-term and two-way. If you see a doctor, you want them to really care about your health and continue helping you until you recover. If you work with a lawyer, you hope they can solve your problem. If you are taking a class, you appreciate a teacher who works with you personally to ensure you succeed. The mindset behind providing a service is one of journeying. The customer should have an excellent experience from the moment they first encounter you all the way to the end of whatever journey you take together.

Ministry is a service much more than a product. The Great Commission doesn't say to just get the Bible into people's hands and then we'll be all done. It calls us to make disciples. Discipleship means building relationships and serving people well. We are to be God's hands and feet in the world sharing the loving message of salvation both through our words and through our actions. Relationships are key. We are sharing God's story and inviting people to explore what the Gospel could mean for their lives. This is much more serious than selling any product. It requires the highest level of care and excellence. We must plan and prepare for how we will serve our audience and journey with them long-term.

It can be easy to have a short-term mindset when it comes to ministry initiatives. Urgent needs are everywhere we look. When we see a need and feel called to respond, we work hard to create the perfect resource or program to address the problem. After a lot of time and effort to make it as great as possible, we launch it into the world for people to find. Then it's on to the next need and the next program. It's easier to design something to be distributed in huge numbers than it is to journey with people for years. Sometimes we prioritize the efficient rather than the effective.

OneHope has been growing tremendously in this space, shifting from a product orientation to a service orientation. We started with a single resource for children called the *Book of Hope,* which we translated into Spanish when we launched our ministry in El Salvador in 1987. We quickly translated it into more languages for more countries. We developed new versions of the *Book of Hope* for other cultures, ages, and specific heartfelt needs. We created films, apps, and websites.

As we started reaching people through new digital media, we began to realize how the relationships with our partners and the next generation needed to change. We started to design programs that allowed us to stay connected rather than reach out one time. Journeying alongside churches, families, and children has shown incredible fruit, but it requires us to think and work differently.

The Gospel is not a product to be packaged and sold, but a way of living that reveals Christ and invites people to begin a relationship with Jesus. We carry living water to a thirsty, broken world. It is the way we serve people and love them that they will ultimately remember. This radically reorients our approach to ministry. It reminds us what we should focus on, like when Jesus gently reminded His disciples they should care about every person. Jesus taught that it was worth leaving the ninety-nine sheep to seek the one lost sheep (Matthew 18:12). Jesus prioritized individual relationships over huge numbers, and we should remember to do the same.

CRAFTING THE JOURNEY

I watched a documentary about the re-opening of a Michelin 3-star restaurant in New York City. The attention to detail was like nothing I had ever seen. Everything was planned and nothing left to chance. Waiters practiced how they would set and clear the tables and how they would speak to customers. Chefs cooked the menu over and over again while being timed and evaluated on taste and presentation. The owner himself tested the chairs to ensure their comfort. Because of the restaurant's reputation for excellence, customers made their dining reservations over a year in advance!

"What we're doing here is special, we have the ability to help people celebrate some of the most important moments in their lives," the owner explained. "I don't think we're in the food business… we're in the human connection business."[32]

The team was able to create an incredible experience for their customers because they had clarity on why people were coming to their restaurant: to celebrate special occasions. Knowing the personal journeys of their customers enabled the restaurant to optimize everything they did to meet their diner's needs and expectations. It guided every decision they made from what they served on the menu to how loud the music was and how dim the lights were.

Now think about a completely different dining experience: fast food. These restaurants intersect people at very different moments in their lives. Drive-thrus serve busy people who need inexpensive food fast. Some fast-food restaurants offer indoor playgrounds so parents can take a minute to relax while they eat and their children play. Red and orange are popular colors for decorating because they stimulate the appetite. Chairs are usually hard and uncomfortable to encourage people to eat quickly and leave.

All of these are intentional design choices made because these restaurants also understand the people they are trying to serve. A fast-food restaurant is completely different from a fine

---

32 The restaurant was Eleven Madison Park featured in the Netflix documentary series *7 Days Out,* December 21, 2018, directed by Michael John Warren.

dining establishment in New York. Both are places to get food, so they serve similar purposes. But the experience is totally opposite because of the personal journey that brings the customers through their doors. Knowing what someone expects of you and why they are coming is critical to serving them well.

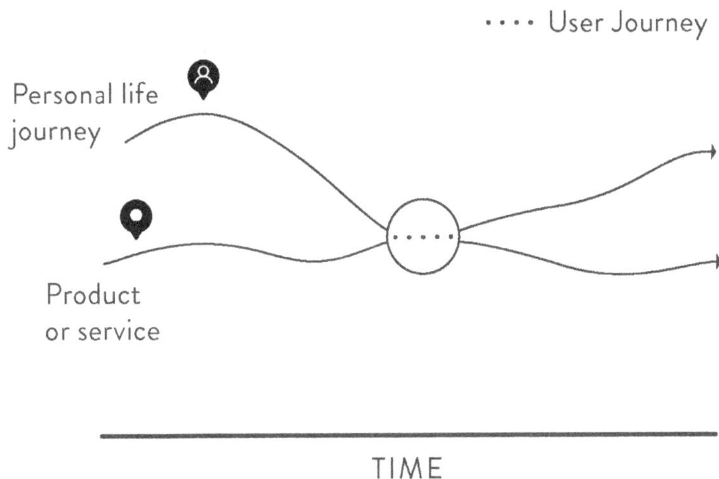

Understanding an individual's life journey creates the critical foundation for the design decisions you will make in your innovation work. Audience segmentation got us started thinking about the unique attributes of the people we are trying to serve. To craft a journey that is personal and compelling for that segment, we must dive deeper into understanding who they are and what they care about.

Creating a *persona* to represent your audience is a great exercise. A persona is a detailed description of a typical person you are trying to reach. It helps us further narrow our focus. Start by giving your person a name, age, and any other biographic information that you identified as part of your audience segment. Then think about their inner life—their thoughts and experiences. What are their goals or desires for the future? What are the things this person is afraid of or anxious about? What do they believe? Who is influencing them? If you are having trouble answering these questions, you should go out and conduct interviews. Choose a few people from your target audience and ask them these questions. Hopefully, they will feel comfortable answering openly and honestly.

Besides their inner life, you should also find out about their actions. Your goal is to understand what they are doing and how it's going. What are they specifically doing to accomplish their dreams? What has been successful? What barriers do they still face? Ask them to share victories and challenges, as both represent opportunities.

If you know what a person's goals are, you can be ready to celebrate with them when they achieve those. If they haven't seen a victory yet, you might be able to help them overcome the barriers standing in their way. All of this information is deeply useful. Don't worry if you can't see the immediate applications to your ministry work. The goal here is understanding and empathy. That is where we must start before we ever consider asking someone to do something.

Take the first step towards them before you invite them to step towards you. Once you have deepened your understanding of your target audience, you can turn your attention towards the journey you will invite them to take with you. You are inviting people into a story they must decide they want to be a part of.

We cannot force people to join us, but we can make it easier for them to participate. This is important no matter who we are reaching, but especially important for those we are connecting to in the digital space. Digital spaces can help us get our message in front of people, but there is a lot of competition.

Just because we can reach people online doesn't mean they will want to reach back. We must put in the hard work to lay out the steps that will naturally build the relationship.

We do this intuitively every day with the people in our lives. You spend time getting to know people and helping them. You know who you can ask for help when you need it. You also know what kinds of requests are appropriate for the level of relationship. For example, you would not ask a casual acquaintance to do something really hard like help you move furniture all day. Nor do we propose marriage to someone we've just met. But for some reason, in our ministry work we can be quick to jump straight to big commitments.

We need to slow down and think about the right first step for our audience to take. How will they encounter us? What will their first impression of us be? What expectations might they bring to the interaction? These kinds of questions help us build our *user journey*.

A user journey describes how people will get from one place to another. It is typically used in digital technology design for apps and websites. But we should think about the user experience in any kind of journey. Where do they start and what steps will lead them to our end goal? If you don't know your end goal, then you know at least one thing you need to work on!

I sketched out my very first user journey when I was sixteen and was hired to build a website for a local law office. I drew a simple diagram on paper showing each page of the website as a different box and lines between them to show how they were connected. My job was to ensure that people could find all the information they were looking for and didn't get stranded on a page with nowhere else to go. My drawing was basic, but it worked for what was needed. This was the early days of websites, where they were primarily just a place for the business phone number and address in case someone wanted to look them up online.

In today's digital world, user journeys have become much more complex. Someone can encounter your ministry for the first time in any number of places. They might meet you through your own content or information others share about you. It may be important to have a presence on multiple social media platforms. In addition you probably have your own website, email list, digital ad campaigns, and more. This doesn't even account for all the things you might be doing to reach people in person.

How are you going to ensure all of those efforts are coordinated and cohesive, following a logical path to move people towards your end goal? That is the work of crafting user journeys.

There is no magical solution to create perfect user journeys. It takes time and effort. This has been a big part of my job with OneHope recently. I have been working with our regional teams to think through their target audiences and the user journeys for each one.

It is like trying to solve a big puzzle. OneHope's work over the years has continued to grow in many different directions, and our teams always have more opportunities than they have time for. It has been very clarifying to see how all those many parts must work together to form the journey we are creating. Sometimes we found areas that didn't make sense and lacked clear next steps for our audience. At other times, we discovered we were investing too much energy in activities that didn't move people towards our goals.

A clear user journey keeps people from leaving in confusion.

Here's the thing about journeys. If you don't plan them purposefully and well, they will still happen—but they will happen accidentally and poorly. A clear user journey is the difference between someone connecting to your powerful message or leaving in confusion.

One helpful framework for mapping a user journey is called the Circular Funnel. It looks like a bullseye with five circles. Everything you do probably falls into one of these stages: Encounter, Explore, Engage, Believe, and Champion. This is not the only way to think about a user journey, but it makes an excellent starting point. Write out everything you do as a ministry and then categorize it into one of these five stages based on where it falls for your user.

CIRCULAR FUNNEL

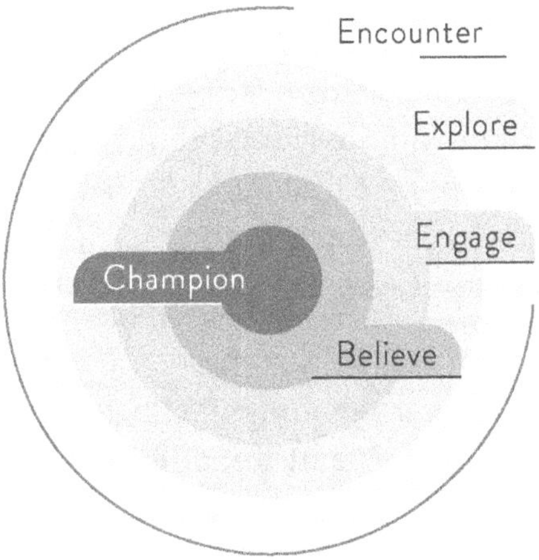

Encounter is when someone first discovers that you exist. It is when they form their first impression of you or your ministry. *Explore* is what happens when they seek out more information about what you do. They might go to your website, social media accounts, or look at anything publicly available about your ministry.

Engage is when they let you know they are interested. They might follow you on social media, leave a comment, or give you their email address to download a resource. At this point, they become known to you. They may have been aware of you for much longer, but you are just getting to meet now.

Engagement may continue and deepen for a long time until they reach the *Believe* stage. This is when the person makes a higher level of commitment. They might make a donation, attend an event, or take some other action that shows they see what you have as valuable for their lives. They are taking a significant step into your story.

Finally, they may become a *Champion*—someone who identifies with your cause. Once they arrive at the champion stage, which is the end goal, the person starts spending their own time and energy to further your mission because it has become something they care about deeply. They share about you with others, partner with you, and perhaps volunteer their time or finances.

Your story has become their story too. Not everyone will become a champion, but everyone should have the opportunity and a clear pathway to take that journey. Each step should build on the one before it, guiding them further into your story and giving them opportunities to deepen their commitment.

Ensure there is always a next step people can take no matter where they enter the journey. You might have heard this referred to as a "call to action." A call to action can be as simple as liking a photo on social media all the way up to inviting someone to give their life to Christ.

Think about what calls to action are appropriate at each step of the user journey. Take into account where that person might be on their personal journey as well. Why will your user want to respond? How does your offering match up with their life and their needs?

Think about the journey from start to finish and look for areas that might feel confusing, as those are likely where you will lose people. Data analytics can help us see this very clearly. Almost everything we do online provides data. You can see where people come from and where they decide to leave. You can see what kind of content gets the most engagement. You can even find out if someone opened and read an email you sent. Use this information to help you understand how the journey looks from the user's perspective. What parts do they find difficult, boring, or irrelevant? If your audience is not responding to your calls to action, take time to consider why. This is humbling but deeply valuable work. We cannot expect people to take a journey we don't even understand ourselves.

Understanding user journeys also helps you prioritize your work and your team's capacity. You can't do everything, so ensure you are doing the most important things.

It is critical to know the change you want to see happen and the path you are laying out for your audience to achieve that change. Which steps need the most attention? Focus on those first. Align and realign your efforts to your user journey. This also helps us ground the work of ministry innovation, which by its nature takes us in new directions. We should be very clear on how those new directions support our overall journey.

You can't do everything, so ensure you are doing the most important things.

This work requires going deep, and it might feel slow. It is not comfortable or easy, and it might show us things we find discouraging or confusing. But ultimately it is the right work. We are entering into people's lives and thinking hard about the challenges they face. We are presenting the Gospel in ways that speak to their deepest needs at their darkest moments. We are inviting them on a life-changing journey to put their trust in Jesus and receive the gift of eternal life!

This is the path we are taking together. It is worth spending the time to get it right.

> Storytellers inspire others to join them on the journey by bringing the right message to an audience they understand deeply.

WHY WE MUST BE STORYTELLERS

» Stories are fundamentally more powerful than facts.

» We have the greatest story to tell in the Gospel message that the world so desperately needs.

» It is better to connect meaningfully with smaller audiences than spread a generic message that few will act on.

» Serving people in love and building lasting relationships should be central to any ministry work we do.

» We turn friends into champions when we are clear about our ministry story and the journey we are inviting others to join.

PRACTICE THE PERSPECTIVE

Take a moment to identify a few of your ministry's most faithful and committed people. They might be staff, partners, volunteers, or donors. Ask them to share their story with you and take time to listen. What led them to you, and what has kept them with you on the journey? Pay attention to key turning points and motivators. Interview several people and consider how you might replicate similar experiences for others.

BROADEN YOUR PERSPECTIVE

Liam's book recommendations:

Selling the Invisible: A Field Guide to Modern Marketing. Harry Beckwith. New York: Warner Books, 2012.

PyroMarketing: The Four-Step Strategy to Ignite Customer Evangelists and Keep Them for Life. Greg Stielstra. New York: HarperBusiness, 2005.

Story or Die: How to Use Brain Science to Engage, Persuade, and Change Minds in Business and in Life. Lisa Cron. Berkeley, CA: Ten Speed Press, 2021.

Start with Why: How Great Leaders Inspire Everyone to Take Action. Simon Sinek. New York: Penguin Publishing Group, 2009.

The Culture Maker's Perspective

CREATE AN ENVIRONMENT WHERE INNOVATION FLOURISHES

WINNIE THE POOH

by A. A. Milne

An Excerpt

"Here is Edward Bear, coming downstairs now, bump, bump, bump, on the back of his head, behind Christopher Robin.

It is, as far as he knows, the only way of coming downstairs, but sometimes he feels that there really is another way, if only he could stop bumping for a moment and think of it.

And then he feels that perhaps there isn't.

Anyhow, here he is at the bottom, and ready to be introduced to you. Winnie-the-Pooh."[33]

• • •

CM

---

33 A. A. Milne, *The Complete Tales of Winnie-the-Pooh*, (1926; repr., New York: Dutton Children's Books, 2016), 1.

THE CULTURE MAKER'S PERSPECTIVE

*"Culture is like the background music that
plays behind everything we do."*

—Tina Seelig, *American educator*

One of the first things I noticed when I started at OneHope was that it sounded like people were speaking an entirely different language. There were many terms I had never heard before. Some were program names or acronyms unique to our ministry. Others were simply phrases I had never used. I had to learn what it meant to "contextualize" a resource and what "pushing back" on an idea looked like. But over time, I have adopted the vocabulary and ways of speaking that seemed strange to me at first. It feels natural after years of being part of this culture. Now I am the person who probably sounds confusing to a new team member.

Every ministry and team has a distinctive character. Collectively as a group, you have your own way of speaking, thinking, and acting. You have habits and expectations that define what is normal. This is critical to understand because organizational culture can either accelerate or cripple innovation.

Culture, broadly defined, is the customs of a particular nation, people, or social group. It is everywhere we go even if we are unaware of it. You were born into a national culture that has shaped what feels right to you. If you have traveled, you have experienced how different the customs can be in another country. You might have felt *culture shock*, which describes the confusion of being in totally different surroundings. Families also have their own culture. Each of us has a distinct way of communicating with our family members as well as shared traditions and experiences that make your little tribe unique.

Within an organization, culture refers to the shared attitudes, values, and practices that characterize you and your co-workers. Workplace culture forms naturally and almost invisibly. You can probably remember jobs where you felt like a great fit with your co-workers and perhaps other positions that were not so great. Culture fit significantly affects whether people enjoy and decide to stay at an organization.

People form culture, but culture also shapes people. Without even realizing it, we will perform to the expectations of our culture and adjust our behavior to ensure we are staying within the norms. People often ask how they can create a culture of innovation within their ministry. The truth is—wherever you are, you already have a culture of innovation. It may just not be a very good one.

You already have a culture of innovation.

We can be like Winnie the Pooh dragged backwards and bumping his head with each step. We know there must be a better way, but we are often unable to take the time to figure out how to change our methods. We are carried along by our organizational culture just like Winnie the Pooh was swept along behind Christopher Robin.

Here's the thing about culture: if we don't intentionally make it, culture creates itself. Rather than letting attitudes towards innovation evolve undirected, we can help purposefully shape a ministry culture where innovation can thrive. Creating culture is powerful. Through it, we influence those around us. Culture can be something we constantly fight against or something that gives us an advantage.

Good cultures of innovation are characterized by diversity, humility, and empowerment. Your ministry culture should enable everyone to contribute in meaningful ways, as well as innovate within their areas of responsibility. We need cultures that are open and supportive of new things. It can't just be you being the innovative one. I have operated alone in the innovation space before, and it is both lonely and ineffective. We need others around us contributing their ideas and supporting the work with their strengths.

Innovation will happen naturally if you have a culture that encourages collaboration and gives people the freedom to change things for the better. To fulfill the Great Commission, we need purposeful ministry cultures that unlock creativity and spark good ideas. From there, we can turn ideas into well-run projects that result in kingdom impact. Are you ready to learn how?

LEADING FROM BEHIND

Culture begins with you. If this sounds like a motivational speech, it is! At times, you might not feel like your individual choices and actions matter. But they do. You are part of a much larger whole, whether that is in your family, organization, church, city, or country. Regardless of your position, you have influence, and you are already contributing to and creating culture around you. Your story is joining with that of others to write history.

The word *culture* refers to the way a society lives—the language, customs, and social habits of a group of people. It includes art, music, fashion, religious beliefs, and more. It is what we say and do as well as the unspoken rules that govern how we behave. Because I happened to be born in the United States, anything I do is automatically "American" and reflects American culture. Because of when I happened to be born, I am part of the

Millennial Generation. We have membership into our culture first and that culture shapes us. But our collective actions also shape how our culture evolves. The world watched and studied the Millennial Generation wondering who we would grow up to be and what we would care about.

Today, Millennials are adults and parents with children of their own. We are employees and business owners, entrepreneurs, and political leaders. There is another generation that has grown up after us—Generation Z—and another generation coming after them. Each will slowly take over more and more cultural spaces, bringing their distinct perspectives and characteristics with them. What they think and how they behave will create new societal realities. This is culture on a broad scale.

Here is a much simpler definition of culture from author and speaker Seth Godin: "People like us do things like this."[34] For example, I am mindful of the fact that Americans tend to have a negative reputation internationally. People like me (Americans) are seen to do things that are rude, loud, and arrogant. Because I am aware of that cultural perception, I am careful to be kind, quiet, and humble when I travel to other countries.

I have been thrilled when people abroad mistake me for someone from France or Spain because it means I have been successful in not living up to their expectations of Americans. My actions don't just change the perception of Americans in their eyes, it represents a change in American culture starting with me. If I can influence other Americans to be polite when they travel, then we will eventually no longer have our bad reputation.

Culture is always changing and evolving depending on our behaviors. However, culture has a very strong pull. It is difficult to act contrary to the norm. I noticed this when my wife and I traveled

---

34 Seth Godin, *Seth's Blog*, July 26, 2013, *https://seths.blog/2013/07/ people-like-us-do-stuff-like-this/.*

to Japan. We were only there for ten days, but it was long enough to change some of our behaviors and attitudes.

People are extremely polite in Japan and conscious of not inconveniencing others. You are not allowed to talk on the phone on public transportation because that would be rude to those around you. We talked more quietly and waited patiently in lines. We found ourselves becoming more aware of how we moved and being careful not to bump into anyone. Even though Tokyo is one of the largest cities in the world, no one ever brushed past us in a crowd.

Japanese culture is also very tidy. The streets are kept clean, and no one would think of littering or leaving trash around. Everyone takes off their shoes inside because it would be rude to get someone's floors dirty. We found ourselves living up to these cultural expectations even when no one was watching or enforcing those rules.

But when we returned home, we adapted back to our American culture almost as quickly. Plenty of people talked loudly on their phones as we rode home on the train, so we did too. We dropped some trash underneath the seat and did not bother to pick it up because the floor was very dirty and others had left trash there too. We quickly became less nice and less clean and less respectful in line with the daily behaviors of those around us.

It was a clear experience of the power of culture to affect the actions of an individual. It also showed how those individual choices collectively create culture.

Culture is present in our ministries. Your team has ways of behaving that set the standard for anyone who joins you. It won't take long for a new staff member to adopt the habits, expectations, and beliefs that have naturally come to form your ministry culture. For example, if someone is treated harshly for making a mistake, what is communicated is "mistakes are not tolerated here." The next time someone does something wrong, that harshness will likely be repeated. Over time, everyone will become less gracious because they learn that "people like us don't make mistakes."

Fortunately, the opposite can also be true. By being kind to our team members when they make mistakes, we can model the idea that "people who work here have grace for one another." That develops a culture with different values and behaviors.

Team culture often comes from the top and is set—intentionally or unintentionally—by those in charge. We naturally look to our leaders to know how we should behave. But it is not just their responsibility. Everyone has the opportunity to contribute to culture.

Culture has momentum.

One question I am often asked is how to lead innovation when you're not the one in charge. Many people feel discouraged because they lack formal authority. They are not the ultimate decision-maker at their organization who can change the way things are done.

Leaders do create culture through the actions they reward as well as the people they hire and promote. But if you really think about it, few of us will ever be the one person at the top: the president, CEO, or senior pastor. Even if you do become the number one leader eventually, you may find your individual actions and choices are not enough to change the entire culture under you.

Culture has momentum and takes tremendous effort to change. Being the boss does not give you absolute control. We don't want a culture of people blindly following where we lead anyway. This doesn't produce innovation. You need everyone's diverse perspectives and contributions. We should not wait until we're in charge to innovate better. Rather, our goal should be to foster the right culture where innovation can thrive naturally within our ministry. Fortunately, we can do that from wherever we are once we become aware of one powerful thing we all have: influence.

"Leadership is influence—nothing more, nothing less," says leadership expert and author John Maxwell. He goes on to say, "True leadership cannot be awarded, appointed, or assigned. It comes only from influence and that cannot be mandated. It must be earned."[35] Influence is earned through investing in people and giving them your time, attention, and care. This is great news because it means you and I can lead our ministries in innovative directions by exercising our influence.

If your ministry culture is not innovative, there are some things you can do to help. Author Clay Scroggins offers practical leadership advice in his book *How to Lead When You're Not in Charge*. Scroggins shares many principles, but here are two that are helpful for culture making.

First, *think like an owner*. We work in ministry, so there isn't really an owner like there would be in a business. But what Scroggins means is to have the mindset of an owner rather than just an employee. This is a biblical principle. The Bible teaches us that we are not just workers in a vineyard but co-heirs with Christ (Romans 8:17).

There is such a difference between the mindset of a worker versus an owner. Workers earn wages, but the land they tend, the fruit they harvest, and all the profits ultimately go to the owner. An owner may work in the fields too, but he invests differently than his workers. An owner cares more deeply about every part of the process. The health of the fields and the way the fruit is picked

---

35 This quote is from John Maxwell's book *The 21 Irrefutable Laws of Leadership: Follow Them and People Will Follow You* (New York: HarperCollins, 2007), 13. You can read a lot of content for free on his blog, *johnmaxwell.com/blog*.

matters because the vines belong to him and he wants them to grow and prosper for years to come.

As members of God's kingdom and co-heirs with Christ, we share in the joy and responsibility of ministry. We should have the mindset of an owner who cares about excellence in every detail. It is not just our name that is reflected in our work but the name of Christ. It is not just our reputation we work for, but the reputation of the Gospel.

This is a critical shift you can make as a ministry innovator that will positively influence those around you as well. A better culture will develop as we all start to take greater ownership of our work and its results.

The second principle is to *practice critical thinking instead of being critical.* It is easy to start blaming others when things don't go well. It is especially easy to blame our leaders. Perhaps they said no to your great idea or yes to a plan you advised against. When things don't go our way, we can quickly become bitter and resentful. We may even secretly wait for failure to happen to prove we were correct. But this is not the right attitude. Our leaders are not our enemies. They also care deeply and want to do what is best.

Avoid the temptation to blame your leaders when innovation is lacking. Grumbling and complaining produce disunity. If we are constantly undermining our leaders by speaking negatively about their decisions, we create a destructive and harmful culture. We also damage our own credibility. Nothing good can get done in this kind of environment. Even if you grow into a leadership position at your ministry, you will be crippled by the toxic culture you fed with your own complaining.

"Choosing to trust your leaders builds trust with your leaders," writes Scroggins.[36] Instead of fighting against their decisions and

---

36 Clay Scroggins, *How to Lead When You're Not in Charge: Leveraging Influence When You Lack Authority* (Grand Rapids, MI: Zondervan, 2017), 198.

making your disagreement louder, work with your leaders and believe that God is speaking to them. This doesn't mean you have to stay silent. If you see a better way, don't be afraid to challenge their thinking. But the way you challenge matters. Approach your leader in a spirit of love and humility. Seek permission to give feedback and ask how you can productively provide it. Be clear that your intention is to improve the team and further the mission.

Faith refocuses our perspective on the bigger picture. Ultimately, God has appointed our leaders, and He is at work through them. We should strive to make our organizations successful even if the ideas we are carrying out are not your own. Whether we understand every decision or not, we can still choose to follow our leaders instead of complaining. We can trust God to bring good results as we serve His kingdom faithfully.

PILOTS, DOCTORS, AND MINISTERS

Matthew Syed begins his book *Black Box Thinking*[37] with a story of a man who drops his wife off at the doctor's office for a minor operation. He takes his kids to run errands and returns in a few hours to pick her up. But he finds out from the doctors that his wife had died due to complications during the surgery. She had not responded well to the anesthesia and the doctors were unable to intubate her, so she went without breathing for too long.

The man was understandably shocked and wanted more details, but the doctors were not helpful and said an investigation would not be conducted without a lawsuit. "These things happen," he was told. "A one in a million chance." But the man who lost his wife was a pilot.

Pilots are similar to doctors because they are also responsible for the lives of hundreds of people every day. But when something

---

37 I highly recommend this book for every ministry innovator. Matthew Syed, *Black Box Thinking: The Surprising Truth about Success* (New York: Penguin Publishing Group, 2015).

goes wrong, their approach is very different. Every airplane has a "black box" designed to survive any kind of incident. Black boxes record everything about the flight: pilot communications, navigation data, altitude, airspeed, flight control inputs, and more. Every time there is a plane crash, that black box is recovered and analyzed by the Federal Aviation Association (FAA). No detail is overlooked because it is a lesson to learn from that has been paid for in human life. The FAA regularly releases new safety regulations based on their discoveries from plane accidents.

Consider the difference between the medical industry and the aviation industry based on these two examples. The medical industry generally assumes that doctors are right and does not typically have procedures to check on medical situations that go wrong. An accidental death may go unexamined and leave families without answers as to why they lost their loved one. This is also a loss to the medical field because they miss the opportunity to gain insight and alter future procedures.

In contrast, the aviation industry has set up its system with practices in place to investigate failures and learn from them when they happen. These two approaches create different cultures for pilots versus doctors. There is more transparency and openness about errors in the aviation industry because pilots have a learning culture. Doctors tend to operate within a performance culture.

When you compare the results of the performance culture of doctors with the learning culture of pilots, the numbers speak for themselves. Syed references studies that show that after cancer and heart disease, preventable medical errors are the third largest killer of people every year in the U.S.[38] The estimated number of deaths caused by medical error "is the equivalent of two jumbo jets falling out of the sky every twenty-four hours," Syed writes.

---

38 According to a 2013 study published in the *Journal of Patient Safety,* preventable medical errors in America were responsible for nearly 400,000 deaths a year. Cited by Syed, *Black Box Thinking,* 10.

In contrast, actual data shows an average of one plane crash per 2.4 million flights.[39]

We are not pilots or doctors, but the work we do in ministry is also life-and-death. We have the serious responsibility of sharing the Good News so people can turn to God and escape eternal judgment. When you think about your ministry, do you have a performance culture or a learning culture? You may not have considered your work in these terms before, but they are critical.

A performance culture tends to cover up mistakes or dismiss them, while a learning culture looks for lessons in mistakes and how to improve for the future. This matters deeply because we are ministers of the words of life. We are representatives of the Gospel and play a significant role in shaping people's perceptions of God.

Our mistakes matter! If we are accidentally turning people away from God through some aspect of what we are doing, that is an issue we cannot ignore. Let me pause here and affirm that God is still sovereign. The work of saving people is not up to us, but up to Him. Ultimately, it is only the Holy Spirit who can bring someone to faith. Yet, mysteriously, God has called us to partner in this work. He has entrusted us to steward the Gospel, so let's be the best stewards we can be.

We must be alert for anything we can learn or change to create the best opportunity for someone to encounter the Gospel. It is God's desire that no one should perish, and that should be our driving motivation also.

Innovation tends to thrive and lead the way in a learning culture rather than a performance culture. The priority in a performance culture is to succeed on an individual level. People want to look good and worry about making mistakes and being punished for

---

39   Syed, *Black Box Thinking*, 9. In 2013, only 210 people died worldwide in plane crashes according to the International Air Transport Association.

them. Because of this, they tend to limit their thinking and their work. They will avoid risky or untested approaches for fear of failure and may hold back their opinions and ideas for fear of criticism.

Remember the man's wife who died in the opening story? There was someone else in the operating room besides the doctors that day. There was a nurse who was alert to the patient's status. As the woman began to go into respiratory failure, the nurse readied a tracheotomy kit that could have saved her life. But the doctors never asked for it. They continued to try to intubate the patient until they ran out of time and her heart stopped beating.

This is a tragic illustration of the results of a performance culture. Perhaps because of her junior status, the nurse didn't feel comfortable or wasn't allowed to speak up even though she had the solution.

This story is painfully sad, but the flatlining of the patient's heart was not the end. The death of his wife prompted Martin Bromiley to become a champion for patient safety and establish the Clinical Factors Group, which is helping make healthcare safer today. The story of his wife's death has gone around the world, challenging and educating doctors, nurses, anesthetists and more. To this day, Martin maintains that it wasn't the clinicians who failed. "It was the system and training that failed them by making it hard to do the right things."[40]

One thing you can do to see if you have a performance culture is to pay attention to the questions being asked. If you don't hear a lot of questions, that is a bad sign. Somewhere along the way, people got the message that questions are unwelcome. They need to look like experts who have all the answers. Eventually, everyone assumes they do have the answers and are already doing things

---

40 Martin Bromiley, *Patient Safety Movement*, https://patientsafetymovement.org/speaker/martin-bromiley/.

in the best way. Performance cultures lack grace and cultivate self-preservation. Ultimately, everyone suffers for it.

Culture does not necessarily follow your mission. You might have the most innovative mission in the world and a team culture that stifles innovation in practice.

Culture does not necessarily follow your mission.

In his book *Think Again*, Adam Grant describes how this happened within America's National Aeronautics and Space Administration. NASA is in the business of innovating space exploration. The very nature of what they do is to try new things and go where humans have never been before.

But NASA has experienced several critical failures that resulted in loss of life and a loss of confidence in their methods. In 1986, the *Challenger* space shuttle exploded shortly after takeoff, and in 2003 the space shuttle *Columbia* broke apart on its way back to Earth killing everyone aboard.

The investigation into the *Columbia* incident concluded that NASA had not demonstrated the characteristics of a learning organization. NASA's vision is to expand humanity's knowledge of space. They are all about learning! But internally they lacked a learning culture of their own.

The failures of those space shuttles were the sensational and tragic result of NASA's performance-driven culture. Fortunately, that is not the end of the story. Grant describes how one woman helped NASA start to dismantle their fatal performance culture and transition to a learning culture.

Ellen Ochoa, a former astronaut herself, was the deputy director of flight operations at NASA who implemented significant safety improvements. One thing Ellen did was ask questions. She wrote them on a card and kept them in her pocket everywhere she went.

Here are the types of questions she would ask:

> » What leads you to that assumption? What might happen if it is wrong?

> » What are you unsure about?

> » I understand the advantages of your suggestion, but what are the disadvantages?

The simple practice of asking "How do you know?" played a big role in changing NASA's culture. Questions opened the door for doubt and discovery. They created an environment where assumptions could be uncovered and critically examined.

Inquiry helped people disagree in healthy ways and work towards better results. As more people asked questions and teams built trust with each other, NASA became a safer place for everyone.

Learning cultures tend to make fewer mistakes and are more innovative overall. Failures will happen. Our ministries are collections of imperfect humans. Even with the best of intentions and planning, things will not always go the way we expect. But when mistakes happen, how do people respond?

It is not shameful to make mistakes. It is only shameful to make mistakes and not learn from them. In a learning culture, leaders don't dwell on what happened or who was at fault, but instead they use failures to inform future actions. People feel comfortable and safe, not worried about their reputation or job security. As a result, they are more open to feedback and correction. It becomes easier to have a posture of humility. People can freely ask questions, suggest new ideas, and work together to find the best solutions.

It is not shameful to make mistakes if we learn from them.

Your ministry culture may have a mix of learning and performance-driven practices. You might notice variation across teams and projects. Leaders create different environments even within the same organization. Every person's expectations and responses contribute to creating the bigger picture.

It is not necessarily easy to identify culture issues and change them. However, this is critical both for ministry innovation and also for our mission as a whole. NASA realized it needed to change its culture for the sake of the astronauts who were entrusting their lives to them. As ministers of the Gospel, we should be willing to change for the sake of those whose lives need to be saved for eternity. If there is anything we could possibly do to help someone better experience Christ, we should be eagerly looking for it.

CHANGING THE CULTURE

Have you ever stopped to think about how weird it is to type? I'm writing right now on an English keyboard, which is in a layout called QWERTY (named because those are the first six letters across the top row). This standard keyboard design was innovative when it was invented back in 1874. It was created to space out the most commonly used letters because the typewriter mechanisms inside (called hammers) tended to get stuck as people typed rapidly. The keyboard design intentionally slowed people down to help the typewriter function properly.

I don't know about you, but I've never needed to use a typewriter. Technology has advanced significantly since 1874! Computers function very differently from typewriters. When I hit the alphabet letters on my keyboard, they no longer activate mechanical hammers to strike paper with an embossed letter loaded with ink. The problem that the QWERTY keyboard was created to solve no longer exists.

The QWERTY keyboard isn't our only option. There's another layout called the Dvorak keyboard that is designed for maximum efficiency of movement. Vowels are primarily on the left, most used consonants on the right, and the most rarely used characters are least accessible. Makes sense, right? Yet no one knows about it.

I've never seen a Dvorak keyboard on a computer, but there are websites where you can try it out. I make this an assignment for my innovation students. I get all sorts of responses ranging from, "This was the weirdest thing I've ever tried; I couldn't stand it," to "This is amazing; I will never see typing the same way again!"

Trying to type in a new layout is challenging because we've all learned QWERTY and have become fast with years of practice. However, just because we can make it work doesn't make it the best solution.

I give you this example as a warning that innovative ideas are not always embraced and implemented. It was easier for hardware producers to sell keyboards people already knew how to type on than to change to a better one that would take time for people to learn. Nearly 150 years later, we're stuck with an irrelevant design that makes typing harder when we could have something better.

People tend to prefer what is familiar rather than what is new. Learning something can feel slow and difficult. The work it would take to change how we do things (like type) often doesn't seem worth it in the short-term. This same attitude can undermine our ministry work.

We all have things we are doing in ministry that are outdated and don't match new realities. But we may be unwilling to change our methods because we've gotten good at those things. Even if what we are doing doesn't work that well, at least we know what to expect. With practice, we get faster and we do see results. Don't be surprised as a ministry innovator if people don't want what you have to offer. You will encounter resistance to innovation because it is human nature to not want to change.

How ideas spread through society is something that has been extensively studied. It turns out that having a popular idea is less about the idea itself and more about who you share that idea with. The theory of the diffusion of innovation was published as early as 1962 and is helpful in understanding how to make our ideas succeed. The innovation diffusion curve (shown below) predicts how people will respond to new ideas.

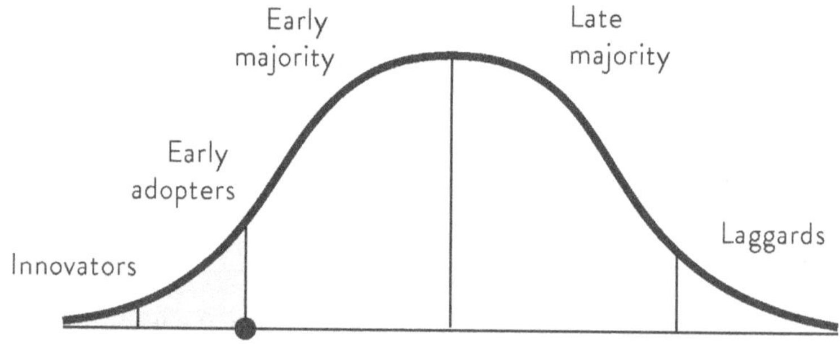

DIFFUSION OF INNOVATION THEORY

If you are the person who is always looking for new ways to do things, you are an innovator and fall in the extreme minority of the population. If you are willing to try new things before others, you are an early adopter. The early majority represents a large chunk of people who are not the first to get on board, but they're not the last. The late majority crowd are the ones who wait for almost everyone else to go first before they eventually join in. The laggards are the very last of the last to adopt an idea.

Business author Simon Sinek has studied this curve and suggests that you will need to persuade 15–18 percent of people in your target audience to adopt your solution in order to reach a tipping point that ensures that idea will spread more widely.[41] Even so, you are not guaranteed to reach everyone. Not every idea will make it through the curve.

This curve helps us understand how we can expect people to respond to innovation within our ministries. You should not be discouraged when people resist your innovations. If they are a laggard, you can expect them to reject anything new. They are not the person you need to convince first. They may never get on board, and that is okay. You need to focus your efforts on communicating with the right people each step of the way.

Look for those who will advance your idea and spread it to others. Each person has a different appetite for change and tolerance for risk. How people respond may also differ depending on the topic. Someone who is a laggard in one area may be an innovator in another. You will need to think about the needs you are trying to meet and who feels those needs most keenly.

Be very careful if you find yourself thinking you don't need others and could do things better on your own. It can be easy to think we know more than others. Innovation is always on the leading edge, so you will naturally be going ahead of others at your ministry. You may see realities they do not yet see. You will steadily grow more proficient at identifying problems and offering solutions. But others at your ministry may not see those same problems or want your great solutions. This can be frustrating. It can also lead us into pride and isolation.

We must be careful not to let knowledge make us arrogant but to instead work lovingly to build up others (1 Corinthians 8:1). Pour out what you know into the lives of those around you and work together to build a ministry culture that supports innovation. Humbly invite others to share your vision and work towards

---

41 Sinek shares this in his TED talk "Start with Why: How Great Leaders Inspire Action," November 2, 2017, *https://www.youtube.com/watch?v=yPLvBju2d8Q*.

it with you. If they do not understand the need, be patient and bring them on a journey of change with you.

It is helpful to think about innovation from the perspective of making change. That is what we are fundamentally asking people to do—change the way they think or behave. "Stop that; do this instead." There are steps we can take to introduce people to a change and help it last. This is a field of study called *change management*. Harvard professor and author John Kotter offers a framework that we can apply to the work of ministry innovation:[42]

1. **Explain why it matters.** You're going to need to help people understand the *why* behind the change you are proposing. What do we stand to gain if we do this? What do we risk if we don't act? Create a sense of urgency around your idea. Be prepared to tell people why it matters and share your vision as well as the reasons you are asking them to take action. Everything might have seemed just fine to everyone yesterday, so you need to explain why today you are asking for change.

2. **Gather wise counselors.** We cannot and should not innovate alone. We need people wiser than we are to speak into our ideas and help us overcome blind spots. There are people both inside and outside your ministry with valuable experience to offer. Invite them to give feedback on the change you are proposing and the best way to go about it. Wise counselors are crucial, and people are often more than willing to help. By bringing people into the journey early on, you give them the chance to help shape the idea and share in your vision. They can become key advocates and champions for the innovation in the future.

---

42 I have rewritten John P. Kotter's points to better apply to ministry and reduced the list from eight points to seven. If you are interested in the original framework, see *Accelerate: Building Strategic Agility for a Faster-Moving World* (Boston: Harvard Business Review Press, 2014), also available for download on his website, *kotterinc.com.*

3. **Plan your journey.** If you don't know where you're going, you will probably never get there. This is a wise principle for many things in life, but particularly for ministry innovation. You may have a general idea of what you want to accomplish, but you need to be clear on what it looks like to reach the goal. What is success? What are the steps you need to take? Without a plan, you just have wishful thinking. Define your objectives and the work that needs to happen, as well the barriers you will have to overcome to make the desired change a reality.

4. **Invite people to join you.** Once you are equipped with a clear vision and plan, you can invite others to join you. People need concrete ways to take action. They may be willing to help, but they need direction. Refer to your plan for the tasks to be accomplished and look for the right people. Share with them why they are uniquely suited for the job you have in mind. People respond to real needs. Continue sharing the vision, especially if the change you are enacting is optional.

5. **Empower people to act.** Once people are in motion, they will need support. A leader who gives ownership and trust creates motivation. Ensure you are available to answer questions and provide resources. Remove barriers that are slowing down the work. Do everything you can to make it easy for people to help you.

6. **Take small steps.** People need to see results and feel that their efforts are succeeding. This is particularly important when the change is new and not guaranteed to work. It is critical to celebrate things that show the project is moving in the right direction. Don't leave this to chance. Actively plan for ways to create and highlight victories. Identify smaller milestones you can work towards on the longer journey. Then celebrate when your team has accomplished them. Take time to affirm the hard work everyone is putting in to encourage the group forward.

7. **Inspire hope for the future.** Accomplishing a major change requires help and intentionality. You will need to sustain forward momentum for your innovation and add energy as you go. One of the best ways you can do this is to share your progress not only with the people who have been involved in bringing about the change, but also with your leaders. Leaders have the authority to either shut down your project or support it. Celebrate what is happening and show them that their trust is producing results. Inspire hope for the future by showing where you have come from and casting vision for where you are going. The more you can make your idea and its impact visible, the more likely it is that the change will last and become permanent.

Follow these steps to introduce people to new ideas and pursue the change you want to see within your ministry. Innovating requires us to be thoughtful and strategic about the journey. Remember that transformation does not happen overnight, nor does it happen alone.

We have to bring others on the journey with us. It may feel like a slow process, but anything worth doing is worth the effort. "If you're creating something great, your time will come," writes author Clay Scroggins. "And if it hasn't come yet, keep working to create something great."[43]

Even when innovation feels hard, I encourage you to remain where you are and stay faithful to what God has called you to. This has been the story of my own journey in ministry innovation. There have been times when I felt frustrated and wanted to quit. I wondered if people at a different organization would value my ideas more or if a business would give me a higher salary for my skills. I wanted people to follow where I led. But God reminded me that the most important thing to do is to follow Him. He is the good shepherd and I am the sheep.

---

43 Scroggins, *How to Lead When You're Not in Charge*, 129.

Sheep make terrible shepherds. Their hooves can't hold a rod and staff. They can't see where to go or defend the flock against predators. I am far better off trusting the Lord to lead me than trying to lead myself. Innovation is not about me or people listening to me, but about what God can do through me.

We should be culture makers who pursue change for the right reasons. "Whatever you do, work heartily, as for the Lord and not for men, knowing that from the Lord you will receive the inheritance as your reward" (Colossians 3:23–24). Changing our ministry cultures is a challenge that is worth doing because we are serving Christ in bringing the Gospel to a hurting world. No calling could be greater.

DESTRUCTIVE PEACE VS. CONSTRUCTIVE CONFLICT

How we disagree is built into the culture of our ministries. Each person has their own way of approaching hard conversations that reflects their personality and the way disagreement has been modeled for them in the past. Conflict is something you will naturally encounter as you pursue new ideas and invite people to change how they do things. Experiencing disagreement is not necessarily a bad sign. Some conflicts are important for our work and should not be avoided. Opposing opinions can clarify our thinking and refine our ideas.

Conflict is something we should expect, especially if we have built a diverse team. Diversity brings differences. A wide range of perspectives represents a wide potential for disagreement. What is important is creating an environment where people can safely express their opinions even if they conflict with someone else's. Loving everyone doesn't mean you always agree with everyone. A learning culture is full of healthy conflict. When disagreement is invited and handled well, it can be a strength that shows our ministry is healthy.

Loving everyone doesn't mean you always agree with everyone.

Almost everyone wants to know the secret behind high-performing teams. Google once studied their many teams to try to understand why some were more effective than others.[44] They set out to investigate every possible factor that might play a role. They looked at team size, location, and skills. They measured experience and education level. They considered dynamics including ethnic diversity, gender, leadership style, and project management processes. In the end, they concluded that none of those things made a significant difference in team effectiveness. Rather, one key thing stood out as the most important trait their best teams shared. The researchers termed it "psychological safety," or more simply put—trust.

Trust is the variable that matters more than anything else. Teams who trust one another will be more successful regardless of any other characteristic. A team of experienced software engineers with advanced degrees might be outperformed by a group of interns depending on the trust levels within the two groups.

Trust is something you might not notice until it is missing. It is often invisible in our relationships, but it is what makes everything work. Trust is the result of feeling known, understood, and accepted. If you trust the people around you, you feel safe with them. You feel valued and know your contributions matter. You will work harder to support your teammates, and they will do the same for you.

---

44 "What Google Learned from Its Quest to Build the Perfect Team," *New York Times Magazine,* February 28, 2016, *https://www.nytimes.com/2016/02/28/magazine/what-google-learned-from-its-quest-to-build-the-perfect-team.html.*

Trust is foundational to a culture of innovation. A feeling of safety is what enables people to speak up and voice both their ideas and their disagreement for the sake of better results. This is the kind of conflict that is healthy. We shouldn't be afraid to disagree over things that truly matter. However, there is a difference between debating about our work versus fighting with people.

As a team, we should challenge each other's thinking because we collectively value the results. If we have built trusting relationships, disagreement will not cause harm. But without a sense of safety, people might misinterpret questions as a personal attack.

Keep watch for when safety has been lost in the group and work to restore it. If people are going quiet and disengaging or comments are starting to seem hurtful, those are clear indicators that safety has been lost. In order to move forward, you will need to reestablish safety. The book *Crucial Conversations* teaches a simple way to do this.

1. **Step Out:** Pause the conversation about the topic and invite a discussion about the conversation itself. Help people take a step back to examine themselves, the tension, and how you got there. Conflict can be consuming. It may be that disagreement is centering around the wrong thing entirely. The best way forward is to pause and talk honestly with each other.

2. **Contrast:** Contrasting is a method to help people refocus. Start by stating what you don't want and then what you do want. Others may feel you don't respect them and question your intentions. So first, intentionally address any concerns that may be creating a misunderstanding. Then clarify your position so people can understand your purpose. For example:

"In this section of the book, I don't want you to feel like I am undermining any of the incredible work your ministry has accomplished or say you have been doing a poor job of building culture. However, I do want to share the tools and ideas I have come across

openly and offer them to you in case they can help your ministry work go even further and be more successful."

3. **Mutual Purpose:** Finally, you need to establish a mutual purpose everyone can agree to before stepping back into the tense conversation. Commit to the group that your intention is to find a way to serve everyone. Try to explore each person's goals, fears, and constraints. There are often underlying motivations people might not be voicing that are leading to the disagreement. Don't assume you know what everyone is thinking. Create space for people to express their deeper concerns, which will reveal opportunities for mutual purpose.[45]

If you can identify the source of the conflict and get everyone working towards the same goal, you will find trust and safety return. Conflict resolution is not an assigned role, but it is a key practice on healthy teams and something we can all take responsibility to do.

It requires courage to disrupt the conversation and resolve tension, but someone must step up or progress will halt. More importantly, relationships may be endangered that are critical to the team.

A culture of innovation makes space for everyone to participate and does not bury disagreement for the sake of preserving peace. Silence sometimes comes from apathy. Disagreeing can feel like too much effort with not enough reward. Discouragement can be another reason for silence. Perhaps opinions shared in the past were ignored.

Fear can also cause people to withdraw. Unknown consequences can make it difficult to go against a group decision or disagree with a popular idea. If you have ever stayed quiet for one of these reasons, you can be certain others on your team have also.

---

45 Joseph Grenny et al., *Crucial Conversations: Tools for Talking When Stakes Are High*, 3rd ed. (New York: McGraw Hill, 2022), chapter 5.

Consensus may feel good at the time, but it is deceptive. If your organizational culture is one where people rarely speak up to add input, it's a dangerous place to be. It means your ministry could be strengthened, but your environment is inhibiting improvement. False peace that covers up disunity endangers your impact.

False peace endangers your impact.

One year, I invited everyone who worked with me to complete a performance review of my leadership. I wanted to learn what I was doing well and what I needed to work on. The feedback was submitted anonymously, and I was surprised that every single person on my team identified the same weakness. They complimented me on being an encouraging leader but pointed out my dislike of conflict. They expressed (in a nice way) that sometimes the work suffered because I was unwilling to tell someone they could do better. I needed to hear this. It helped me realize that harmony should not always be the ultimate goal.

Disagreement can be a way we lovingly work towards better results. By being unwilling to disagree, I was letting my team down without even knowing it. One thing that has helped me in this area is to see there is a difference between challenging a person's idea and disapproving of that person. We should be able to disagree with ideas and provide feedback without anyone feeling personally attacked. In fact, we must learn to do this and invite others to sharpen our innovations through their critiques.

Our ministry work is too important to allow false harmony to weaken our impact. We all have blind spots and don't know everything. That is why we must surround ourselves with people who see what we don't and invite them to speak into our work. Share the truth with one another in love and humility. It isn't easy to disagree, but we must strive to create a culture where this can happen. Affirm arguments not for their own sake, but for quality's sake and for the sake of the non-believers we are reaching with the Gospel. If we have planted and watered the seeds of trust, we can reap the fruit of healthy conflict in our work.

YOUR MINISTRY IS YOUR PEOPLE

Before I joined OneHope, I had a pretty good idea of what I wanted to do with my life, and it involved never staying in one place for long. My wife and I discussed a plan to move to a new city every two to three years. We would sell all our furniture and start over—find new jobs, make new friends, and explore new places. We thought this would keep our lives interesting.

In our life plan, it never mattered much where we would work. I thought a job was just what someone did to pay their bills and that fun happened outside of work. I was unfamiliar with the idea of vocational work—a purposeful career that I could truly enjoy.

Then God led us both to OneHope, and after two years we discussed whether it was time to move on. It wasn't. After three years, then five, we were still there and still growing. Each year that passed we evaluated and still felt called to what we were doing. The mission of the ministry is part of what has kept us in place, but just as important are the people we get to work with. The community we have joined at OneHope is precious and not easily replaced. People are the reason we have stayed far longer than I imagined.

Your ministry is your people. Everything you are able to accomplish depends on your team. Attracting the right people to join you and keeping those people for years to come is vital to your ministry's effectiveness. Organizations must be intentional to care for their people and build a healthy culture where they will want to stay. The management book *Love 'Em or Lose 'Em* teaches twenty-six principles for how to care for people well that results in an engaged team culture. Here are seven of the most helpful principles reframed for ministry application.[46] These practices are designed for people in leadership positions. But if you are not currently in charge of anyone, that is okay. You should still learn these ideas and look for ways to apply them as you grow in influence.

Who You Say Yes To

How your ministry hires and promotes people communicates your values more strongly than words. Team engagement and retention actually starts with the hiring process.[47] We should be careful to consider culture fit as an essential aspect of who we say yes to. Inviting someone to join your team or move up in leadership is an important decision. It signals to your entire team who you consider worthy of your confidence. One of the leaders I have learned much from at OneHope evaluates people based on two things: skill and will.

Skill includes the specialized knowledge and experience a person brings to the job. We often think first about a person's qualifications, but it is not the only thing we should consider. Skills are external and visible, while a person's will is internal. Will represents motivation and commitment. You should ensure the people you add to your team align with your mission.

Aim for people who score highly in both skill and will. If you cannot have both, prioritize will over skill. Skills can be taught and experience gained with time, but a person's attitude is not easy to change. Character is an area where we cannot afford to compromise.

---

46 These concepts are the same as what the authors share, but note that I have rewritten the titles to better apply to ministry. Adapted from Beverly Kaye and Sharon Jordan-Evans, *Love 'Em or Lose 'Em: Getting Good People to Stay*, 6th ed. (Oakland, CA: Berrett-Koehler, 2021).
47 Kaye and Jordan-Evans, *Love 'Em or Lose 'Em*, chapter 8.

If we fill our organizations with people who are highly competent but lack integrity, our ministry culture will begin to suffer. The absence of character is not worth even the best of skills. Instead, look for people who live out God's kingdom values. Seek team members who show evidence of the fruits of the Spirit. Even if they have things they need to learn, with your help they can grow their skills.

Invite People to Stay

When someone leaves an organization, they may have an exit interview. This is usually an opportunity to express why they are leaving so leadership can learn from the situation and improve in the future. This is a beneficial practice.

But why do we wait until someone is quitting to have these kinds of honest conversations? By the time someone is asked, "What would make you stay?" it is often far too late to repair the damage. *Love 'Em or Lose 'Em* suggests that organizations implement regular "stay interviews."[48] These are like an exit interview but conducted even when someone is not thinking of leaving.

Being intentional to deepen relationships with our team members strengthens individual motivation and organizational culture. Research shows that the top reasons people stay at their job have little to do with pay or benefits. People value meaningful work, a supportive leader, and being recognized, valued, and respected.

Leaders can talk with their people one-on-one and ask a few simple questions. For example: *What do you love about your job? Are we using your skills in the best way we can? What would keep you here? What might make you want to leave?*

Courage and humility are needed to ask questions like this, but you will be richly rewarded for doing so. Not only will you learn

---

48 Kaye and Jordan-Evans, *Love 'Em or Lose 'Em*, chapter 1.

more about each individual on your team, but simply having this conversation communicates that you care deeply. Take time to listen well. Invite people to be honest and respond to them openly and honestly as well. People want to be understood and valued by their leaders. It doesn't cost anything to listen, it only requires making space to do so.

The Cost of Losing People

If expensive technology equipment went missing from your offices, how would you respond? Perhaps you would conduct an investigation to find out what happened and implement new security practices. In ministry we carefully count the cost of each activity to be wise financial stewards. But we can sometimes overlook our greatest asset: our people. When they decide to leave, how do we respond?

A talented employee is worth far more than technology equipment.[49] We typically do little to investigate why team members choose to leave, nor think about how we can prevent it in the future. Our people represent our most significant investment, and replacing them is costly.

When you lose a team member, people must spend time to search for and hire the right replacement. Projects might have to be delayed until someone can be found. Your team may experience lost productivity from the dissatisfied person and lose team morale after they exit. Training a new employee also takes time. When I started at OneHope, someone told me it would be over a year before I would really be useful to the organization. I didn't believe them then, but I do now.

Since being hired, I have seen dozens of people come and go from our ministry. I have helped with interviews and training and have seen how steep the learning curve can be. It takes a long time

---

49 Kaye and Jordan-Evans, *Love 'Em or Lose 'Em,* chapter 14.

for people to settle in and apply their skills effectively to projects. When someone leaves with all their knowledge and skills, we should be very alert to why that is and work to avoid turnover in the future. Replacing someone represents a real expense that is far more costly than you might expect.

Cultivating Connections

How can we create a ministry environment where people want to stay? One key is in having a culture of true connection where people are linked together.[50] People are naturally social and want to connect with each other and be known. Working alongside one another should give us a chance to learn about each other's lives, passions, and families. Much of this will happen naturally, but our ministry culture should also encourage deepening connections.

At OneHope, we call ourselves a ministry family. It is an important value for us that every team member feels like they are part of that family and genuinely cared for. I feel so fortunate in this environment. There is no one I don't consider a friend—I care about each person and want to get to know them better. It is very hard to think about leaving your friends who have come to feel like family. On the other hand, it is very easy to leave a workplace where everyone is a stranger.

Have you considered how you can encourage connections within your organization? This is especially important if you are a large ministry. It can be difficult for people to get to know others outside their team, especially if they are working remotely.

How can you connect people to others and create opportunities for them to build relationships? Meals are some of the best ways for people to connect. Could you sponsor a lunch once a month? What about an event where people can bring their families?

---

50 Kaye and Jordan-Evans, *Love 'Em or Lose 'Em*, chapter 12.

Consider non-work activities that are lighthearted and help teams bond. Sometimes we focus only on the work and not on the relationships that ensure the work gets done. But building team culture is essential. Time spent cultivating connections is never wasted. It will pay you back many times over in creating a deeply engaged culture that people will not want to leave.

Reconsidering Rules

When a new team member joins, you will experience a valuable window of time when they are unfamiliar with your processes and rules. They have fresh eyes to see what might not make sense. They will ask questions about things you may never have thought about. Your team may have adapted to methods that have grown inefficient or complicated with time. You tend to think "this is just the way things are" without considering that they could be different. But a new team member doesn't have the same assumptions, and this can be a great strength.

Rather than shutting down a new person's questions and observations, welcome them. Leverage their perspective. We should have a willingness to change things that don't work well, but sometimes we are truly blind to problems. Invite not just your newest team members but all of your team to speak into how things could be improved. This sparks creativity and leads to a culture of high ownership and engagement. This can only happen if people see that rules can be reconsidered.[51]

If our default attitude is that everything is fine and nothing can be changed, then people have little motivation to make suggestions. People want to help, but they will quickly lose heart if they speak up and are not listened to. If someone raises a concern, don't just dismiss it. Hear them out, explore the issue further, and be willing to collaborate on solutions that make your ministry better.

---

51 Kaye and Jordan-Evans, *Love 'Em or Lose 'Em,* chapter 17.

A culture of innovation empowers everyone to contribute, and it can free your ministry from being held hostage to rules that might no longer serve you well.

Of course there is a difference between changing your methods and changing your mission. Think about the kind of rule that is being questioned and what the consequences would be of revising it. Few rules are unchangeable. Many can be adjusted or even removed.

Find out the reason someone is challenging the rule and seek to understand the heart of their concern. Even if you are not able to take action, you can listen well and share why a process is in place.

Open conversations help your team members better understand your ministry and how they fit in. Whether the rule changes or not, your people will feel valued and trust will begin to flow in both directions.

The Value of Affirmation

Compensation is what people earn. Pay is what they deserve in exchange for their work. But recognition and encouragement are a gift. You don't have to be someone's boss to tell them how much you appreciate their contribution. Affirming someone doesn't cost anything. So why don't we do it more often?[52]

Affirmation is something we need to take time for and build into our culture. Our ministries should be characterized by a spirit of encouragement and positivity. We should be quicker to praise one another than we are to criticize. This does not mean we hand out empty compliments or withhold honest feedback. In fact, situations where constructive criticism is needed are opportunities for encouragement. Consider opening with, "I'm really impressed by how you…" or "You've really grown in the way you. . ." before you give the rest of your comments.

---

52 Kaye and Jordan-Evans, *Love 'Em or Lose 'Em*, chapter 18.

We can all take time to tell people why we enjoy serving with them and affirm the skills or character qualities they bring to the team. It often only takes one person who is intentional about building others up for this attitude to spread.

Positivity and praise are contagious. There are so many ways we can encourage people. We can praise someone privately one-on-one or publicly in front of their peers. It might happen spontaneously or we might need to purposefully plan for it, such as taking time to write a note of encouragement.

People have specific ways they like to be affirmed. It may be verbal compliments, spending quality time, acts of service, or gifts.[53] See what works for different people or even ask them to tell you how they like to be encouraged. You won't know if you don't ask! Beyond individual interactions, think about ways to build celebration into the rhythm of your ministry.

Take time to highlight victories and work done well. Celebrate people on your team and the milestones in their lives. Create special moments to commemorate accomplishments and give God the praise for what He is doing through your team.

Mentoring Future Leaders

Mentorship is all about helping people be the best they can be. Think about who has had a powerful influence on your life. Perhaps one person set an example you admired or helped you walk through a difficult time. Maybe a leader at work helped you build skills or believed in you at a critical moment. Hopefully you have had the chance to do the same for someone else.

Mentorship has a powerful impact on people and culture. It strategically deepens relationships and gives people a reason to stay and grow at your ministry. Mentoring others is a selfless act, but

---

53 If you want to explore this more, consider reading Gary Chapman's book *The 5 Love Languages: The Secret to Love that Lasts* (1992; repr., Chicago: Northfield, 2015).

it does pay off in producing your ministry's future leaders. The book, *Love 'Em or Lose 'Em* uses the word *mentor* as an acronym to help us remember what we should do.[54]

» **Model**—Show others how you hope they will work. Be alert to what your own example is communicating and invite people to come behind the scenes with you. Show them your thought process. Invite them to join you in real situations and see the interactions for themselves.

» **Encourage**—Watch for what the person is doing right and ensure they know you notice and appreciate their efforts. Take time to get to know them so you can celebrate their successes, both in work and in life.

» **Nurture**—Help others develop their strengths and grow in their areas of interest. Regularly ask them what they enjoy doing and how they want to continue to be inspired. Find ways to align their passions with the mission and look for others who can guide them in areas where you are not an expert.

» **Teach about the Organization**—A key way you can help someone you are mentoring is to offer the wisdom you have about the organization itself. You know many things others do not. Why does your ministry function the way it does? How can you best present your ideas to those in power? Who are the key people you need to convince, and how do you approach them? Your hard-earned insights can make the journey easier for others. Be generous with your knowledge and help them avoid mistakes you may have made in the past.

» **Release**—Mentorship prepares others to exercise authority on their own. We need to yield power and empower others to lead. We sometimes don't get to this critical step. Releasing authority downwards creates ownership and responsibility.

---

54 Note that I have slightly reworked these ideas to help them better apply to ministry. Adapted from Kaye and Jordan-Evans, *Love 'Em or Lose 'Em*, chapter 13.

People rise to meet a challenge and prove that they are worthy of trust. Step back to make space for others to solve problems. Ultimately, our goal should be to put ourselves out of a job by empowering others to stand on their own.

As you work to build a culture of innovation within your ministry, consider how to invest in your people and engage them so they can build culture alongside you. Which of these seven points is already a strength for you? Which ones might you need to work on? Your team is your path to fulfilling your mission.

Your people are your greatest gift. Be intentional to ensure everyone in your ministry feels supported and cared for. Connect them to your ministry's purpose, to each other, and to mentors. Listen to your people and help them know they are in the right place to give their best for the sake of the Gospel.

DOING OUR BEST WORK TOGETHER

Remember our definition of culture: "people like us do things like this." Our ministry cultures have two essential elements: the people you have on your team and the way those people work together. We must consider both as we seek to create a culture of innovation.

You can have the best people in the world, but without defining helpful ways to work together, you will fail to leverage your team's strengths. Every team has rhythms and rituals. Rhythms are the patterns and habits you establish for your work. Rituals are events or actions that have special meaning to the team.

When I led OneHope's Innovation Team, I wanted clear rhythms and rituals. We worked in five-week cycles where each member of the team focused on one project at a time. We met weekly to review progress and share updates. At the end of each project, we prepared a final report and shared it with the team and our leaders. We were an unusual team in that we never extended our timelines beyond the five weeks. We delivered the results and moved on to the next project. These were our work rhythms.

One of our team's rituals was that after completing a project we would leave the office and meet at a coffee shop to debrief. Before we started that meeting, we would all learn a new board game and play it together. This was a ritual to remind us of the importance of learning new things and staying open to change. It was also a ritual that built community—which is one of the five types of rituals that form workplace culture.

5 Rituals for Workplace Culture: [55]

1. **Creativity** rituals help your team generate ideas or understand the vision for change with a new project.

2. **Community** rituals bond people together and make them feel known and connected.

3. **Transitions** are wonderful opportunities for rituals. You can celebrate the completion of a project, a team member changing roles, or other milestone accomplishments.

4. **Conflict** rituals are designed to help people with communication when there are disagreements or tension to navigate.

5. **Performance** rituals help a team stay focused and get work done.

Rituals can be carefully designed or may emerge naturally on your team, but either way they should reflect your group's unique personality.[56]

There is no one right way to build culture. My own experience with the Innovation Team is just an example, and it is not ideal for

---

55 Kursat Ozenc, *Rituals for Work: 50 Ways to Create Engagement, Shared Purpose and a Culture that Can Adapt to Change* (Hoboken, NJ: Wiley, 2019).

56 We'll talk broadly about designing moments like these that can function as your team's rituals in the section on Crafting Memories in the chapter "The Host's Perspective."

everyone. In fact, the team operated this way for just over a year before adapting our rhythms and rituals to meet new needs within the organization.

As I reflect back on that specific model as well as the way our team operates today, I see that there are five areas to thoughtfully design around. You will always need some sort of process for prioritizing projects, communicating, executing work, evaluating success, and collaborating with others. You should explore what methods work best for your ministry in each of these areas.

Prioritization

What is the most important work to do? You need a process to define project priorities because you should not say yes to everything. Your team's capacity will always be limited. Establish rhythms to help you evaluate requests and focus your attention on the most important tasks first.

Keep your team's long-term goals in mind because it is easy to get distracted by what appears urgent. Just because something has a quick deadline doesn't mean it is the most important.

Seek input if needed. On the Innovation Team, we regularly met with leaders from different departments to examine requests and prioritize them together. If needed, we would suggest breaking larger projects into smaller ones that could be accomplished within our five-week cycle. Other teams have intake forms to fairly assess every request and help them decide what to take on. Choose what works for you, but be sure to have something in place to help you make decisions and identify the right work to carry forward.

Communication

Good communication is the glue that holds a team together. All teams need to connect regularly. But there are many ways to communicate. You can gather a group for a meeting or send a quick message. The medium matters. No one wants to waste time in a meeting that could have been an email, but many emails would have been better as face-to-face conversations.

Think also about your group. Who needs to be included? What is the best format for sharing information and gathering responses? For some conversations to go well, everyone needs to come prepared, while other meetings can be informal. You should establish communication frequencies that help your team stay connected but don't tire everyone out.

COMMUNICATION PURPOSE: ____________________

Type	Location	Group Size	Format	Frequency
Meeting or conversation	Online	Large group	Informational (leader or only one person shares)	Daily
Long text (emails, documents)	In-person	Small group	Collaborative (everyone shares or responds)	Weekly
Short text (direct messages)	Hybrid	One-on-one	Facilitated (group works together towards a goal)	Monthly
Audio/Video Message			Open (no guidelines)	As Needed

The chart above can help guide you in crafting your communication rhythms. Select one option from each column or come up with your own options to fit your team. For example, I sometimes need to share important updates with leaders in our organization, but their schedules are difficult to coordinate. It might take two months to find a meeting time that works for everyone.

So instead, I've discovered I can send an audio or video message. They can watch or listen on their own time and it still feels personal like a one-on-one informational meeting. I don't do this very often, only as needed.

But for a team that is working closely on a project, I would choose very different options. Meetings would certainly be needed, and it might be best to coordinate in-person if possible, rather than online. Daily collaborative meetings help everyone pass on the latest information and problem solve as a group.

Once you've defined the meeting type, location, group size, format, and frequency—create an agenda. You should always have a plan for how you will facilitate your team's time together. Know your communication purpose and work with your team to experiment until you find what works. Meeting rhythms help set expectations and build a culture of connection. People prefer consistency, so you don't have to re-create your agenda every time. Once you establish good patterns, keep following them as long as they serve your team well, and be open to changing them when they don't. Good communication takes planning, but it pays off in team alignment.

Execution

How do you practically accomplish work? Every team will have a different way for projects to move through their process. Your choices may have evolved over time, but it is always beneficial to consider your underlying approach and ensure it helps you achieve your best results.

CM

PEOPLE

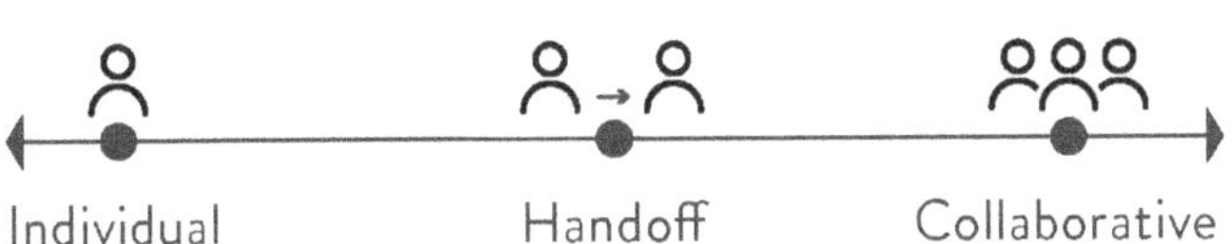

The first thing to consider is how you utilize your **people**. Some teams take an individual approach with each project assigned to one person who carries it out from start to finish. In other teams, projects are passed through many hands with each person completing a portion of the work and handing it off to the next person to move forward. Other teams may break up a project and assign team members to work collaboratively on different portions simultaneously. The approach you choose depends on the type of work you do and the people available.

Consider how work moves through your team and anticipate key moments in this process. Think about the life cycle of a project including how things get started, finished, or handed off in the middle. Transition points like this are areas where work can tend to get stuck or sidetracked. Do your best to define ahead of time how approvals, feedback, and key decisions will be made. You cannot plan for every possible situation, but working without a plan wastes time and energy. Processes help people move forward confidently.

FOCUS

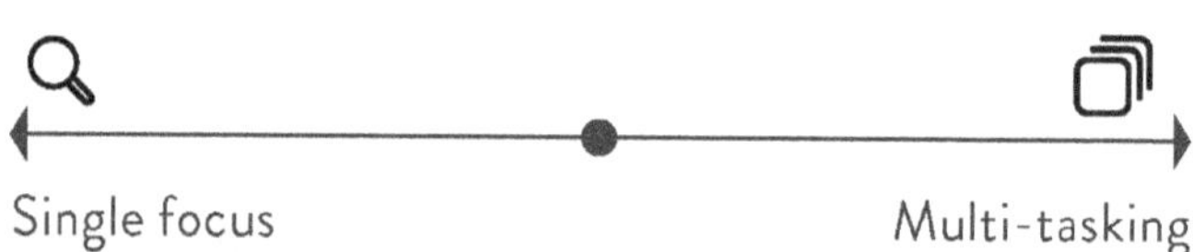

Focus is how we divide our attention between tasks. When I led the Innovation Team, we had a single-focus approach and intentionally took on only one project at a time for each team member. But most teams tend to multi-task, carrying responsibility for many projects each with its own tasks and deadlines. Some people thrive on variety and love having a lot going on all the time. But for others, a clear and simple focus is key.

Productivity is lost when you are constantly changing between tasks. This is called a *switching cost*—the natural delay that results when switching your thoughts from one project to another.[57] We've all experienced this. You are in the middle of answering an email when someone stops by to ask you a question. Or you're on a Zoom meeting when a chat message comes in. It is impossible to focus on more than one thing at a time.

The more you switch, the more time you lose. It's not just the time you spend in conversation or typing out the answer to a quick question. Distractions break your focus. You have to get oriented to the new subject, respond to the need, then reorient to what you were doing before. Getting back on track can take longer than you expect. This isn't only a problem when dealing with distractions. It applies whenever you are switching between projects or types of tasks.

In a busy season, it might not be possible to only carry a single project, but how you divide your days and weeks can help you avoid the costs of frequently changing their focus. Each person can schedule their work and protect time to focus on important tasks.

TIMELINE

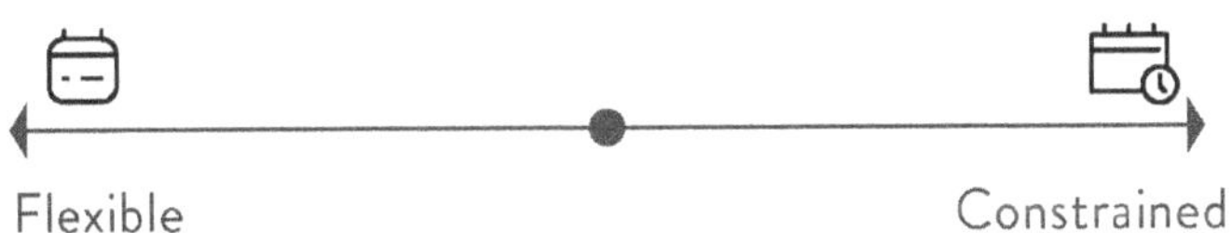

The kind of work you do often dictates the **timelines** you have to accomplish it. For example, an events team is highly deadline-driven. Everything has to get done by a specific date, so

---

57 Switching costs is a concept explained in the book *Scrum* by Jeff Sutherland and J. J. Sutherland. Scrum is a project management method that advocates for single focus as the best way to accomplish complex tasks. It teaches a detailed way of breaking down projects into achievable portions. Jeff Sutherland and J. J. Sutherland, *Scrum: The Art of Doing Twice the Work in Half the Time* (New York: Crown Business, 2014).

timelines are constrained and there is little flexibility. Other teams have the freedom to set their own deadlines and move them if needed.

It can seem like projects always take longer than we think. Generally speaking, the time required corresponds to our familiarity with the task. If you have an assignment with the same type of requirements as a project you or others on your team have done before, the approach will be clear. You roughly know what needs to get done and approximately how long it will take. You can set a constrained timeline and reasonably expect to meet it so long as nothing major goes wrong.

If you have new work, however, it can be difficult to set a timeline. You don't know what kind of challenges you may encounter or how long it will take. It is better to have a more flexible timeline that allows you to figure things out, problem solve, and re-do work as needed. Flexible timelines are especially important if you are learning a new skill or trying a new platform or method.

There are exceptions to every rule of course. It can be valuable to set deadlines on new work. Constraints add urgency, which helps drive results and limit time spent going in an unfruitful direction. If something is new and not guaranteed to work, deadlines can create healthy checkpoints to decide whether to continue, or cut losses and try something else. Work can tend to drag on, so we need to be aware of how that displaces other projects. Time is a limited resource, so we should be strategic in how we spend it.

EMPOWERMENT

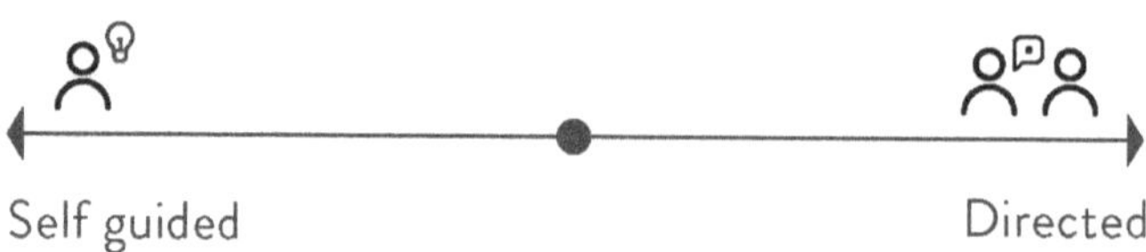

How much freedom does each person have to pursue their work in the way they think is best? This is **empowerment**. A self-guided approach encourages people to take action on their own. They have the freedom to explore, and there is no right or wrong way to accomplish the work so long as it gets done. A directed approach steers people towards a proven method to follow for best results and may discourage experimentation.

People have different ways they prefer to work and leaders do too. Every team has to figure out their balance. A high level of empowerment can be motivating to some and discouraging to others. Some people prefer being told exactly what to do, but others will see too much direction as micro-management. The project may also dictate the approach. When a task is well-defined or has a quick deadline, there might not be room to experiment. In these cases, a self-guided approach might not be possible or useful.

Your cultural context may also dictate the approach that works best. Every culture views authority and decision-making differently.[58] Leaders need to be aware of the cultural expectations of their team in addition to individual preferences. It should always be our desire to support people in the best way so they can do their best work. Communicate expectations and constraints so people know what is needed and how they can succeed. Remember not to leave anyone unsupported or under-resourced, even if they are working on their own.

In general, innovative work requires some level of empowerment. To do new things or do old things in new ways, people need freedom. Encourage your team to exercise creativity and independent thinking as much as possible, while guiding and supporting them towards excellence.

---

58 Leading and decision-making are two of the eight aspects of culture that author Erin Meyer describes in her book *The Culture Map*. You can read more in the section How Culture Shapes Your World in the chapter "The Beginner's Perspective."

Evaluation

We can often be so busy working, we don't take time to step back and evaluate how we are doing. Are we succeeding? Does the team feel motivated? Sometimes we fail to ask these questions until we receive negative feedback or are experiencing problems. But evaluation is a key rhythm to build into a healthy team culture.

It is important to create regular opportunities to examine both the big picture and the smaller details. On the Innovation Team, we reviewed our work every month using an activity called *Four Helpful Lists*.

We made a list of what went right, what went wrong, what was missing, and what confused us about our projects. The conversation helped us identify specific things to change the following month, and taking time to talk openly as a team was a healthy practice. Sharing honestly with each other improved how we worked together and helped team members feel heard and supported.

FOUR HELPFUL LISTS

⊘ Right   ⊗ Wrong

⊙ Missing   ⊙ Confusing

Creating space to evaluate reinforces a learning culture. Make time to hear from your team internally as well as from those you serve externally. Make it easy for comments—both positive and negative—to reach the right people on the team.

Ultimately, we are all on a learning journey. It takes humility to ask others what we could be doing better, but we should want to know and invite people to tell us the truth in love. It is impossible not to improve if we have set up pathways for evaluation and are open to hearing what people have to say.

Collaboration

We get more done working together than we could ever accomplish alone. But collaboration is something that needs definition to happen well.[59] People don't just accidentally collaborate—it takes planning and organization.

Partnerships are formed when we share similar priorities. You may find your mission and activities align with that of another ministry's and want to work together to solve a problem. Or collaboration may be internal—your team working with another team on a joint project. Priorities and passions may bring us together, but partnerships need to be strengthened with actions that build trust.

One of the first things you need to do in any collaboration is set clear expectations. Define the purpose that is driving the partnership and ensure priorities are aligned. This is important not just at the start, but along the journey as well.

Keep realigning and reminding each other of your shared goals to keep the collaboration on track. Consider the other areas we have discussed in the specific context of the partnership and

---

59 A helpful model for collaboration is the Collective Impact framework described by *John Kania and Mark Kramer* in "Collective Impact," *Stanford Social Innovation Review*, winter 2011, https://ssir.org/articles/entry/collective_impact.

create rhythms that help you work together. How will you communicate? Make sure you have a shared vocabulary to help you avoid miscommunications. Information and resource sharing is also critical to effective collaboration. Define how this will happen and how your teams will continue to stay in touch and problem solve together. Take time to connect and get to know one another so you come to care about the people on both sides of the partnership. Don't underestimate the power of relational connections to getting work done.

Execution is the area where collaboration can fall apart if there are not clear expectations. Ensure both sides know how the responsibilities are being divided. Be honest with each other about how it is going and any difficulties that are slowing the work. Transparency is the best way to build trust—plus it opens the door for each side to help the other if needed. If we hold back from our partner, they will hold back from us too. But modeling humility and integrity will multiply grace.

Finally, be sure to evaluate throughout the process. Check in with your team on how the collaboration is going and dialogue about ways it can be improved. Have the courage to bring that feedback to the partner and ask them to do the same. It can be difficult to have honest conversations when working across organizations or teams. But we can anticipate this and build evaluation into the collaboration process from the beginning. Making space for these conversations before problems occur may even prevent them from happening.

Partnerships can be a real testing ground and force us to clearly define how we will work together. But by being aware of the principles we have discussed, you are well prepared to collaborate gracefully.

A culture of innovation takes careful investment. You cannot have the fruit without putting in the effort. Without careful examination and pruning, trees grow in unintended directions. It is the same in our ministry work. We all figure out how to navigate these areas, even if we are not being intentional about them. But it is worth taking the time to consider where we are and design rhythms and rituals that will move us forward.

Your culture carries your ministry forward.

Building culture might feel like slow or even nonessential work compared to the urgent ministry to be done. But it is your culture that carries your ministry forward. We can work hard to accomplish our goals, but what have we gained if we burn out our people in the process? It is not good to struggle with poor communication and frustrating processes. It is even worse when people feel hopeless because they cannot have honest conversations about the problems they see.

Our work suffers when we don't have healthy organizational cultures. But when we pour energy into caring for our people, they will far exceed our expectations. Like trees, the fruit we produce from our ministries will only be as good as the health of our ministry. Innovators are culture-makers who help cultivate healthy ministries that can produce good fruit for God's kingdom.

CM

Culture making is spiritual work. Your ministry culture should be life-giving, because our mission is to bring life to the world. We must be careful to ensure that the Gospel has penetrated our lives and work so we can minister to others with integrity.

The inside of our ministries should reflect the same beauty and freedom of the Gospel we preach to others. Ultimately, this is the work of the Holy Spirit. Ask God to give you insight and creativity and He will answer you. He is the master innovator who will work through you and your ministry culture to spread His message of redemption.

Culture Makers create an environment where innovation can flourish for kingdom purposes.

WHY WE MUST BE CULTURE MAKERS

» Innovation is not just the responsibility of ministry leaders. We can all contribute to a culture of innovation by exercising our influence.

» Innovation thrives in a learning culture where people feel safe, are open about mistakes, and prioritize the mission over personal pride.

» Innovation suffers in a performance culture where people are fearful for their reputation and hesitant to take risks.

» We should be gentle with one another, but quick to sharpen each other's ideas because ministry is too important to remain silent.

» Your ministry culture is determined by your people and the rhythms of how they work together.

PRACTICE THE PERSPECTIVE

Consider if your ministry has a learning culture or a performance culture. If there is evidence of a performance culture, model humility and a genuine desire to learn from others. What can you do to get honest feedback and make changes in response? If you have a learning culture, ensure those good practices are passed on. Take time to mentor people who are new and encourage others to do the same.

BROADEN YOUR PERSPECTIVE

Liam's book recommendations:

Love 'Em or Lose 'Em: Getting Good People to Stay, 6th ed. Beverly Kaye and Sharon Jordan-Evans. Oakland, CA: Berrett-Koehler, 2021.

Crucial Conversations: Tools for Talking When Stakes Are High, 3rd ed. Joseph Grenny et al. New York: McGraw Hill, 2022.

Think Again: The Power of Knowing What You Don't Know. Adam Grant. New York: Viking Press, 2021.

How to Lead When You're Not in Charge: Leveraging Influence When You Lack Authority. Clay Scroggins. Grand Rapids, MI: Zondervan, 2017.

Shape Up: Stop Running in Circles and Ship Work that Matters. Ryan Singer. Basecamp, 2022. This book can be read digitally for free at *https://basecamp.com/shapeup*.

The Host's Perspective

UNLOCK INNOVATIVE COLLABORATION
ON YOUR TEAM AND OTHERS

A TALE OF TWO TABLES

A Parable

"**R**ight this way, let's get you seated. Sorry you had to travel so far to get here. I so appreciate you taking the time!"

The host led the way a couple steps ahead of his guest, opening the door to a cozy room with a small round table surrounded by four comfortable chairs. The table was set with a clutter of differently shaped bowls, mismatched plates, colored glasses, and an equally diverse array of food. It all looked freshly set down and hot.

"And here we are," he gestured towards the chair opposite one which was already occupied by a thin man with dark hair who seemed out of place among the brightly colored furnishings. The new guest, a man with a bold presence and strong jawline to match all his other lines, took his seat.

He let out a deep sigh, "Ahh . . . it's good to sit down every once in a while, eh? Thank you for pestering me, endlessly, to make time for a normal evening for once. What with this awful wretched conflict going on, I've barely had time to take my boots off, much less enjoy a home-cooked meal. Right?" He said half to the host, half looking across at the man who had been seated when they entered. "I don't believe we've met, how are ya?"

"Yes, nice to meet you. Couldn't agree more, I haven't had a night's peace in . . . oh, I don't know how long," the thin man replied through a grimace.

"Well, plenty of time to get acquainted over dinner," the host said cheerfully. "I am afraid I got carried away in the kitchen and made too much of everything, so I hope you're hungry."

The night progressed uneventfully as the meal and conversation moved forward pleasantly. The host asked questions about their families, their childhood, and the things they valued most in life. As stories flowed, they found they had a tremendous amount in common, despite never having met. The two guests laughed heartily, and there were even a few moments of solemn pain and shared empathy as they talked—one of losing a father and the other, a brother.

The conversation naturally shifted towards the darker topic of the conflict that had veiled the region of late.

"If I could just kill every one of 'em this whole thing would be over and I wouldn't have to see any more of this ruin," said the larger of the two guests, thumping his fist on the table. "It would be better to just have it be over and done with."

"Mmm, I can certainly understand that. Is that why you're fighting in this mess?" the host responded. "Getting rid of the other side completely and having the whole thing be over with. . . those aren't necessarily the same thing," he observed.

"I just want it over with. Seems like if they didn't exist at all, that would be the quickest way," the larger man replied.

"But of course there are other ways to end the conflict," the host put forward. "The upcoming peace talks for instance?"

The thin man scoffed, "Those brutes would never opt for peace; they crave war! The talks are a sham, probably a setup for yet another betrayal."

The large man laughed, "Ha! I couldn't agree more. I don't know what they want, but they are truly despicable."

The host was quiet for a moment, then said. "If they did offer peace, hypothetically speaking, do you think we should take it?"

"Ridiculous!" the two guests answered in unison. They both looked at each other surprised, then laughed.

The thin man spoke up after a pause, "Well, hypothetically speaking, if they wanted peace, I would take it. I want this to be over."

The large man too was thoughtful and after a moment, slowly said, "Despite everything they've done. I would also."

The night was quiet and it felt still in the room as the three reflected on the echoing phrase, *"everything they've done."* Each recollected some private or personal horror they had endured and still lived under its shadow.

The host spoke up, breaking the silence at last. "Well," looking from one man to the other, "you two are my dear friends and guests tonight. Let's not dwell on the past. We can hope that the talks are more than just talk. I had planned for this to be a time of refreshment, not depression. Who knows where God may lead us. Let's pray and leave it up to Him, eh?"

The host opened his hands and prayed aloud,

> *"Lord of lords. King of kings. Prince of peace. I pray you would have your way with us and this conflict. You know it better than we know ourselves, so we lift this burden to you. Your hands are greater than ours, so we trust you with it. We love you. Thank you for this evening. Amen!*

Ah, well, now that that's all in the *right* hands, let's think about the future and the new possibilities it may bring … like dessert for instance!" He stood up and gestured to the incredible tray of sweets, dried fruit, baked cookies, and thickly cut banana bread.

The two guests smiled at their host and began to eat again. The conversation skillfully directed towards the happier, brighter pieces of life they hoped would someday dwarf the sad and broken fragments.

As the night grew late, the two new friends said their goodbyes to their kind host, walking off in opposite directions down the dark road. The host pulled the door closed, the dinner a success, but his night not quite finished. There was still the tidying up and dish washing to do!

But he felt refreshed and hoped his guests too would sleep more peacefully than they had for a while, the evening having lightened the present struggle they carried.

The following month, a new table had been set. This table was long and dark, splitting the room down the middle. A sense of foreboding hung in the air, each half of the room tense as two sides of the terrible conflict met to decide the fates of many.

The room was cold and the light was harsh. Security was tight and unwelcoming, each person thoroughly searched before entering. There was no trust on either side. A tall thin man entered the room from the right in a dark uniform with gold cords and sharp yellow accents. He headed towards his seat at one end of the table.

As he reached for the chair to pull it out, the doors at the opposite end of the room swung open and a large muscular man with a square jaw entered dressed in a pale-gray uniform trimmed in blue like the sky.

The two made eye contact and paused, the first mid-motion, the other mid-step. The others in the room froze, eyes wide. The already-tense atmosphere seemed ready to explode. It was as if time had forgotten itself in the anticipation, watching to see what would unfold.

Slowly, as the seconds remembered to move, a smile broke out on the thin man's face and the large man grinned broadly, almost embarrassed. The two moved past their designated seats and down the table towards one another to shake hands.

"I suspect these talks will go better than I'd hoped," the thin man said.

"Yes," the other replied firmly. Inhaling deeply, he breathed it all out in relief. Still clutching the thin man's hand, he said, "Let's make some peace happen ... and then I think we'll need to pay our mutual friend a visit to celebrate."

• • •

THE HOST'S PERSPECTIVE

> *"A guest never forgets the host who*
> *has treated him kindly."*
>
> —*Homer, Greek poet*

What would you do if you had the opportunity to have Jesus over to your house for dinner? I'm sure you would want the evening to be memorable, the food delicious, and the conversation special. You would think through every detail to make the experience perfect. Nothing would be left to chance.

The New Testament shares stories of people who hosted Jesus and His disciples as they traveled. People opened their homes and invited Jesus into their lives. Mary, Martha, and their brother Lazarus were some of the people who became close friends of Jesus through the time they spent together.

Inviting someone to share your table is a powerful act of hospitality. When we host others, we care for them as we do for our own families. Jesus Himself demonstrates the power of hosting when He washed the feet of His disciples. He also broke bread and ate with them—instructing them to do this regularly. He could have chosen anything to become His followers' ritual. But the act of coming to a table and sharing a meal was what He chose for us to remember Him by.

Every opportunity we have to host people is a chance to show the love of Christ. What does this have to do with ministry innovation? More than you would expect. Every time you are with a group of people you have the choice to adopt the host's perspective—creating an experience that demonstrates Gospel values.

A host's perspective is key to the work of ministry innovation because we cannot solve our biggest challenges alone. The kingdom problems and opportunities we face are too big. We must collaborate to innovate. A host helps people collaborate well and focuses their energy in the right direction.

We must collaborate to innovate.

Ministry innovators can learn to be facilitators who activate others to give their best. Facilitation is a powerful way you can lead and serve. The host steps forward knowing that every interaction is a valuable opportunity. Great results come from well-designed experiences.

Well-facilitated gatherings take effort to plan and execute. But they are worth it. The most valuable part of any ministry is its people, which means the most valuable thing we have is people's time and attention. We should strive to steward our people, partners, and their contributions in the best way possible to ultimately lead others into powerful encounters with Jesus.

TOGETHER AS ONE

Innovation thrives in diversity, but diversity also brings challenges to navigate. Each person is different and brings their own expectations, communication style, and way of working. Effective teams leverage these differences to create strength, but this does not happen by itself.

Think about when you are invited to someone's house for a gathering. You walk into a room of people you don't know but who have also been invited. You instinctively look to the leader of the gathering to know what to do. The host is the guide who moves you through the event from beginning to end. A good host connects people together and helps them find areas of similarity or interest to talk about. A host is also alert to areas of difference among their guests and helps gracefully navigate any potential tensions.

A host does not need to be the team leader, but they are always a servant leader. They serve the team by creating an environment that brings out people's best contributions. A host sees each person's individual strengths and plans ways for everyone to work together effectively. You may already have someone like this on your team—someone who can empathize with many different perspectives, or perhaps a peacemaker who can negotiate your team out of conflict. That person may naturally exhibit the qualities of a host, but anyone can learn this skill.

One of the most practical areas where a host's perspective is needed is in any kind of meeting. Meetings gather people together for a purpose. They are incredible opportunities for innovation, but we often don't take enough time to plan for them well. Getting the right people in a room is only the first step. What you do with them once they are there is when the real work begins.

Too often we stop at just scheduling time together assuming that the meeting will take care of itself. That is where we are wrong. I have found that the most successful meetings are the ones that have a host dedicated to planning and conducting the gathering.

As the host, you set expectations and keep the group moving forward to accomplish their purpose. You don't have all the answers, but you do know how to plan a group's time so that they can discover the answers together. Hosts are the most visible to everyone, but the least important in terms of contributing content to the meeting. This is good news because it means you can host any kind of meeting. You do not need to be the expert in whatever the subject is, you just need to learn to be an expert facilitator to make any meeting a success.

Planning Your Purpose

Before you gather anyone together to do anything, ensure you know your purpose. Your purpose guides every decision you will make. I learned this principle from a book called *The Art of Gathering* by facilitator and strategic advisor Priya Parker. Parker has built her career in the field of conflict resolution through group dialogue. She helps people who disagree get together in an environment where they can seek understanding and resolution. Her book's tips for designing gatherings are widely applicable from planning business meetings to birthday parties.

Parker emphasizes that every meaningful gathering has a strong and specific purpose. Why are you getting *these* people together? The purpose must be clearly defined from the start. We often confuse the *type* of an event with its *purpose*.

A birthday party is a type of event, but its purpose is to celebrate a milestone in someone's life. Who that person is and how they feel about that milestone should guide you in creating a more specific purpose for their party. A weekly team meeting is a type of event, but its purpose is not just to take up time in our week. Perhaps it helps us align our work, increase communication, or solve problems together.

Your purpose determines who you gather and points you towards the best format and agenda for the time together. For example, if your goal is to serve pastors in your city, you might decide to host a citywide pastor's conference. This generally tells us who should be included (pastors in this city) and what they are being invited to (a conference). However, this is not a strong specific purpose that helps us plan a meaningful event. A purpose might be "to create an opportunity for the community to show appreciation for pastors and their families," or alternatively, "to help pastors who don't usually work together share ideas for how to reach the city." These are two very different purposes that would result in very different decisions and plans. From the venue you select to how many people you invite and what you include on the schedule—everything is built around your purpose.

Purpose determines the kind of conference you end up with and helps you plan an event that accomplishes it. I realize this sounds basic, but it is surprising how often we skip the step of defining our purpose and communicating it clearly. We tend to jump straight into planning and execution.

We often let our constraints drive our decisions rather than being guided by our intended purpose. Practice slowing down at the beginning of your process and looking at the bigger picture.

Creating Safety and Trust

To accomplish your stated purpose, you must establish an environment of trust where people feel safe to contribute. Every gathering has its own opportunities and risks. You are mixing different personalities, perspectives, and opinions together in one place. No two groups of people are ever the same. Even the same group of people can act very differently depending on the day, time, and their mood.

Hosts serve a critical role in equalizing the environment so each participant feels comfortable. Many factors impact a group's feeling of safety. In your gathering, you may have people of different cultural backgrounds, authority, and expertise. Some people may know each other, while others will be new to the group. Some people are used to leading, while others will be shy to share their opinions.

A good host anticipates these differences and establishes guidelines for interaction so the group can function harmoniously.

For example, in some gatherings I have set a "no phone" rule to help people stay focused. Phones can be very distracting, and checking them while someone else is talking can be rude and disrespectful. I communicate this to the group at the start of the meeting and invite everyone to put their phone in a box. This saves me the trouble of having to enforce the rule during the meeting and potentially cause embarrassment. At the end, everyone gets their phone back and even those who initially complained about the rule usually see that it makes the group more productive.

It is important to consider what rules you need to establish for your gathering. Don't have too many rules, but carefully choose which guidelines are needed to ensure the group can do their best work. People feel safer when they know what is expected of them and have boundaries in place to guide collaboration. Save the group from miscommunications and hurt feelings by communicating the guidelines clearly and holding the group accountable to those values.

The primary job of a facilitator is to help people to work together. In order to do that, people need to get to know each other. Do not underestimate the need for human connection. It can be easy to skip things like introductions and icebreakers in your agenda, but these are critical to establishing a friendly environment.

The host builds trust among the group by helping people connect. This is particularly important at the start of the gathering when everyone feels awkward, as well as in transitions between activities. These are important moments the host must intentionally guide. Work to ensure everyone enjoys the time together and leaves with a positive impression. Be friendly and help them connect to you as well as to each other. Fill in awkward silences and lighten the mood if you need to.

As the host, you are not there to be in the spotlight. But you are uniquely positioned to create a positive environment where people are able to bring their best.

Producing Participation

Bringing a diverse group of people together to accomplish a shared purpose only works when everyone participates. Having different perspectives represented in a room is useless unless those perspectives are able to be voiced. As a host, one of your primary responsibilities is to help people engage. There will always be people who speak too much and people who are shy to contribute. But a host ensures no individual takes over the conversation.

As the facilitator, you have unique permission to gracefully interrupt when someone is dominating the conversation. Invite others to share their thoughts. Everyone has something valuable to contribute, so ensure everyone has a chance to be heard. Communicate this value to the group ahead of time so they can all share in the responsibility of listening well.

Hosting requires empathy and alertness. Pay attention not only to the group's conversation, but also to their body language. Facial expressions and nonverbal cues communicate loudly if you look. You can usually tell when someone disagrees even if they don't say anything. Invite them to share their opinions.

You should also watch for anyone who might feel uncomfortable or confused. People may have questions but feel embarrassed to ask. Be sure to make space for clarifications and ensure everyone is on the journey with you.

If you have planned a long meeting, know that it will be difficult to stay focused the entire time. You should monitor people's energy levels and take breaks when needed. Use the power of your words to encourage the group. Help them know they are moving in a positive direction and their contributions are appreciated and valuable. If the group is getting stuck or disagreeing, you might need to adjust your plans.

Be willing to adapt and exercise flexibility. While your agenda is important, your people are more important. Your first priority should be helping them give their best towards the shared purpose. If needed, sacrifice your schedule. You can always plan another meeting or follow-up conversation.

Finally, know that hosting requires humility. It is not about you and your plans. You may be the most visible person as the facilitator of the gathering, but the group is not there to follow you. You are there to serve them. They will listen to you, but your opinion is not the one that matters.

The strength lies in the group and in each person who comes to the table. Your role is to set the table and serve the group by directing their energy and efforts towards the shared goal. People will quickly come to recognize the value of this skill set and invite you to help them further.

CRAFTING MEMORIES

Think back on your life. What moments stand out as truly special memories? Take a minute and recall a few . . . maybe you thought of your wedding, a graduation, or a trip you took with friends or family. Often these memorable moments are the most carefully planned moments in our lives.

Just consider how much time, effort, and money is spent planning a wedding. Indian weddings literally last for days. My Brazilian friends tell me you invite the whole town to celebrate a wedding. Wedding planning is a multi-billion-dollar industry worldwide dedicated to ensuring every single moment is as perfect as it can be. It requires multiple people working together to create an experience that honors the special couple and everyone who joins them. So it is no mystery that we remember those days well.

I never bothered to think much about what my wedding would be like and left all the planning to my wife. But I remember being unexpectedly moved by all the people who came to support us. I didn't even know many of them, yet they took time to be with us and see us off into our first steps of life together. One of the most special parts of the afternoon was when people took time to toast us and speak words of affirmation and blessing for our future. I still get choked up thinking about it. Yet that was such a simple thing. No special equipment was needed—just people together in a heartfelt moment. It made me wonder why we don't take time to bless and affirm each other more in our daily lives.

Most days are unremarkable. You probably don't remember much about what happened last week or last month or even last year. Weeks blur together and time seems to slip by. One of my leaders told me once that "the days are long, but the months are short." I have found this to be true particularly as an adult.

When I was a child, every year was memorable and different. I had new teachers, new friends, and new experiences. Every birthday was a major milestone. The leap between age nine to ten felt enormous! But now it feels like birthdays are very close together. A whole year passes quickly because I am mostly doing the same kinds of things every day.

Picture your usual daily life as a flat line. When you have a great experience, the flat line jumps up to make a peak. If you have a negative experience, it drops down creating a valley.

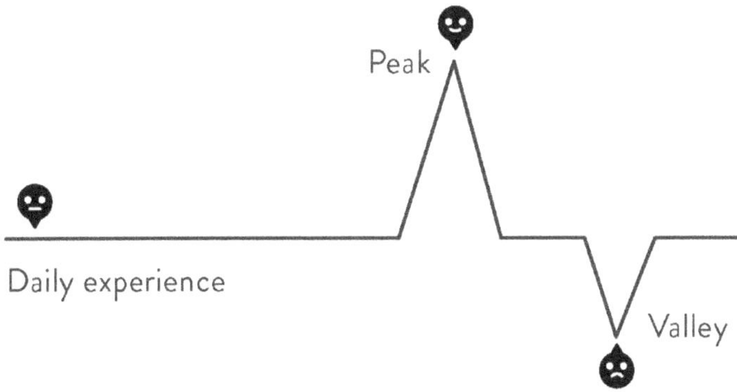

The language of peaks and valleys is helpful as we think about creating memories. People tend to remember what breaks the pattern of their everyday, mundane experiences—for good or bad.

People tend to remember what breaks the pattern.

Jesus Himself created powerful moments throughout His ministry so people could better understand the kingdom of heaven. He performed miraculous healings, cast out demons, and multiplied food to feed thousands. He told stories that communicated the power of the Gospel in a way people could more easily understand. Jesus's disciples lived with Him through some incredible peaks and some very low valleys.

We are engaged in that same work of helping people understand the Gospel and how it applies to their lives. As we journey with people through their lives, we will get to celebrate their peaks and comfort them in their valleys. Most importantly, we can be alert to opportunities for them to encounter Jesus personally.

Memories don't have to be limited to miraculous, once-in-a-life-time moments. Crafting memories is a powerful tool available to us all if we know how to use it. Brothers Chip and Dan Heath teach this in their book *The Power of Moments.* This concept of peaks and valleys comes from their book.

They describe four types of moments we can create: Moments of Elevation, Moments of Insight, Moments of Success, and Moments of Connection.[60]

---

60   If I had the space, I would have highlighted all four types of moments because they are all applicable to ministry work. It is well worth reading the whole book. Chip Heath and Dan Heath, *The Power of Moments: Why Certain Experiences Have Extraordinary Impact* (New York: Simon & Schuster, 2017).

Let's look at the first two types of moments and their potential applications to our ministry work.

Moments of Elevation

Teaching Sunday School to six-year-olds is challenging work! They are just old enough to reason with, but they don't always listen. Their individual personalities are really starting to emerge, meaning there are lots of ways they can upset one another and their teachers.

I taught Sunday School classes with my mom, who is one of the most creative and inspiring people I know. The weekly lesson guides provided were often disappointing. While the activities were simple to conduct, they were boring and never engaged our students' imagination.

We decided to do things differently. One Sunday, we were teaching the lesson of Jesus miraculously feeding the crowd of 5,000. When the children arrived, they were greeted by the unfamiliar smells of fish and freshly baked bread. We had stopped by our local market on the way to church and picked up two fish and some loaves, just like in the biblical story.

The children were excited to see and touch a real fish! We broke the bread and ate it together as we told the story. Certainly we could have done an easier activity, such as coloring pictures of fishes and loaves. But real fish and bread helped the children participate in the story in a powerful way and make a memory. They couldn't wait to tell their parents what had happened. We created a moment that broke the typical pattern of a Sunday morning.

Moments of elevation rise above our typical experiences by breaking our expectations. They form peaks. These moments transform an experience from ordinary to unexpected. In doing so, it activates our brain in figuring out how to respond to the new situation. The vivid experience leaves a strong memory.

My mom and I broke the pattern often with our Sunday School class. One day, we tiptoed around the church because we heard there was a giant in the building. We glimpsed a life-sized drawing of Goliath's outline in a dark hallway and quietly snuck away hoping he hadn't seen us. Another week, students arrived to find my mom in the classroom at the top of a ladder imitating Zacchaeus when he was up in a tree.

These creative activities made our Sunday School class the most popular at church. But most importantly, we hope it helped those children experience Scripture for themselves and grasp the wonder of those Bible stories.

We can plan for and create moments of elevation in our ministry work. To do so we first need to understand the expectations we need to break. What do people anticipate from their interaction with you?

We can easily slip into ministry routines, repeating patterns that seem to work. This isn't bad, but it creates a habit in our audience. They may start to have a flat-line experience instead of peak moments. The great news is that once you recognize the habit, you can embrace the opportunity to interrupt the pattern in a surprising way.

Sometimes people interrupt us as well. For example, when someone has a complaint about us or something we have done. Chip and Dan Heath describe this as a "pit moment" in their book.

But even negative experiences present opportunities. When someone complains, you also have the chance to break their expectations in a good way. People remember great service even if it was initiated by a problem. Practice empathetic listening and go above and beyond to fix the problem.

Every experience creates a lasting impression of your organization. As Christians, we also represent Christ and should be intentional to leverage every moment to reflect the love of God to others.

We have learned about two ways to create moments of elevation. But which should you focus on: creating a peak or filling a pit? Which is more effective?

Imagine a rating scale of 1–7 for your ministry. The people you interact with have the chance to score you between a 1, being "very bad," and 7, being "very good." When considering the ratings, you have limited team capacity and resources to respond. You face two choices:

1. **Eliminate all the negatives:** You can focus on all the areas that score low (1–3) and aim to make them a 4, which is average.

2. **Elevate the positives:** You can take all the good scores (4–6) and aim to make them a perfect 7—the best score you can get.

Which should you choose? Chip and Dan Heath extensively studied businesses that took different approaches. Research showed that elevating the positives was nine times more beneficial than eliminating the negatives.[61] This is surprising!

---

61 For purposes of the study, the overall revenue of the businesses was used as the measure of success. Heath and Heath, *The Power of Moments*, 59.

It can be easy to spend all our time fixing problems and not spend any time improving what is going well. However, it is much more valuable to focus on creating spectacular experiences, even if there are still some flaws to work out.

Moments of elevation are what create fans who tell others about your work. We don't remember "not-bad" experiences (in other words the 4–6 ratings). We remember and share amazing experiences (the 7's). Focusing on filling in the pits just brings people to average, which means we have met their expectations. We should aim to exceed their expectations. How can we make something extraordinary rather than ordinary?

Moments of elevation create fans who tell others about your work.

This is not easy, and we may need to fight to make it happen. Not everyone will see the need to create a moment of elevation. They may be perfectly satisfied with the work as it is. It would have been easy to say that bringing in fish and fresh loaves of bread for our Bible lesson was "over the top" or "too much trouble." That's probably what other Sunday School teachers thought. Why couldn't we just teach the Bible story the *normal* way? The pressure to "be reasonable" will persistently threaten to drain the awesomeness from the peaks you aim to create.

There will always be logical excuses not to make an effort. Creating moments of elevation may require time, cost money, or be a risk that may not work. Businesses know the value of creating peak moments though. Disney designs exclusive experiences at their theme parks that create special moments for families on vacation. Apple unveils each new device they create and makes getting it an event worth celebrating. The Gospel is worth far more than a family vacation or a new phone.

As ministry innovators, we should be willing to go where others have not gone before for the sake of the Gospel. Creating moments requires us to push past resistance and fight for something exceptional and different.

How can we elevate a person's encounter of the Gospel and make it the most special moment they have ever experienced? Peaks do not build themselves. It is worth the effort to make our presentation of Christ meaningful and memorable because there is nothing in this world more deserving of elevation than Christ.

Moments of Insight

Another way to create a powerful experience is by helping someone have a moment of insight. An insight is a new realization that comes not from someone else but from within our own heart and mind. We cannot guarantee that an insight will occur, but we can create an environment with all the right conditions.

OneHope has a program called *God's Big Story* that we developed for children in Africa. We created it to share Scripture with children who cannot read. Each week, a teacher shares a Bible story and gives each child a small card with a picture on it to help them remember the story. Collecting the story cards motivates them to come back each week for the next card.

The stories start in the Old Testament and continue into the New Testament with the death and resurrection of Jesus. There are sixteen cards to collect, and when lined up in the right order they unlock a secret. The children can flip all the cards over and see that they form a picture on the back like a puzzle. This picture shows how we fit into God's bigger story of salvation.

This creates a powerful moment of insight. It connects everything they have been learning about the Bible to their own lives.

It helps them see that the Gospel message is for them personally. Millions of children have been reached through this program, and it has spread from Africa to Latin America, to Asia, and around the world.

Moments of insight must be intentionally designed. They don't happen accidentally. Chip and Dan Heath tell a story of how teachers were led to a moment of insight. The teachers were asked to write down what they hoped their students would remember years after taking their class.

One by one the teachers read their dreams and goals to the group. They said things like, "I want my students to learn that math is actually fun," and, "I hope they will feel more confident connecting with other people and talking about ideas." All the teachers expressed worthy goals, but the next assignment was to look at their lesson plans and identify what would lead their students towards those ends. The teachers struggled to do this, and many had a powerful moment of insight.

They realized that nothing in their lesson plans would really accomplish the dreams they had for their students. Most of their plans focused on teaching information students needed to pass their tests. They had not spent a single minute planning experiences that would accomplish what they said they wanted students to remember years later.

It was as if they were leaving for a trip and they were already lost. They had a vehicle, gas, and a destination—but no map to plan how they would get there. It can be the same for us in ministry. We have dreams and goals for those we are reaching with the Gospel. But have we spent enough time and effort planning how that experience will truly change their lives in the way we hope?

A church service is a type of gathering you may be involved in designing. Yet we often fall back on an expected routine, rather than carefully examining the pattern to see if it is helping us meet our goals. For example, rather than hoping people feel connected to the church community, why not design a Sunday specifically focused on helping people make friends? Use some of the time to help people connect one-on-one and break down the barriers of age or culture that might be standing in the way.

If evangelism is a priority, what about making space for people to practice sharing their testimony to help them feel equipped and confident? There are many ways we might reimagine church services to create powerful moments of insight and elevation if we stop and look.

The ultimate moment of insight is realizing what the Gospel means for your life and choosing to follow Christ. That is the purpose behind each one of our ministries. It is a worthy purpose, and we should use every tool and resource available to us to accomplish it.

Think about how you can create moments of insight for the people you are reaching. Look through your ministry plans with new eyes to see how what you are doing is connecting people personally to Jesus. If you struggle to find those connections, think about how you can create them.

We sow the seeds and God brings the growth, but we should still do everything we can to give those seeds the best chance to grow. By considering each person and carefully crafting moments for them, we can make the most of every opportunity we are given to share the Gospel.

THE HIDDEN POWER OF FACILITATION

It had been a long week. Brightly colored sticky notes cluttered the windows and walls. Elaborate drawings were taped up around the room, and the whiteboard was an inky mess of shapes, arrows, and illustrations. The team worked tensely, nervously checking the clock.

"Alright, ten minutes left till we start the first interview!" I said. "Let's run through the prototype again and make sure we're ready."

Everyone anxiously watched the screen while we clicked through each button on the fake app we had pulled together in just the past twelve hours. It wasn't quite perfect, of course. It was only designed to look like the real thing. Some places weren't clickable, and all the content was made up. But it would be enough.

Everyone breathed a sigh of relief, but there wasn't much time to celebrate. I quickly ran to meet our first guest—a nine-year-old. He would be the first of five children we would interview that day and ask to give an honest first impression of our fake app. They were the experts now because our project was intended to help children better engage with Scripture digitally.

Our team of eight had spent the past four days in a room together thinking up ideas for this monumental task. The best thing we could do now was hear from the children themselves because none of us knew exactly how things looked from the eyes of nine- to twelve-year olds.

The whole team watched from the room next door as the scene unfolded on live video. The children clicked the buttons we had just carefully tested and paused to watch the video of a young person sharing how Scripture taught her the importance of relying on God. Then the comments started rolling in. "That was funny!" "She seems nice!" "What is this here for?" "So cool!" "Will there be more tomorrow? I would watch that again!"

We carefully took note of each response and what surprised us. Some comments were expected, while others we would never have imagined. After just five interviews, we had all the feedback we needed to make some key decisions about how to move forward.

The team ended the week feeling tired but confident about the next steps needed to create an engaging digital Scripture experience. We had just completed our first sprint.

Sprint is a book by Jake Knapp that lays out a method to solve problems and tests ideas in just five days.[62] A sprint gathers a team of seven to ten people for a focused period of brainstorming and work, at the end of which you test your idea on your target audience by using a prototype—like the fake app we showed the kids.

Sprints create valuable moments of insight that save you from going the wrong direction. We all tend to get attached to our own ideas and the solutions we think are the best way forward. But by testing those ideas early, it is easier to let them go if needed— before spending a lot of time and money on them. It is also so valuable to hear from the people you are trying to serve, rather than assuming you know what they want or need.

A sprint requires a facilitator to host the five-day experience, and every person who is invited has a specific job too. For example, one person is "the Decider," who is the final authority on decisions and helps the group move forward when there is a disagreement. Defining roles is critical to keep the group focused since everything has to be done in just a few days. If you follow the plan, you are guaranteed valuable insights on how your best idea will be received.

The secret to a sprint's success is the effectiveness of facilitation and focus. It is an intentional plan to support collaboration. All the activities have already been designed and arranged. All you have to do is learn to lead those activities and get the right group of people to focus on the problem you want to solve.

Here is a brief outline of the sprint schedule:

Day 1: Map. The team defines their long-term goals, maps out their vision for how they want to serve their audience, and establishes a shared understanding of the problem to solve.

---

62 Jake Knapp, *John Zeratsky*, and *Braden Kowitz*, *Sprint: How to Solve Big Problems and Test New Ideas in Just Five Days* (New York: Simon & Schuster, 2016).

Day 2: Sketch. The group works towards a solution by researching ways other organizations have solved similar problems. Using all those ideas as inspiration, each person in the group sketches out a proposal showing a drawing of how the problem could be solved.

Day 3: Decide. The team reviews their sketches and chooses one solution to focus on. Once everyone's feedback has been considered, a more detailed sketch is created, and the group plans how to create a prototype.

Day 4: Prototype. The group works for the entire day building the prototype to test their idea. A prototype is not a finished product, but rather the bare minimum needed to collect honest impressions and feedback from real users.

Day 5: Test. Five people from the target audience are brought in to use the prototype and give their opinions. One person from the team interviews each person while the rest of the group observes and takes notes. After the interviews are completed, the team reviews what they learned and how they should move forward.

When I started facilitating sprints, I felt like I had a new superpower to help people. I didn't really do anything other than explain the activities, keep people on track, and answer questions. But it was like magic. At the end of the sprint, people had clarity and could move forward in their work more confidently. Plus, everyone had fun and felt purposeful contributing their skills to build something together. It broke the script of the ways we usually worked together and created memorable moments.

What I was experiencing was the hidden power of facilitation. Sprints teach one method of leading a group over multiple days to solve a specific kind of problem. But you can apply the same facilitation skills to any meeting or presentation. Sprints are not the solution for everything. It is difficult to get a team to commit five full days to this process, plus there are many projects that don't require prototypes and interviews. Rather, a sprint's true value is in excellently hosting people to solve a problem collaboratively.

We often think that by simply putting brilliant people in a room together, we will get brilliant results. But the truth is that much more is needed. People dislike being without direction and leadership. Not having a plan wastes time and makes everyone feel uncomfortable. Inevitably, someone has to step up and lead. With a good host, even the most ordinary group can produce extraordinary results. You just need a well thought-out agenda and a host dedicated to facilitating the time well.

With a good host, the most ordinary group can produce extraordinary results.

Remember, you don't need to be a subject matter expert to facilitate—you just need to practice facilitation. By starting with sprints, you can learn many activities that you can use or modify to meet different needs and time constraints. Always be on the lookout for new activities and tools you can try to help people collaborate better. Even a simple brainstorming activity can really help a meeting be more creative and productive.

As a facilitator, you are not responsible for a group's results, but you are responsible to help people make the most of their time together. Plan with the values of a host in mind: communicate a clear purpose, create an environment of safety and trust, and help everyone participate and give their best. Look for opportunities to create moments that break the script or lead to insights.

Hosting is a sacrificial role but a powerful way you can lead and serve, modeling Christ's humility and love for others.

Hosts create meaningful experiences and enable people to bring their best to collaboration.

WHY WE MUST BE HOSTS

» Innovation thrives when diverse people collaborate, which requires an environment of safety and trust.

» Hosts unlock innovative potential by facilitating groups towards a shared purpose and helping participants engage effectively.

» Facilitation is a valuable skill set that requires investment, but it always pays off.

» People tend to remember moments that break the script of their everyday lives.

» Creating powerful experiences is a skill you can learn to help others have meaningful Gospel encounters.

PRACTICE THE PERSPECTIVE

Implement the values of a host in the next meeting you organize. Know your purpose, create an environment of safety and trust, and plan for participation. Even if you are not in charge of the meeting, you can always offer to help the organizer—they probably won't say no!

BROADEN YOUR PERSPECTIVE

Liam's book recommendations:

The Power of Moments: Why Certain Experiences Have Extraordinary Impact. Chip Heath and Dan Heath. New York: Simon & Schuster, 2017.

Sprint: How to Solve Big Problems and Test New Ideas in Just Five Days. Jake Knapp, *John Zeratsky*, and *Braden Kowitz*. New York: Simon & Schuster, 2016.

Electronic Propaganda Society. Podcast hosted by Mathew Sweezey. *https://mathewsweezey.com/podcast/*.

The Art of Gathering: How We Meet and Why It Matters. Priya Parker. New York: Penguin Publishing Group, 2018.

The Learner's Perspective

ENSURE YOUR INNOVATION REMAINS
RELEVANT TODAY AND TOMORROW

THE PERFECT MAN

A Parable

Upon a high mountain, unique in all the world, lived the Perfect Man. Each day, he reminded himself, "I am perfection. I can do no wrong."

People came to this man often seeking help, wisdom, or guidance. They toiled up the mountain for the promise of perfect advice.

A wealthy man approached, "Perfect Man! I must know how to invest my money. Will you help me?"

"I refuse," the Perfect Man replied. The wealthy man retreated down the mountain disappointed.

The next day, a widower approached, "Perfect Man! Will you help me? I must know how to go on in life without my wife."

"I refuse," the Perfect Man replied. The widower retreated down the mountain disappointed.

The next day an artist approached, "Perfect Man! I want to be the greatest artist in the world. How should I paint? Will you help me?"

"I refuse," the Perfect Man replied. The artist retreated down the mountain disappointed.

And so it went each day. Many people approached with many problems, but the Perfect Man refused to help any of them.

A bit further on was a small hill, not extraordinary in any way. On it a Good Man sat calmly and quietly. One day, the wealthy man passed by looking disappointed.

The Good Man called out, "Excuse me, sir. You seem sad. What's the matter?"

The wealthy man said, "I was hoping the Perfect Man would tell me how to invest my money. I have heard he does no wrong, but he refused to help me."

The Good Man replied, "Well, I'm not perfect. But I might be able to help you. What if you invested a little and saw how it went, then invested more in the things that did well? Surely through steady, careful attention and practice you could make secure investments."

"It's kind of you to offer, but I'm not interested in *your* advice. I want to do it perfectly." He walked on.

The next day, the widower passed by looking depressed. The Good Man called out to him, "Sir, you seem upset. Are you okay?"

"Well, my wife passed away, and I was hoping the Perfect Man would tell me how to bear my grief and go on with life."

"I can't say I'm perfect, but I've experienced loss," offered the Good Man. "I'm afraid it never gets easier, but there is still much good in life. Perhaps we could sit and talk for a while. You might discover there are still things that give you hope, and over time life won't feel so bleak."

"No, thank you. I only wanted his help; otherwise, I can't be sure it's right," the widower answered before shuffling off.

The following day, the artist passed the hill looking distressed. The Good Man waved and said, "Hello, you seem unwell. Are you alright?"

The artist turned and said, "I want to be the greatest artist in the world and I hoped that the Perfect Man would tell me how to paint. But he refused."

The Good Man replied, "I'm no artist myself, but surely painting what you love and practicing are a good place to start. Perhaps we could learn together and improve gradually if we help one another."

The artist replied, "I'm not interested in that. I wanted to be like the Perfect Man and have it done right now." And so she continued on.

The Good Man stood up from his hill and climbed to visit the Perfect Man on his mountain. "Perfect Man! I need your help. These people who come to see you—the wealthy man, the widower and the artist—they needed help. Why did you refuse them?"

The Perfect Man replied, "How should I help them? I know nothing of art, or grief, or money. Were I to try to help them and fail, I would no longer be perfect."

The Good Man answered, "Well, then you would never help anyone! There is no perfect answer to these sorts of things!"

"And so I haven't," the Perfect Man replied, staring off into the distance. "They can help themselves." He was indifferent to the struggle and sorrow of those who strove to be like him, but would never be.

At the bottom of the mountain, the Good Man put up a sign to save future travelers from seeking the Perfect Man's advice.

There is no effort without error.

The Perfect Man knows no effort

and therefore knows no error.

Endeavor. Err. But endeavor still.

• • •

THE LEARNER'S PERSPECTIVE

"The learning and knowledge that we have, is, at the most, but little, compared with that of which we are ignorant."

—Plato, Greek philosopher

I wanted to be a scientist when I grew up. One of my favorite teachers in high school taught me physics, and he brought to life what could have been a really boring subject.

We explored the way the world worked by conducting experiments. We tried to build the fastest mouse-trap powered car and float the most pennies on a raft made of aluminum foil, and we competed to see who could drop an egg from a tower and not have it break. We tested theories and learned through both our successes and our failures.

Scientists know that their knowledge is incomplete, and so they actively look for ways their beliefs might be incorrect. Scientists are always trying to disprove themselves. First, they form a hypothesis (a best-guess explanation based on evidence) and then test it in all the ways they can to see if it proves true. They are the first to question their own findings. Even after they are confident of their theory, they invite their peers in to check their results and look for flaws.

Assuming they are wrong is the attitude that is the key to their success. It is only discouraging to be wrong when you are not expecting it. Scientists can celebrate every failed experiment because that failure still brings them understanding. They are one step closer to knowing how the world really works.

The mindset of a scientist is so helpful for our ministry work. The learner's perspective reminds us that there is so much we don't know yet. We must strive for a clear and accurate understanding of the world and the people we are trying to reach.

We should be the first to doubt our own assumptions. We should be the first to ask hard questions and carefully examine what we believe to ensure it matches reality. Will this "great idea" really help people encounter the Gospel in the best way?

We should not press forward blindly hoping we are going in the right direction, but carefully take each step with our eyes open and minds ready to learn. A learner's perspective helps take some of the uncertainty out of innovation. It frees us from pursuing perfection and instead helps us try new things in small, calculated ways.

I've heard ministries say they cannot afford to innovate because it is too risky. They worry about getting it wrong and wasting their time and money for nothing. The truth is, we cannot afford *not* to innovate. The world is changing so fast that what worked yesterday will not work tomorrow. Nothing is guaranteed except change.

Innovation can actually be very methodical and deliberate, just like science. We don't have to wait for a once-in-a-lifetime idea or a flash of inspiration that may never come. Innovation is not a mysterious power of creativity that some are blessed with and others are not. Innovation is a discipline you can learn and consistently practice to move your ministry forward.

You can test ideas, learn from the results, iterate, and try again—each time getting closer to a solution and learning more about the world. When you approach it this way, innovation is not unsafe or risky.

Innovation is not unsafe.

Certainly, it would be easier if someone just told us what to do. We live in a world that idolizes experts. We look to people hoping to discover their secret to success. Maybe that's even why you picked up this book!

We want to be experts too and spend time cultivating our own knowledge so we can be the person with answers to give. But expertise can be overvalued, and perfection is impossible. Becoming an expert learner is the most effective way to help you reach your goals.

THE WORK OF UNLEARNING

My wife and I were lost. We were in Bali, Indonesia, looking for a restaurant located in the middle of a rice field. It looked easy to get to in the photos online, but we had missed a turn somehow.

Hot and tired, we trudged to the top of a hill to ask directions at a nearby resort. The helpful lady informed us to go back down the hill, turn left, and look for a small dirt road leading off into the rice field. We retraced our steps down the hill and my wife immediately turned to the right.

"Where are you going?" I asked.

"I'm following the directions," she said looking equally confused. Somehow she had heard the lady say "turn right" and I had heard her say "turn left."

Only one of us could be correct, and I was certain it was me. But my wife was just as certain, and as a peacemaker, I followed her to the right. We ended up getting trapped in a huge street parade that was moving the other direction. By the time we made our way through we discovered my recollection was correct after all and the road we were looking for was back the way we had come.

It is rare that two people hear the exact opposite thing, but it is true that we are often wrong without knowing it. As humans, we like to be right. Our minds are constantly working to understand the world around us and fit new experiences into the patterns of our past observations. This is how our brain keeps our bodies safe—by ensuring we are constantly aligned with the truth of how the world works. That is why we don't decide one day that cars aren't real and step into oncoming traffic to test this idea.

When you were young, your parents probably taught you important things like not to touch a hot stove or jump from high places. If you did those things anyway, you experienced the painful consequences and hopefully didn't repeat the mistake. Our brains are very good at processing information and experiences to help us learn.

We most often think about learning as adding new information to what we already know. But sometimes new information conflicts with a belief we already hold to be true. When this happens, we face a choice: unlearn something we believe to be true or reject the new information as false.

You should know that your brain will most likely try to reject new information and hold on to what you already believe. Author Kathryn Schulz explores the very interesting topic of how people view and respond to error in her book *On Being Wrong*.

It turns out that even in the face of concrete facts, our minds may try to find ways to invalidate or ignore those facts to preserve our existing beliefs. "With error as with disaster, we screen out unwelcome information to protect ourselves from discomfort, anxiety, and trauma," Schulz writes.[63]

---

63 Kathryn Schulz, *On Being Wrong: Adventures in the Margin of Error* (New York: HarperCollins, 2010), 229.

Denial can be a go-to response when someone tries to tell us we are wrong. It can be easier to deceive ourselves and hold our position than it is to change our mind. You can imagine how this tendency increases along with the importance of the belief.

The more core a belief is to a person's identity, the more likely they will be to defend why that belief is right and refuse to consider an alternate position. This is a critical thing to be aware of in ourselves and others. There is a cost to admitting we are wrong, and it is a cost we do not like to pay.

Right now, you and I are both wrong about all sorts of beliefs we hold, we just don't know it yet. However, ministry is too important for us to live in ignorance or denial. We must not be satisfied with making errors or mistakes and not knowing it.

As ministry innovators, we need to be actively seeking out areas where we might be wrong so we can correct our thinking and methods. Some mistakes may be pointed out to us, but others we will need to locate on our own. This takes courage, but it is worth doing to fulfill our calling to the Great Commission.

Sometimes our good ideas won't work as well as we expect. In his book *Black Box Thinking,* author Matthew Syed describes a program called "Scared Straight."[64] Started in the 1970's in the U.S., the program aimed to keep teens from falling into a life of crime.

Students were taken on a field trip to a prison and got a chance to talk with criminals who were serving life sentences. The program was created with the belief that teens would be discouraged from committing crimes once they saw first-hand the life that would await them in prison. They would be scared into living a "straight" life within the law.

The program was highly praised for its effectiveness and became popular in schools across America. The only problem was that

---

64 Syed, *Black Box Thinking,* chapter 8.

it was actually having the opposite of the intended effect. But nobody knew or cared to look into the results. Years later an independent researcher discovered that the research validating the program was incomplete and biased towards making the program look good. The truth was that the teens who went through the program were not deterred from committing violent crimes. In fact, some of them were more likely to end up in prisons like the one they had visited.

Despite the best of intentions, the educators, politicians, and policemen who promoted the program were making the problem of crime worse. The scary thing is that the program is still active in some places despite several decisive research studies proving it is counterproductive. This is a tragic example of innovation gone wrong with serious consequences for everyone involved. Lives were forever changed, not just for those students but for their future victims and their families.

This is not a ministry example, but it reminds us that the work we are doing in ministry is much more serious than this. Evangelism and discipleship is also life-or-death work. We are sharing the Good News of how people can be saved from an *eternal* life sentence. Through our ministry programs, we are connecting people to God and shaping their perspective on this life and the next.

Ensuring our methods are right and that we are accomplishing what we intend should be a priority. We cannot afford to be ignorant of our mistakes and blind spots. The learner's perspective helps us diligently seek out our errors so we can fix them. It is the mindset we need to become more effective.

The learner's perspective is the active approach of relentlessly challenging information. Rather than being satisfied that your viewpoint is correct, you continually seek more up-to-date information. You strive to recognize the assumptions you have about people, their lives, values, and desires and how those intersect with the solutions you are offering.

Test your ideas to see if they work, and adjust them when they do not. It's not a bad thing to be wrong. Getting something wrong doesn't mean we have failed, it just means there was something we didn't understand or anticipate. It is great to find that out! It means we can realign our understanding and our actions with reality.

Remember that the Gospel message we bring to the world may be hard for people to hear. We are fundamentally telling people what they believe about God is wrong, and this has many implications for their lives. People will resist this. It is difficult to change minds and hearts. Only the Holy Spirit can give someone the eyes to see God's truth.

So remember to be gentle as you minister. Be willing to walk with people through their hard questions and their natural resistance to change. Pray that they will see the Gospel as the Good News it truly is. Pray that they will have an undeniable encounter with Jesus that will forever change the way they see. Work hard to see this happen, but at the end of the day entrust everything you are doing into God's hands, which is where this work belongs.

CELEBRATING FAILURE

I had a first-grade teacher who gave students a report at the end of each day with a happy face or a sad face to represent their behavior. I never understood why I often received sad faces, but it felt like a tremendous failure that I wanted to avoid. My mom later learned the reason. The teacher said it was because I finished assignments too quickly and then would go back to my reading, which wasn't allowed. I was tremendously upset at the time, but when I reflect back on it today, being an avid reader has been a good thing for my life.

Our perceptions of failure affect many areas of our lives. We often associate being wrong with getting in trouble. But sometimes getting in trouble has little to do with right or wrong (like my story with reading), or being wrong is actually a step towards progress. The reaction we have towards failure reveals a lot about us and the way we think. It can be traced back to two fundamentally differing views of error.

"Errors expose the real nature of the universe or they obscure it," writes Kathryn Schulz in her book *On Being Wrong*. "They lead us towards truth or away from it. They are either abnormalities that we should try to eliminate or inevitabilities that we should anticipate."[65]

In other words, how we view making errors and mistakes dictates how we respond to making mistakes. Either it's the worst possible thing that could happen or it's something that will certainly happen and we need to be prepared to learn from it.

What is your natural way of thinking about mistakes? Do you go out of your way to avoid them at all costs, or do you accept them as a natural part of life and learning? On a practical level it makes sense to have a positive view of failure. After all, you will not go through your life and ministry being perfect. Only Christ was perfect. We should expect to make lots of mistakes and be prepared to have grace for ourselves and others in the work we do.

This is especially important in innovation where we are often trying something for the first time. Changing our view of failure is one of the most freeing things we can do to unlock innovation in ourselves and others.

For some reason we tend to think that when we face a problem all we need is a solution. We will come up with an idea, make a plan, execute the plan, and it will solve the problem, and our work will be done. Unfortunately, things rarely go this smoothly. When was the last time your plans worked perfectly? It seems a little arrogant to expect that they would. We are not God, so we cannot see into the future. "You don't know what you don't know," is a true saying.

---

65 Schulz, *On Being Wrong*, 40.

When plans fail, a truth is being revealed that we did not understand. We should be open to learning this lesson so that we can act differently in the future. It is not shameful to try something innovative and have it go poorly. After all, it's only the first time we've tried it! Avoid the temptation to cover up failure out of embarrassment or fear of punishment.

Failure is not the end point; it is the beginning point. Failures give us lots of useful information. We can't go back in time to make our mistakes never happen. But we can move forward armed with new understanding. Failures can be fresh starts for a new and wiser version of ourselves. Failing is a huge success if it propels the work into the future.

Failures can be fresh starts for a new and wiser version of ourselves.

This makes sense on an intellectual level. But it is challenging to put this perspective into practice in our ministries. It is discouraging to fail in ministry because we want to be good stewards of our resources. People give us their time and money because they believe in us. We want to prove ourselves worthy of that trust by producing good results.

There is tremendous pressure not to fail. There is a pull to do things that are guaranteed to succeed. But ironically, if success is guaranteed, then that idea has been proven effective enough times that it is no longer innovative. Innovation, by definition, means trying untested things to create new value.

Your ministry's attitude towards risk and its tolerance for failure will determine much of what you are able to do as an innovator. Some innovations will not succeed the way we hope, but we must be willing to accept failures and learn from them. Intolerance for failure stifles innovation before it has even begun. If we give in to the pressure to only do what is guaranteed to work, our ministries will never be able to innovate.

Let's not run away from our failures or hold ourselves to such a high standard that we never risk making a mistake. Hopefully your ministry culture is not one that pins the blame on a specific person when failure happens or slams the door shut on future innovations because something did not go as expected. Mistakes are natural and point us towards the places we need to learn and grow more. Let's be courageous to try new things and be persistent in the face of failure.

Success is never guaranteed. But we have God on our side, and He promises to equip us for our calling. Your value does not come from how right you are or how well you perform, but from Christ, who establishes our worth before God. It is His work that we are joining, so we should feel complete freedom to reflect God's infinite creativity in our work. Innovate, fail, learn, and try again. Trust God with the results since He is the one who spoke all of creation into being and is tireless to pursue the lost for His kingdom.

FASTER AND SMALLER IS BETTER

Every few years my wife and I try to improve some part of our home. We have gradually improved how our home serves us room by room. This has meant many trips to the store and lots of furniture assembly.

One day I found myself struggling to bolt together our new dresser. The tool included in the box was small and not great for the job. I knew I could probably find a better solution in my personal collection of tools, but for some reason I was too lazy to change my process. With each screw I installed, I was closer to the finish line and had less incentive to change my methods.

But the work was slow and painful. Finally, in frustration I got my power drill and quickly finished the job. The work went so much faster with the right tool. I was ashamed it had taken me so long to innovate my approach.

This story illustrates *sunk cost*—a business term that describes investments made that cannot be recovered. Sunk costs encourage us to keep going in the same direction because the more we sink our time, effort, or money into something, the harder it is to change course. We are invested in that particular solution and changing later represents giving up all the energy, resources, or time spent in the wrong direction. This thinking is totally natural, but it can put us into dangerous positions. It may force us to keep going with something that might not be headed in the right direction.

Failure is an effective way to learn, but it can be expensive. We don't want to see things fail that we have put a lot into. Fortunately, there are ways to minimize the impact of failure—not by avoiding it, but by seeking it out. One of the best things we can do as ministry innovators is to test out our ideas as soon as possible to see what we need to adjust. This makes it much easier to try new things and take risks.

Some of the most successful businesses embrace the approach of failing fast and often. This is because failure is much easier when you are at the beginning of the journey than when you are further down the road. When you haven't put too much behind an idea yet, you are much more willing to make changes or even abandon a solution that will not ultimately work.

Start small and test quickly. I wish I had known this principle at the beginning of my career. I was new to both technology development and innovation when I first started at OneHope. I was given a project called MyStory. The goal was to create an app that would enable Christian teens to record their testimony and share the video with their friends. It seemed like a great idea.

We spent over a year working with a team of developers to build the app. We were sure it would meet a need and planned ways to promote it to our partners and to teens at youth events. But when we finished the project and launched the app, we found that nobody really wanted it or used it. It didn't accomplish the results we expected and was a failure. As one of my first innovation projects, it was a big disappointment.

What did we miss? We all cared about the app and did our best, spending time to get every detail as perfect as we could before release. But ultimately our efforts didn't matter because teens didn't download and use the app. What if I could have found out this would happen in just a few days instead of after an entire year of development? I didn't know it at the time, but that is the purpose of a prototype.

The word *prototype* comes from the Latin roots *proto*, meaning "first," and *typus,* meaning "figure or impression". A prototype is a first form or first impression that comes before the real thing. Before jumping straight into the work and expense of developing the MyStory app, we could have created a prototype to test our idea.

Innovators should be able to do almost anything with almost nothing.

A prototype is anything that helps us get feedback from real users. For example, I could have created a flier talking about the app and asked teens what they thought. Would they download it? Do they ever share their testimony with their friends? What kind of content do they feel comfortable publishing online and where? These questions and a few others might have helped us figure out that convincing teens to use the app was going to be a challenge.

We could have made different decisions before hiring a team of developers to build the project. Notice that zero coding skills would have been required to make the prototype flier.

Innovators should aim to be able to do almost anything with almost nothing. This is the power of prototyping. It helps us get to the early phase of discovery quickly before investing more time and effort. I have used prototypes that are extremely simple (like the flier example) and others that have appeared almost as functional as a real app. Prototypes aren't just for technology solutions either. You can develop prototypes for products, experiences, and even physical spaces. The key is not that the details are perfect but that they are just enough to help you get feedback.

The reason that prototypes are effective is that you are putting your idea in front of people to see what they think. Watch to see if they understand the idea. Ask if they would use your solution. If not, what are the barriers that would keep them from it? Surprisingly, you don't need to talk to that many people.

Jake Knapp's book *Sprint* suggests that conducting just five in-depth interviews with people in your target audience is enough to get you most of the feedback you need. Five people are usually able to spot 85% of the problems.[66] You could conduct many more interviews, but you will hear similar comments and repeating themes. *Sprint* lays out a plan that enables a group of people to take something from idea to prototype in just five days. It is a great method because it helps you move quickly and learn even more quickly.[67]

Smaller and faster is better. The quicker you can bring an idea to life and try it out, the easier it will be to make changes and try again. This is the process of iterating. When you are taking this approach, it won't even feel like failure. It will feel like experimentation.

---

66 Knapp, *Zeratsky*, and *Kowitz*, *Sprint*, 198.
67 Read more about sprints and how to conduct them in the Hidden Power of Facilitation section in the chapter "The Host's Perspective."

Experiments are exciting! You create an idea, set up a test, and find out what happens. The learner's perspective helps us be scientists for our ministries. It doesn't entirely remove risk from our work. But exploring an idea with a prototype is often more than enough to show whether it will provide results. We can help ensure we are at least going in the right direction and take the first few steps forward.

GROWING IN THE RIGHT DIRECTION

Prototypes help us test an idea inexpensively and quickly, but what comes after the prototype? How do we move our ideas forward while ensuring we are still heading in the right direction?

Let's revisit my app example. Imagine that my prototype had revealed that teens really were interested in a way to share their testimony with their friends. Equipped with that information, we could decide to move forward with development. But this time, we don't work for a year in isolation building the app exactly the way we think it should be and unveiling it to teens in hopes they will love it. Instead, we work quickly to build the next step: the *minimum viable product* or MVP.

An MVP follows the same principles as a prototype in that it moves us forward inexpensively and quickly. But instead of being a representation of our idea like a prototype, this version needs to be "viable"—it needs to work. It should be functional while being the simplest it can possibly be. Just useful enough and no more.

It will feel uncomfortable to put an MVP out into the world. We typically like to perfect our work before letting anyone else see it. But our goal is to get our product into the hands of users as quickly as we can so we can find out what they think.

To do this, you will have to focus on only the most essential aspects of your idea. It should be the bare minimum to accomplish your goals. This will be challenging because it means you have to say "no" or "maybe later" to lots of features you would like to have. But if those features are not core to your purpose, they do not belong in the MVP.

This might sound like a strange way to work, but this approach has been proven and is popular in the business world. There is an entire method around creating new companies to do this called *lean startup*. It focuses on developing MVP's to get businesses up and running quickly so entrepreneurs can learn which direction they need to go.

People who like this approach often refer to "lean thinking" to indicate that we should keep things as small and fast as possible until we determine the best next step forward. If you've ever been curious how top technology companies like Google, Facebook, and Amazon became so successful, this is it. They create space for new ideas, test those ideas, and move forward only what works.

This points us towards another helpful principle for innovation: follow your strengths, not your weaknesses. When you see your audience responding well to something you are doing, examine that more. What is it that people are enjoying? How can you accelerate or improve it? Be willing to pivot towards the things your users find most valuable even if it is not something you planned for. Remember, incongruity—the unexpected—is an opportunity for innovation.[68]

Observe how people are using your product or service and work to build on its strengths. Of course, if you see an obvious problem, you will need to fix that. But in general, it is more effective to focus on improving core strengths than adding new features. Your MVP is the core of your experience. So if it is not meeting a need, adding features won't fix it. A bicycle with square tires doesn't

---

68 Incongruity is one of Peter Drucker's seven sources of innovation. For a quick overview, refer to the section Making Sense of It All in the chapter "The Beginner's Perspective."

become more desirable with a bell, reflectors, and a helmet hook. It's not fun to ride, so the extra features are irrelevant.

Make the most of the momentum you already have rather than focusing on what your ministry, outreach, or product doesn't have. There may be time in the future to add what you think is missing, and your audience will welcome that if they feel you have already made something valuable for them.

Building minimum viable products helps us stay focused, which is critical because we have limited time and money to dedicate to our projects.

One of the most common complaints I hear about technology development is, "If we only had more funding, we could make something really good!" The reality is that our ministry budgets will always be limited. We need to learn to work within our constraints to produce things that are excellent. The best way to do that is by simplifying.

Simplify to the primary purpose and build that first. As you find problems, try thinking in new ways. Rather than immediately asking, "How can we fix what isn't working?" consider first, "Can we *remove* what isn't working?" Eliminate anything that is cluttering the experience or that no one is really using. This gives you and your team more time to focus on what is proving valuable to your audience.

To iterate effectively, you will need access to data about how people are using your product or service. Plan for ongoing research from the beginning. Data is key. It helps us construct an accurate picture of what is happening rather than needing to guess. Data unlocks insights we might not gain any other way. Analytics can be overwhelming, however, so ensure you know what you are looking for. If you are having trouble interpreting your data, the best thing to do is go straight to your users and ask them.

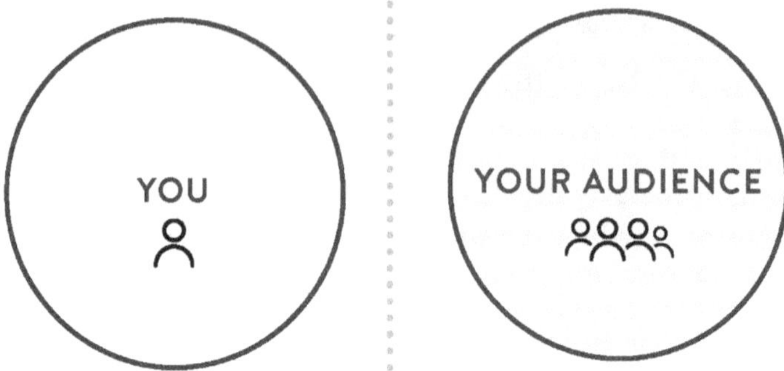

Our solutions are never separate from the people we are trying to serve. Most of the time, we are building things for people who are not like us. So we cannot rely on our own experiences and preferences to guide our work. We must put our products into the hands of the people they are intended for and bring them on the journey with us. They will see what needs to be changed—all we have to do is listen. The better we are at listening and learning, the faster we will be able to create something innovative and valuable.

You and I as part of the Global Church face challenging problems. We need methods for discipleship in digital spaces; ways to plant churches in areas that are hostile to the Gospel; better approaches to making Scripture accessible and understandable; and much more! These challenges can seem overwhelming.

But I am confident that none of these problems can withstand the creative force we bring by starting small and learning quickly. By embracing the learner's perspective, we maximize our time and resources and minimize the risk of innovation to find new ways to advance God's kingdom.

WHY WE'RE NEVER FINISHED

Early in my career at OneHope, I helped build an app to go with a book we were producing for young children. The illustrations for the book were in a fantastic animated style with bright colors. The content had a storybook rhyme to it, communicating how God had rescued us to be part of His kingdom. We wanted to make the book digital somehow, so we came up with an idea for an app that would include all the content and some games to go with the stories. I helped create the games and project managed the development team to build and launch the app on time. Through this project, I learned that launching an app is only your first step.

After release, we found many things to fix. But I quickly discovered a bigger problem. The project budget only got us to launch, and we lacked money to make continuing improvements. We treated the entire project like a product. The release became our focus, but we didn't consider how we would work through the app to serve children and families long-term. We released it into the app store like we might put a book on a shelf for people to find.

Our product was a final destination rather than an entry point. You can probably still find it in the app store, but it hasn't been updated in years. Unfortunately, this can happen often in ministry.

The pace of technology development and change is unrelenting. If we treat our digital initiatives like products, we are setting ourselves up to fail. It takes a tremendous amount of effort to keep an app or website functioning properly. One of the advantages of digital products is that they are dynamic. We can make changes whenever we need to. A book might go to print with spelling errors, and those cannot be corrected, but an e-book can be updated any time.

The ability to make changes to what we have released digitally is an advantage. But if our teams are not thinking about this and are not structured to respond, it is a lost opportunity. It may even become a liability. Just consider what might happen if someone downloads my outdated app today and finds it doesn't work correctly. What kind of impression will they form of OneHope? They may think we create terrible products and don't care enough to fix them.

Now let me tell you a different story. At about the same time I was working on my app, OneHope was assembling a team to figure out digital Scripture engagement for young children. We had the opportunity to partner with YouVersion, the creators of the world's most popular Bible app, to create something innovative for children.

Together, we came up with an idea to share the Gospel through interactive stories spanning from Genesis to Revelation. Our team came up with a launch plan and strategies to market the app to families.

When it was released, the *Bible App for Kids* was downloaded more than a million times in its first week alone! It quickly became the number one children's app on the app store. The initial release created demand for more content. We launched with just six stories but had a plan for a total of forty. We worked with church partners and individuals to sponsor new development and added interactive elements and games. We recorded audio so children could listen to the Scripture stories. An accompanying curriculum was developed with engaging videos churches could use for their Sunday School classes.

Later, the app was translated and downloaded around the world— even in places where Bibles are illegal. The stories are on YouTube as well, where they are reaching millions more. The results of this project blew us away, and the app continues to be one of our main digital programs for children.

Many times I have met someone for the first time, only for them to say, "My kid loves that app! We use it every night before bed. Your ministry made that?" The app has gone much further than we could have ever imagined. So what made the difference? Why did the *Bible App for Kids* succeed when my first app failed?

It's an interesting case study because the circumstances were really similar. Both apps were even put out by the same organization.

But in one case, I was working on an app we treated like a product. Once it was done, we were done. In the other case, we worked in partnership on a digital program we treated like a service.

The *Bible App for Kids* was able to do amazing things because we thought long-term. We assembled a team to be dedicated to the project for years. They were able to give the app their full attention and had a project budget to add features over time. We still started small. We released an MVP of just a few stories and then built on that. We gathered feedback and built on the app's strengths. We fixed bugs and made improvements along the way.

Other teams contributed their ideas and skills to the project as well. They helped develop innovative resources around the app that met a real need for our church partners. We didn't try to do this all at once. We knew we were on a journey to serve families long-term. Because of that, we had the right attitude, team structure, and expectations that allowed us to build something great over years.

Approaching digital initiatives as services, rather than products, is key to success. This is the reason we are never really finished. Our work is not done when we launch something. We must be effective at listening, watching, and understanding who we are trying to serve. Then we must be willing to make changes based on what we learn throughout the project.

Our work is not done when we launch.

Data helps us learn. In digital ministry, there are many data points that show how people are using what we have created. In fact, we can quickly become overwhelmed by all the numbers available. The important thing is not to gather as much data as possible, but rather to focus on the right data.

"What we measure and how we measure determine what will be considered relevant, and determine not just what we see, but what we—and others—do," writes Peter Drucker.[69]

In other words, measure what matters because people will focus their action towards changing those numbers. If a church wants to grow their Sunday School, they would need to start by counting how many children attend each week. Attendance is their key metric. Then they would need to take into account what affects that metric such as adult attendance (families usually come together), the topics taught each week, how children like their teachers, and more. By putting this data together, we can gain insights to help us make decisions.

Making the right improvements starts with measuring the right things. But sometimes our data can distract us or lead us in unfruitful directions. Let's look one more time at my example of the *Bible App for Kids*. How do we know the app is a success? One metric we use is the number of downloads. This indicates that people want the app. We celebrate every time we reach a major milestone. The last time I looked, the app had been downloaded more than 75 million times! But if downloads is the only number we care about, we would be in trouble.

Don't get distracted or fooled by the wrong data—what some call "vanity metrics." Many people install apps that they never open or use. It is easy to market an app and get people to download it. There are even systems in place that advertise to users in other apps and reward them for downloading yours. But most often they will uninstall without ever opening it. One data point, such as downloads, doesn't tell the entire story.

Our goal is for children to engage with Scripture. So we care more about metrics that show how long people use the app and how many times they return to it. We do everything we can to

---

69 Drucker, *The Daily Drucker*, 81.

improve those numbers. We celebrate downloads, of course, but we recognize that this one number doesn't guarantee we are meeting our mission. Research puts us in touch with reality. When that reality is not the one we hoped for, we know we need to make changes.

Don't be overwhelmed or discouraged by the fact that you will never be finished. The work of ministry is an incredible opportunity to model Christ's example of serving others. Jesus lived with and journeyed with His disciples for three years. He did not just reach out to them one time; He developed a relationship that grew and deepened over time.

As we minister to others, it is important to think in terms of years instead of minutes or seconds. We live in a fast-paced world, but believing in Jesus and growing our faith in Him is a lifelong pursuit. By thinking with a service mindset, we think long-term in the context of a relationship.

Jesus taught His disciples through sermons, parables, experiences, and miracles. Yet they still didn't understand His death when it happened. The people closest to Christ thought His ministry had failed when they saw Him on the cross. It wasn't until He rose from the dead, walked with them again, and explained everything to them that their eyes were opened to the truth of the Gospel.

It may be similar for many you are trying to reach for Christ. It will take more than a single encounter, a single explanation, or a single program. You should be prepared to walk with them and serve them as Christ taught us to do. There are many things to learn and even things we must unlearn as we do this.

As we grow in our understanding of how best to communicate the Good News to a broken world, let us do so like Jesus himself. Let us be servants humbly journeying with those who have yet to see the truth.

Learners guide ministry in new directions by testing ideas quickly and gaining knowledge from both successes and failures.

WHY WE MUST BE LEARNERS

» We are always wrong about something, but we don't always know it. So we need to be humble and aggressive learners.

» Failure is a valuable opportunity because it indicates that some area of our thinking does not align with reality.

» It is not shameful to make mistakes, but it is a waste if we do not learn from them.

» We can keep from going the wrong direction by quickly testing our assumptions and ideas through prototypes and minimum viable products.

» Our work is never really done because there will always be ways to grow our successes and continue serving people.

PRACTICE THE PERSPECTIVE

Rather than seek to be an expert at your ministry, make it your goal to be an expert learner. When you are asked for your opinion, don't just rely on past experience. Offer to help connect with the target audience directly for their feedback. Be the first to admit you don't know the right direction, and lead the way in asking questions and experimenting.

BROADEN YOUR PERSPECTIVE

Liam's book recommendations:

Scrum: The Art of Doing Twice the Work in Half the Time. Jeff Sutherland and J. J. Sutherland. New York: Crown Business, 2014.

The Lean Startup: How Today's Entrepreneurs Use Continuous Innovation to Create Radically Successful Businesses. Eric Ries. New York: Crown Business, 2011.

Hacking Growth: How Today's Fastest-Growing Companies Drive Breakout Success. Morgan Brown and Sean Ellis. London: Virgin Books, 2017.

Afterword: Keep Going

As I wrote this book, I couldn't escape the feeling that I might be missing something important. I wanted to be able to provide you with a guarantee—a promise that if you practice the seven perspectives described in this book you will see success in all your endeavors. I wanted to be able to give you the magic formula for ministry innovation. But I don't think there is one.

I believe the approaches and ways of thinking I have shared in this book will make you a more effective ministry innovator and better kingdom collaborator. It will shape you into the innovator you need to be to solve the complex problems you face.

However, I cannot guarantee that you will see immediate success. This has been my own story in ministry innovation. In many areas, I am still waiting to see results from the seeds I have planted and cultivated over years of effort. I have sown into many people, projects, and processes, but I have never seen my work produce an extraordinary transformation. I have to warn you not to expect to see the fruits of your labor either.

Do we work for the fruit? Or do we work to faithfully serve God? Ministry innovation is different from business innovation. Many ideas and approaches I have included in this book are from a business context, where innovation is promoted for its guarantee of success. It is sold to us with the promise that if you innovate, your business will profit. Innovating will help you sell more products, attract more customers, and build a bigger brand. But those are not our goals in ministry.

Jesus has already warned us that the way to life is hard. The gate is narrow and few will find it (Matthew 7:14). We work to reach the whole world with the Gospel, even knowing that most will reject our message. We do the best we can, but the Holy Spirit is the only one who can move people to believe.

I am not the first writer to wonder and worry about whether my work will be helpful in the great conversation. Where success comes from has been a central debate among human authors for thousands of years. Across the span of classic literature, there is an ongoing rivalry between poets and philosophers.

Poets follow a tradition of seeking divine inspiration. The epic poems by Homer, Virgil, Dante, and Spencer all begin by appealing to God or some sort of divine muse. Poets seek inspiration from supernatural sources of goodness, truth, and beauty and depend on those for their success.

The philosopher, on the other hand, believes that there is no need for supernatural revelation. Philosophers such as Plato, Aristotle, Cicero, Descartes, and Hume focused on making sense of the world through human logic. They believed all truth could be attained through reason. The philosopher's tradition of inquiry and observation has led to many of humanity's great advancements over the years.

So who is right—the poet or the philosopher?

A great amount of human wisdom has been shared in this book that would naturally fall into the philosophy category. My goal has been to teach you the perspectives needed to practically pursue innovation in your ministry. There are many things you can go out and do today to increase your chances of success. You should be a philosopher who takes the very best the world has to offer, learns from it, and uses it for ministry.

However, you also need to be a poet who acknowledges that human wisdom will never be enough. God is the author of all creation and the ultimate source of truth. To build on any other foundation is foolishness.

Our ministries are powerless and fruitless if God is not at their center. It is only by drawing near to God that we can move closer to reality because God is the source of reality! My prayer for you is to become the ultimate *poet-philosopher* who steadfastly seeks guidance from God, while also doing everything in your power to steward your skills and intellect to further His mission.

God rewards the faithful servants who multiply what has been given them to invest. We are called and equipped for this mission, so "let us run with perseverance the race marked out for us, fixing our eyes on Jesus, the pioneer and perfecter of faith" (Hebrews 12:1–2, NIV).

Fix your eyes on Christ, not on what the world calls success. Make space to be Spirit-led and be sensitive to listen for God's voice. Be prayerful about your projects and seek divine direction. He is the ultimate Innovator. See God's hand at work both in successes and in the valuable lessons we learn through our failures.

Fix your eyes on Christ, not on what the world calls success.

If you feel alone, ask God to send you like-minded people to join you. Even Jesus did not minister alone. He built a team around Him and commissioned them to build His church according to their talents and abilities. They faithfully continued in partnership and collaboration for the Gospel. Paul planted seeds and Apollos watered them, but ultimately God is the one who brings the growth (1 Corinthians 3:6).

All our efforts must be rooted in Scripture's truths and in God's values. The kingdom economy is not like the business economy. We are not creating profit margins, but seeking to save souls for eternity. This work is not easily measured. How will we know if our innovations are a success? In many cases, only God will know because only He sees the heart and the transformation occurring there.

We are simply called to be faithful. Even if we never see the fruit of our labor, we can trust that God is still at work through us in ways we cannot even imagine. Because of Christ, victory over death is assured and mankind has the opportunity to walk with Jesus every day. This is the Good News we bring to a lost and broken world.

Acknowledgements

I say, "I wrote a book," but in reality nothing about this process was an individual effort. Bringing this book to life was a picture of the body of Christ in action. I would like to thank:

My amazing wife, constant companion, and supporter of dreams. Without your fiery tenacity, inhuman focus, and dedication to God, this book would not exist.

My mom, who not only modeled innovation and inspires me daily, but who also covered this project in prayer from start to finish.

My leaders at OneHope who give me tremendous opportunities to learn and grow in service to God.

A special thanks to my advance readers around the world:
Rachel Adyamo, Erika Andujar, Kurian Babykutty, Godwin Bategeka, George Childs, Khainza Suzan Joan, Jonivah Katusiime, Arun Meshach, Shanely Niemi, Becky Ogden, Heather Pubols, Miriam Thomas, and Sydney David Walusimbi.

Editorial Team:
Marisa Antonaya, Lani Savage, Patti Savage, Lois Stück

Design and Layout Team:
Jason Anscomb, Jeanne Elizabeth, Wayne Kehoe, Patti Savage

I would also like to thank my Innovation Launchpad graduates for their depth of thought in engaging with this content and sharpening my thinking in every area of ministry. This book is for you and all the other kingdom innovators like you.

Index 1: Authors, Books, and People

A

Actionable Gamification: Beyond Points, Badges and Leaderboards   **83, 101**

Allen, James   **65**

Art of War   **168**

B

Bahcall, Safi   **70, 101**

Beckwith, Harry   **169, 181**

Black Box Thinking: The Surprising Truth about Success   **147, 192, 270**

Bromiley, Martin   **195**

Brown, Morgan   **289**

C

Cascades: How to Create a Movement that Drives Transformational Change   **20, 45**

Chou, Yu-Kai   **83, 86, 88, 101**

Cron, Lisa   **156, 181**

Crucial Conversations: Tools for Talking When Stakes Are High   **207, 233**

The Culture Map: Breaking Through the Invisible Boundaries of Global Business   **126, 147**

Do/Scale: A Road Map to Growing a Remarkable Company   **68, 101**

Drucker, Peter F.   **134, 141, 147, 280, 286**

E

Einstein, Albert   **57**

Electronic Propaganda Society (podcast)   **261**

Ellis, Sean   **289**

F

Ford, Henry   **59**

Fortune Magazine   **135, 138**

G

Gandhi, Mahatma   **19**

The Goal: A Process of Ongoing Improvement   **95, 101**

Godin, Seth   **187**

Goldratt, Eliyahu   **95, 101**

Grant, Adam   **93, 196, 233**

Greer, Peter   **45, 165**

Grenny, Joseph   **208, 233**

H

Hacking Growth: How Today's Fastest-Growing Companies Drive Breakout Success   **289**

Hausmann, Ricardo   **26, 27**

Heath, Chip and Dan   **248, 250, 253, 261**

Homer   **239, 291**

Horst, Chris   **45, 165**

Hoskins, Bob   **154**

Hoskins, Rob   **45**

How to Lead When You're Not in Charge: Leveraging Influence When You Lack Authority   **190, 204, 233**

I

Innovation and Entrepreneurship   **141, 147**

J

Jobs, Steve   **151**

Jordan-Evans, Sharon   **211, 233**

K

Kaye, Beverly   **211, 233**

King, Martin Luther Jr.   **11, 19, 153**

Knapp, Jake   **257, 261, 278**

Kotter, John   **202**

Kowitz, Braden   **257, 261, 278**

L

The Lean Startup: How Today's Entrepreneurs Use Continuous Innovation to Create Radically Successful Businesses   **280, 289**

Loonshots: How to Nurture Crazy Ideas That Win Wars, Cure Diseases, and Transform Industries   **70, 101**

Love 'Em or Lose 'Em: Getting Good People to Stay   **210, 218, 233**

Luther, Martin   **19**

M

Mandela, Nelson   **19**

Maxwell, John   **45, 190**

McKeown, Les   **68, 101**

Meyer, Erin   **126, 129, 147, 227**

Mission Drift: The Unspoken Crisis Facing Leaders, Charities, and Churches   **45, 165**

N

Noah   **157**

O

Ochoa, Ellen   **197**

On Being Wrong   **269, 273**

P

Parker, Priya   **242, 261**

The Power of Moments: Why Certain Experiences Have Extraordinary Impact   **248, 261**

PyroMarketing: The Four-Step Strategy to Ignite Customer Evangelists and Keep Them for Life   **160, 181**

R

Reinventing the Organization   **74**

Ries, Eric   **280, 289**

S

Satell, Greg   **20, 45**

Schulz, Kathryn   **269, 273**

Scroggins, Clay **190, 191, 204, 233**

Scrum: The Art of Doing Twice the Work in Half the Time **225, 289**

Seelig, Tina **184**

Selling the Invisible: A Field Guide to Modern Marketing **169, 181**

Shape Up: Stop Running in Circles and Ship Work that Matters **233**

Sher, Barbara **23**

Sinek, Simon **153, 181, 200**

Singer, Ryan **233**

Sprint: How to Solve Big Problems and Test New Ideas in Just Five Days **257, 261, 278**

Start with Why: How Great Leaders Inspire Everyone to Take Action **154, 181, 201**

Stielstra, Greg **161, 181**

Story or Die: How to Use Brain Science to Engage, Persuade, and Change Minds in Business and in Life **181**

Stroh, David Peter **57, 62, 101**

Sun Tzu **168**

Sutherland, Jeff **225, 289**

Suzuki, Shunryu **112**

Sweezey, Mathew **261**

Syed, Matthew **147, 192, 270**

Systems Thinking for Social Change: A Practical Guide to Solving Complex Problems, Avoiding Unintended Consequences, and Achieving Lasting Results **57, 62, 101**

U
Ulrich, Dave **74**

V
Voltaire **52**

Y
Yeung, Arthur **74**

Z
Zeratsky, John **257, 261, 278**

Zook, Chriz **65**

Index 2: Concepts and Keywords

A

accomplishment (gamification core drive) **84**

advertising **160, 166, 169**

affirmation **216, 247**

Africa **124, 129, 143, 253**

agenda **126, 223, 242, 245, 257**

Airbnb **143**

algorithms **81, 168**

Alpha **123**

Amazon **74, 280**

American culture **129, 133, 186**

analytics **168, 178, 281**

apathy. *See also* peace, false **138, 208**

Asia **129, 254**

assumptions **32, 113, 119, 124, 134, 142, 146, 151, 197, 215, 267, 271, 288**

audience segmentation **162, 164, 173**

authority **19, 76, 129, 189, 191, 204, 218, 227, 233, 257**

avoidance (gamification core drive) **89**

B

Bible

    and Emmaus road **140**

    and Great Commission **22, 170**

    and OneHope **155, 253**

    and Peter **99**

    and Solomon rebuilding the temple **8**

on God's love **159**

on ownership **191**

on partnership **34**

on peace **29**

on purpose **155, 205, 292**

on uniqueness **114**

on unity **12, 29**

on wisdom **54**

on wonder **145**

teen opinions on **30**

Bible App for Kids **142, 285**

black hat motivators **86, 89**

Blue sky innovation **69**

Body of Christ **9, 11, 16, 17, 28, 30, 34, 44**

book recommendations **45, 101, 147, 181, 233, 261, 289**

boundaries **55, 72, 244**

brainstorming **69, 257**

branding **167, 291**

C

change

and management **202**

positive **100, 115**

transformational **18, 20, 45**

changes in meaning (source of innovation) **144**

children **25, 29, 55, 61, 85, 117, 120, 142, 154, 171, 249, 253, 256, 284, 286**

soldiers **154**

Chile **125**

China **129, 144**

Christianity **115, 122**

and gamification **90**

and non-Christians **22, 122**

and teens **30, 276**

as a global movement **22**

denominations **29**

in Africa **144**

Christ's Body. *See* Body of Christ

Church. *See* Global Church

Circular Funnel framework   **177**

Clinical Factors Group   **195**

collaboration   **29, 33, 186, 230, 260, 292**

communicating (dimension of culture)   **127**

communication   **64, 72, 151, 166, 221, 231, 242**

community   **18, 26, 29, 124, 136, 167, 210, 219, 242**

compensation, vs. pay   **216**

conflict   **29, 33, 89, 126, 130, 133, 209, 241**

    constructive   **205**

    healthy   **205, 209**

    resolution   **208, 242**

consensus   **130, 209**

core drivers   **83, 87, 90**

courage   **114, 165, 208, 212, 230, 270**

COVID-19 pandemic   **137, 144**

creativity rituals   **220**

cross-connections   **27**

cultural intelligence   **133**

culture

    American   **129, 133, 186**

    and affirmation   **216**

    and decision making   **130**

    and disagreement   **130**

    and evaluation   **128, 228**

    and innovation   **185, 207, 216, 219, 230, 232**

    and leadership   **129, 189, 227**

    and mentorship   **217**

    and ministry   **186, 190, 205, 209, 214, 231**

    and perception   **125, 126, 187, 188**

    and persuasion   **132**

    and scheduling   **131**

    and trust   **126**

    building   **65, 207, 231**

creating **186**

definition **184, 187**

differences in **133, 188**

eight dimensions of **127**

learning **193, 205, 229, 232**

performance **193, 232**

workplace **72, 185, 189, 215, 220**

D

deciding (dimension of culture) **129**

decisions **19, 61, 64, 72, 76, 82, 95, 97, 129, 164, 172, 191, 221, 243, 286**

demographics (source of innovation) **143**

denial **270**

design choices **81, 82, 173**

intentional **172**

destructive peace **205**

digital initiatives **282, 284**

digital marketing **169**

digital platforms **86, 137, 169**

disagreeing (dimension of culture) **130**

disagreement **29, 33, 130, 151, 192, 205, 209, 220, 257**

discipleship **8, 17, 22, 99, 140, 170, 239, 248, 271, 282, 287**

discipline **18, 54, 267**

disunity **16, 29, 191, 209**

diversity **25, 27, 34, 44, 133, 186, 205, 240**

E

education **56, 58**

El Salvador **171**

empathy **15, 120, 123, 133, 146, 174, 241, 245, 250**

empowerment **73, 85, 186, 227**

empowerment (gamification core drive) **85**

encouragement **216**

engagement **65, 71, 155, 178, 211, 215**

Enneagram **118**

epic meaning (gamification core drive) **84**

evaluating (dimension of culture)   **128**

evangelism   **25, 90, 92, 255, 271**

expectations   **31, 113, 127, 146, 175, 184, 227, 230, 250**

   cultural   **188, 227**

expertise   **113, 145, 243, 268**

F

Federal Aviation Association (FAA)   **193**

Facebook   **68, 80, 280**

facilitation   **222, 240, 245, 255, 258, 260**

failure   **272**

   and innovation   **274**

   and success   **84**

   celebrating   **266, 272**

   fear of   **194, 272, 274**

   learning from   **75, 193, 274, 276, 288, 292**

feedback   **128, 130, 192, 197, 202, 209, 216, 224, 230, 233, 277, 278**

flatness   **70**

founder's mentality   **66, 74**

Four Helpful Lists   **228**

France   **187**

G

gamification   **83**

   applied to ministry   **90**

Germany   **133, 144**

Global Church   **12, 18, 28, 44, 282**

Global Youth Culture research study   **29**

goals, long-term   **61, 221, 257**

God

   and collaboration   **33**

   and community   **24, 29**

   and empathy   **15, 32**

   and Global Church   **14, 29**

   and Gospel   **14, 15, 61, 90, 145, 159, 194, 272, 293**

and Great Commission   **23, 117**

and Noah   **158**

and OneHope   **117, 210**

and Paul (apostle)   **162**

and teens' view of   **29**

and unity   **18, 29**

relationship with   **13**

God's Big Story program. *See also* OneHope   **253**

Good News. *See also* Gospel   **8, 14, 66, 90, 120, 162, 193, 241, 272, 287, 293**

Google   **68, 74, 206, 280**

Google Maps   **79**

Gospel

and empathy   **15, 120**

and gamification   **91**

and Global Church   **14, 281**

and innovation   **8, 44, 137, 219**

and Jesus Christ   **9, 16, 61, 91, 155, 171, 179, 205, 248, 252, 254, 272, 287, 293**

and love   **15**

and OneHope   **162, 283**

and unity   **16**

message of   **180, 253, 271**

Great Commission   **22, 90, 92, 117, 162, 170, 186, 270**

growth, and organizations   **65, 75**

growth mindset. *See also* learning culture   **267**

H

hackathons   **24**

HCD (Human-Centered Design)   **121, 124**

hierarchies   **19, 70, 130**

Holacracy   **75**

Holland   **129**

Holy Spirit   **22, 44, 123, 138, 154, 194, 231, 272, 291**

homelessness   **58**

humility   **57, 93, 100, 114, 135, 140, 186, 192, 197, 209, 212, 229, 246**

I

IDEO **121, 124**

incongruity (source of innovation) **142, 280**

incumbent organizations **65**

India **19, 246**

Indonesia **268**

innovation

    and changes in meaning **144**

    and culture **185, 207, 216, 219, 230, 232**

    and demographics **143**

    and disagreement **209**

    and diversity **28, 44, 240**

    and empathy **133**

    and expertise **113**

    and failure **274**

    and flat organizations **71**

    and Henry Ford **59**

    and incongruity **142, 280**

    and leadership **189, 191**

    and learning culture **194**

    and market structure **143**

    and ministry **8, 11, 202, 215, 230, 267**

    and new knowledge **145**

    and process need **142**

    and scaling organizations **69**

    and systems thinking **54, 76**

    and the unexpected **141**

    and trust **206**

    and wisdom **54**

    constraints on **69**

    defining **7**

    seven sources of **141**

Innovation Launchpad **16**

Innovation Team. *See also* OneHope **53, 221, 224, 228**

Instagram **82, 166**

insurgent organizations   **65**

intentionality   **66, 114, 203, 224**

Internet   **13, 26, 80, 133, 145, 160**

interviews

    exit/stay   **212**

    motivational   **93**

    research   **30, 122, 174, 256, 278**

isolation   **23, 98, 201**

J

Japan   **130, 188**

Jesus Christ   **12, 23, 82, 84, 99, 116, 123, 140, 145, 159, 171, 178, 239, 249, 287, 292, 293**

    and Gospel   **9, 16, 61, 91, 155, 171, 179, 205, 248, 253, 272, 287, 293**

    and love   **15, 29, 33, 159, 171**

    and ministry   **8, 17, 23, 33, 44, 92, 99, 123, 140, 191, 240, 250, 287**

    and ownership   **191**

    and perfection   **273**

    and Peter   **99**

    and success   **275, 292**

    and unity   **18**

K

kids. *See* children

kingdom values   **12, 28, 140, 212**

    love   **15, 28, 34, 44, 54, 159, 171, 180, 192, 209**

    See also humility, unity

L

Latin America   **116, 126, 129, 254**

leadership   **68, 76, 87, 95, 130, 190, 209, 211, 217, 227, 241, 259**

leading (dimension of culture)   **129**

lean thinking   **280**

learning culture   **197, 205, 228, 232**

M

marketing   **169**

    digital   **168**
    teams   **98**
market-oriented ecosystem   **74**
markets   **143, 167**
market structure (source of innovation)   **143**
meaning
    changes in (source of innovation)   **144**
    epic (gamification core drive)   **84**
mentorship   **87, 217**
micro-management   **227**
Minecraft   **85**
ministry
    and audience segmentation   **162, 164, 173**
    and building culture   **231**
    and collaboration   **29, 33, 229**
    and community   **210**
    and COVID-19 pandemic   **137**
    and disagreement   **205**
    and discipleship   **8, 22, 99, 170, 239, 248, 271, 281, 287**
    and diversity   **27**
    and failure   **274, 278**
    and gamification   **90**
    and goals   **61**
    and hackathons   **25**
    and hierarchies   **19, 22**
    and innovation   **8, 28, 62, 70, 185, 202, 204, 215, 219, 267, 270**
    and leadership   **76, 191**
    and learning culture   **193, 197, 232**
    and networks   **20, 24**
    and OneHope   **29, 53, 70, 73, 117, 125, 142, 144, 155, 159, 162, 170, 176, 184, 210, 213, 219, 253, 276, 282**
    and organizational culture   **184**
    and organizational structure   **73**
    and partnership   **12, 33, 44, 229, 284**
    and scale   **67**

and success   **7, 62, 84, 98, 142, 155, 192, 275, 290**

and systems   **62**

and the why   **95, 154, 160, 202**

digital   **92, 169, 175, 285**

marketing   **166**

ministry culture   **186, 190, 198, 201, 205, 211, 214, 219, 231, 275**

ministry innovation   **11, 33, 119, 133, 138, 162, 179, 197, 202, 204, 240, 290**

miscommunication   **33, 73, 126, 151, 230, 244, 268**

mission

and missional calling   **117**

and OneHope   **29, 117, 155**

and organizations   **53, 62, 76, 98, 178, 196, 212, 216, 229, 232**

God's   **12, 16, 23, 28, 44, 91, 159, 292**

mission drift   **165**

moments, designing   **246, 254**

motivators   **86, 89, 91**

movements   **14, 20, 23**

MVP (minimum viable product)   **279, 285**

MyStory   **276**

N

NASA   **196**

networks   **12, 20**

network theory   **20**

new knowledge (source of innovation)   **145**

New Zealand   **128**

Nigeria   **129, 144**

non-Christians   **22, 122**

O

Octalysis framework   **83**

OneHope   **29, 53, 70, 73, 117, 125, 142, 144, 155, 159, 162, 170, 176, 184, 210, 213, 219, 253, 276, 282**

online course   **16, 63**

online ministry   **92, 137, 160, 174**

online missionaries   **98**

organizational structure   **19, 53, 63, 70, 73**
organizations
  flat   **70**
  incumbent   **65**
  insurgent   **65**
  large   **53, 64, 69, 75, 214**
  scaling   **68**
  tall   **70**
  wide   **70**
outreach. *See also* Alpha, online missionaries   **90, 154**
ownership   **71, 85, 90, 191, 203, 218**
ownership (gamification core drive)   **85**

P
partnerships   **12, 33, 44, 229, 284**
peace
  destructive   **205**
  false   **209**
performance rituals   **220**
persuading (dimension of culture)   **132**
philosopher   **52, 292**
pilots   **193**
Plato   **103, 266, 291**
poets   **291**
praise. *See* affirmation
pride   **18, 33, 138, 140, 201**
prisons   **103, 270**
process need (source of innovation)   **142**
productivity   **213, 224**
prototyping   **258, 277**
psychological safety. *See also* trust   **206, 243**

R
retention   **211**
rhythms and rituals   **220, 230**
risk   **201, 232, 274, 276, 279**

S

scarcity (gamification core drive)   **87**

Scared Straight Program   **270**

scheduling (dimension of culture)   **131, 133**

Scripture engagement   **25, 29, 125, 155, 284**

Scripture. *See also* Bible   **25, 140, 142, 155, 250, 255, 286, 293**

service mindset   **170, 287**

smartphones   **78, 134, 143, 145, 166**

social influence (gamification core drive)   **86**

social media   **80, 86, 98, 134, 151, 160, 178**

solutions, long-term   **57, 60, 170, 285**

South Africa   **19**

South America   **116**

Spain   **187**

span of control   **70**

sprint   **257, 278**

Starbucks   **67**

startups   **64, 68, 74**

    lean   **280, 289**

storytelling   **9, 151, 155, 159, 169, 180**

structure. *See* organizational structure

success

    and diversity   **26**

    and failure   **84, 142, 266, 275**

    and ministry   **7, 97, 165, 203, 290**

    and scale   **64, 66, 69**

    organizational   **22, 64, 66, 74, 97, 135, 144, 155, 192**

    team   **206, 218, 221**

Sunday School   **120, 141, 249, 252, 286**

sunk cost   **276**

switching cost   **224**

Switzerland   **133**

system design   **73**

systems   **57**

    and authority   **77**

   and gamification **83**

   creating **78, 82**

   examining **63, 77**

   symptoms **58, 60, 100**

systems thinking **54, 58, 60, 76, 93**

T

tall organizations **72**

teams

   culture of **189, 195, 211, 227**

   leaders **64, 241**

   members **71, 189, 214, 216, 220, 224, 228**

   small **64, 67**

technology

   and COVID-19 pandemic **137**

   digital **78, 81, 160**

technology development **79, 276, 281, 283**

TED talks **23, 154, 201**

teens **30, 270, 279**

Tencent **74**

tension **54, 61, 69, 208, 220, 241**

the unexpected (source of innovation) **141**

traffic **59**

transformation, life **18, 204, 293**

transparency **193, 230**

trust **206**

   and branding **167**

   and conflict **209**

   and cultural differences **126**

   and innovation culture **206**

   and leadership **191, 203, 218**

   and networks **22**

   and partnerships **230, 274**

   and teams **206, 216, 219**

   creating **197, 207, 244**

dimension of culture **126**
  in God **17, 158, 179, 192, 205, 272, 293**
Twitter **80**

U

Uber **143**
United States **19, 126, 128, 129, 130, 131, 132, 133, 186**
unity **12, 15, 18, 29, 191**
unlearning **268, 287**
unpredictability (gamification core drive) **88**
User Experience (UX) **79, 82**
User Interface (UI) **79, 82**
user journey **175**

W

white hat motivators **86, 91**
why, start with **153, 159, 168, 202**
Wikipedia **84**
wisdom **8, 54, 138, 144, 218**

Y

YouTube **78, 80, 112, 134, 284**
YouVersion **284**

Z

Zappos **79**
Zoom **138, 225**

Liam Savage is passionate about helping the Global Church innovate in order to fulfill the Great Commission. Liam currently serves as the Director of Innovation for OneHope, an international nonprofit that reaches the next generation with God's Word.

He is the creator of the Innovation Launchpad, an online learning journey that raises up innovators for ministry. Liam is a kingdom collaborator and leader with Indigitous, a global movement that activates believers to digital missions.

Liam's innovation work is grounded in his study of theology at Biola University and Knox Theological Seminary. He holds an executive MBA from Quantic School of Business and Technology, and is currently pursuing his doctorate in missiology and PhD in organizational leadership at Southeastern University.

liamsavage.co

Want to grow your perspective?

Take the Innovator's Quiz

---

greenskyinnovation.com

www.ingramcontent.com/pod-product-compliance
Lightning Source LLC
Chambersburg PA
CBHW071304140726
47996CB00005B/1621